Pan Tadeusz Or, the Last Foray in Lithuania; a Story of Life Among Polish Gentlefolk in the Years 1811 and 1812 • Mickiewicz, Adam

PREFACE 1
INTRODUCTION 1
LIST OF THE PRINCIPAL CHARACTERS IN "PAN TADEUSZ" WITH NOTES ON POLISH PRONUNCIATION 5
BOOK I.—THE FARM 6
BOOK II.—THE CASTLE 15
BOOK III.—FLIRTATION............... 22
BOOK IV.—DIPLOMACY AND THE CHASE 30
BOOK V.—THE BRAWL 39
BOOK VI.—THE HAMLET............ 47
BOOK VII.—THE CONSULTATION 53
BOOK VIII.—THE FORAY 59
BOOK IX.—THE BATTLE 66
BOOK X—THE EMIGRATION. JACEK 73
BOOK XI.—THE YEAR 1812 82
BOOK XII.—LET US LOVE ONE ANOTHER! 88
NOTES 96

Publisher's Note

Purchase of this book entitles you to a free trial membership in the publisher's book club at www.rarebooksclub.com. (Time limited offer.) Simply enter the barcode number from the back cover onto the membership form on our home page. The book club entitles you to select from millions of books at no additional charge. You can also download a digital copy of this and related books to read on the go. Simply enter the title or subject onto the search form to find them.

Note: This is an historic book. Pages numbers, where present in the text, refer to the first edition of the book and may also be in indexes.

If you have any questions, could you please be so kind as to consult our Frequently Asked Questions page at www.rarebooksclub.com/faqs.cfm? You are also welcome to contact us there.

Publisher: General Books LLC™, Memphis, TN, USA, 2012. ISBN: 9781153810852.
Proofreading: pgdp.net

❧ ❧ ❧ ❧ ❧ ❧ ❧

PAN TADEUSZ
  OR
  THE LAST FORAY IN LITHUANIA
All rights reserved
PAN TADEUSZ
  OR
  THE LAST FORAY IN LITHUANIA
  A STORY OF LIFE AMONG POLISH GENTLEFOLK
  IN THE YEARS 1811 and 1812
  IN TWELVE BOOKS

BY
  ADAM MICKIEWICZ

TRANSLATED FROM THE POLISH BY
  GEORGE RAPALL NOYES

1917
  LONDON AND TORONTO
  J. M. DENT & SONS LTD.
  PARIS: J. M. DENT ET FILS
  NEW YORK: E. P. DUTTON & CO.

[pg v]

PREFACE

The present translation of Pan Tadeusz is based on the editions of Biegeleisen (Lemberg, 1893) and Kallenbach (Brody, 1911). I have had constantly by me the German translation by Lipiner (ed. 2, Leipzig, 1898) and the French translation by Ostrowski (ed. 4, Paris, 1859), and am deeply indebted to them. The English translation by Miss Maude Ashurst Biggs (Master Thaddeus; or, The Last Foray in Lithuania : London, 1885) I did not have at hand until my own version was nearly complete; after that I consulted it only very rarely. I do not think that I am under obligation to it in more than a half-dozen scattered lines of my text. (Perhaps, however, my use of foray as a translation of zajazd is due to an unconscious recollection of the title of Miss Biggs's volumes, which I looked over several years ago, before I had even formed the plan of my own work.) In my notes, however, my debt to Miss Biggs and her collaborators in her commentary on Pan Tadeusz is important; I have striven to indicate it distinctly, and I thank Miss Biggs heartily for her kind permission to make use of her work.

To my friend Miss Mary Helen Sznyter I am grateful for aid and advice in the rendering of several puzzling passages. But my greatest debt I owe to my wife, whose name, if justice were done, should be added to my [pg vi] own as joint translator of the volume. Though she is entirely unacquainted with the Polish language, nearly every page of the book in its phrasing bears traces of her correcting hand. The preparation of the volume for the press and the reading of the proof have been made easy by her skilful help.

Berkeley, California ,
December 9 , 1916.
[pg ix]

INTRODUCTION

"No European nation of our day has such an epic as Pan Tadeusz . In it Don Quixote has been fused with the Iliad . The poet stood on the border line between a vanishing generation and our own. Before they died, he had seen them; but now they are no more. That is precisely the epic point of view. Mickiewicz has performed his task with a master's hand; he has made immortal a dead generation, which now will never pass away. ... Pan Tadeusz is a true epic. No more can be said or need be said." 1

This verdict upon the great masterpiece of all Slavic poetry, written a few years after its appearance, by Zygmunt Krasinski, one of Mickiewicz's two great successors in the field of Polish letters, has been confirmed by the judgment of posterity. For the chapter on Pan Tadeusz by George Brandes, than whom there have been few more competent judges of modern European literature, is little more than an expansion of Krasinski's pithy sentences. The cosmopolitan critic echoes the patriotic Pole when he writes: "In Pan Tadeusz Poland possesses the only successful epic our century has produced." 2

Still more important than the praises of the finest literary critics is the enthusiastic affection cherished for [pg x] Pan Tadeasz by the great body of the Polish people. Perhaps no poem of any other European nation is so truly national and in the best sense of the word popular. Almost every Pole who has read anything more than the newspaper is familiar with the contents of Pan Tadeusz . No play of Shakespeare, no long poem of Milton or Wordsworth or Tennyson, is so well known or so well beloved by the English people as is Pan Tadeusz by the Poles. To find a work equally well known one might turn to Defoe's prosaic tale of adventure, Robinson Crusoe ; to find a work so beloved would be hardly possible.

Pan Tadeasz is so clear and straightforward in its appeal that but few words of explanation in regard to its origin are required. Its author, Adam Mickiewicz, was born in 1798, near Nowogrodek in Lithuania. His father, a member of the poorer gentry of the district, was a lawyer by profession, so that the boy was brought up among just such types as he describes with so rare a humour in the Judge, the Assessor, the Notary, and the Apparitor. The young Mickiewicz was sent to the University of Wilno 3 (1815-19), where he received a good classical education, and, largely through his own independent reading, became well acquainted with French, German, and Russian—even with English literature. On leaving the university he obtained a position as teacher in the gymnasium at Kowno (1819-23). Though even as a boy he had written verses, his real literary career began with the publication in 1822 of a volume of ballads, which was followed the next year by a second book of poems, containing fragments of a fantastic drama, The Forefathers , and a short [pg xi] historical poem, Grazyna . These volumes reflect the romantic movement then prevalent in Europe, of which they are the first powerful expression in Poland. They were in large part inspired by the poet's love for a young woman of somewhat higher station than his own, who, though she returned his affection, was forced by her family to marry another suitor.

In 1833 Mickiewicz was arrested as a political criminal, his offence being membership in a students' club at the University of Wilno that had cherished nationalistic aspirations. With several others, he was banished from his beloved Lithuanian home to the interior of Russia; the following years, until 1829, he spent in St. Petersburg, Odessa, and Moscow. During this honourable exile he became intimate with many of the most eminent men of letters in Russia, and continued his own literary work by publishing his sonnets, beyond comparison the finest ever written in Polish, and a romantic poem, Konrad Wallenrod , based on the stubborn resistance of the Lithuanian folk in the fourteenth century to their German foes, the Knights of the Cross, and showing in its style marked Byronic influence. The poem unfortunately admitted, or rather invited, an application to the resistance of the Poles to the Russians; Mickiewicz, fearing with reason the anger of the Russian authorities, succeeded in obtaining, just in time to save himself from serious consequences, a passport permitting him to leave the country.

Arriving in Germany in 1829, Mickiewicz travelled through Switzerland to Italy. His residence in Rome, with its sacred associations, and the meeting with new friends of a deeply religious temperament, brought about within him a new birth of Catholic faith that [pg xii] strongly affected bis later writings, notably Pan Tadeusz. In Rome also he became intimate with the family of the rich Count Ankwicz, for whose daughter Eva he conceived an affection that is reflected in the passion of Jacek Soplica for the Pantler's only child. On the outbreak of the insurrection in Warsaw, at the end of the year 1830, the poet meditated returning home to join the national forces; but he delayed his departure, and never came nearer the scene of action than Posen and its vicinity. The grief and discouragement caused by the failure of the insurrection, instead of crippling Mickiewicz's powers, seemed to spur him on to new activity. During 1833 he wrote a continuation of The Forefathers , in an entirely different tone from that of his youthful poem of ten years before. The action is based on the persecution by the Russian authorities of the Polish students in Wilno; the lovelorn Gustaw of the earlier poem is transformed into the patriotic martyr Konrad. In this same year he settled in Paris, along with many other Polish exiles or "emigrants," who were made homeless by the downfall of the national cause, and who, if the truth be said, were split up into bitterly hostile factions. Mickiewicz was now beginning to assume the role of prophet and seer. For the reproof and instruction of his fellow-countrymen he composed his Books of the Polish Nation and of the Polish Pilgrimage, a mystical work, written in biblical prose, and intended to bring comfort and harmony to the distracted exiles. In Paris also, in the course of about fourteen months (1832-34), he wrote Pan Tadeusz, his greatest poem—and (with insignificant exceptions) his last.

The story of Mickiewicz's closing years may be passed [pg xiii] over very briefly. In 1834 he married; his wife was subject to attacks of insanity, and all his later life was saddened by the struggle with misfortune and poverty. In 1840 he was called to a newly founded professorship of Slavic literature at the Collège de France. His lectures as holder of this chair are the only literary work of great importance that he produced during this last period of his life. Soon after the completion of Pan Tadeusz he had become absorbed by a religious mysticism that caused him to turn entirely aside from poetry. In 1841 he fell under the influence of Andrzej Towianski, a teacher who announced himself as the prophet of a new religion. His acceptance and promulgation of a doctrine which was pronounced heretical by the Catholic Church, and which inculcated a religious reverence for Napoleonic traditions, made it impossible for the French government to retain his services in a government institution, and in 1844 he was deprived of his professorship. The accession to power of Napoleon III. filled him with new hopes. In 1855 he journeyed to Constantinople, wishing to aid in the war against Russia, and there he died of the cholera. His remains, first laid to rest in Paris, were transferred in 1890 to the cathedral at Cracow. 4

Pan Tadeusz was not the result of a momentary inspiration, but grew gradually under the author's hand. On December 8, 1832, he wrote to a friend: "I am now at work on a poem of life among the gentry, in the style of Hermann and Dorothea . I have already [pg xiv] jotted down a thousand verses." He had evidently planned a village idyl of no great length, probably based on the love of Thaddeus and Zosia. In a draft of the first book that is still preserved, Thaddeus sees on the wall a picture of Joseph Poniatowski at the battle of Leipzig (October 19, 1813), "riding a mettled steed" but "stricken with a mortal wound." Thus the action of the poem could not have taken place earlier than 1814. Later, Mickiewicz threw back the time of his action to the autumn of 1811 and the spring of 1812; thus, by giving his poem a political background in the invasion of Russia by Napoleon, he transformed his village idyl into a national epic. The Monk Robak, or Jacek Soplica, and not his commonplace son Thaddeus, now became the real hero of the poem. 5 Nor was this hero wholly a product of the writer's invention. There has recently been discovered a petition by Mikolaj Mickiewicz, the father of the poet, praying the authorities to grant him protection from one Jan Soplica, "a man of criminal sort," who had slain the uncle of the petitioner and was now threatening to kill the whole Mickiewicz family and burn their house. With the character of this person the description of Jacek Soplica's early years agrees as closely as his name. Mickiewicz even mentions his own kindred as the ancestral enemies of the Soplicas (page 45). Yet one of that hated family he now made the hero of his greatest poem. By introducing him in the guise of Father Robak, repentant and striving to atone for past misdeeds through heroic service to his country, he infused into his poem a [pg xv] romantic charm. The mystery surrounding this figure connects Pan Tadeusz , an epic that is truly classic in its dignified elevation and restraint of feeling, with Konrad Wallenrod , a romantic tale conceived in the spirit of Byronic passion.

In the work of Mickiewicz as a whole two characteristics predominate: a great intensity of feeling, which sometimes sinks into sentimentality, and at others rises into lyric fervour; and a wonderful truth, not only to the general impressions of his experience, but to the actual concrete facts of it, even to such trifles as the names of persons and places. Thus The Forefathers , despite all its fantastic elements, reproduces many incidents in which the poet himself was concerned. Furthermore, in certain works, as in his early tale Grazyna , Mickiewicz had shown a wonderful ability suddenly to detach himself from passing currents of emotion and to rise into regions of Olympian calm, giving to his work a classic, rounded completeness worthy of Grecian art. All these aspects of his genius are present in Pan Tadeusz . Echoes of the poet's personal emotion are heard in Jacek's tale of his passion for Eva; and an ardent love of country permeates the poem and breaks out again and again with lyric force. On the other hand the book is faithful to reality in its picture of Lithuanian manners and customs; the great romantic poet is at the same time the first realistic novelist of Poland. Minor details beyond number are introduced from the writer's personal recollections; "even the Jew's playing of the dulcimer the poet had heard in St. Petersburg from the famous Silbermann." 6 Through the whole book runs a humour [pg xvi] not often found elsewhere in Mickiewicz; the reports of the debates in Jankiel's tavern and in Dobrzyn hamlet are masterly in their blending of kindly pleasantry with photographic fidelity to truth. The poet sees the ludicrous side of the Warden, the Chamberlain, the Seneschal, and the other Don Quixotes who fill his pages, and yet he loves them with the most tender affection. In his descriptions of external nature—of the Lithuanian forests or of the scene around Soplicowo on the moonlight night just before the foray—Mickiewicz shows a genius for throwing a glamour of poetic beauty over the face of common things such as has never been surpassed. Finally, the whole poem is perfect in its proportions; from its homely beginning, with pictures of rural simplicity and old-fashioned hospitality, it swells into rustic grandeur in the panorama of the hunt, and at last reaches the most poignant tragedy in the scene about the death-bed of Jacek Soplica: then, lest the impression should be one of total sadness, the narrative concludes with the magnificent epilogue of the last two books, full of hopes of rescue for Poland, full of gaiety and courage. A large epic calm pervades the whole. The age-long conflict between Pole and "Muscovite" is the theme of the epic, but the tone is not that of passionate hatred and revolt such as fills The Forefathers ; human kindliness breathes through the whole work; not indignation and rebellion, but faith, hope, and love are at its foundation.

This brief introduction may fitly close with some verses that Mickiewicz wrote as an epilogue for Pan Tadeusz , but which he never finally revised and which were never printed during his lifetime. Since his death [pg xvii] they have most frequently been inserted as a prologue to the poem rather than as an epilogue.

"What can be my thoughts, here on the streets of Paris, when I bring home from the city ears filled with noise, with curses and lies, with untimely plans, belated regrets, and hellish quarrels?

"Alas for us deserters, that in time of pestilence, timid souls, we fled to foreign lands! For wherever we trod, terror went before us, and in every neighbour we found an enemy; at last they have bound us in chains, firmly and closely, and they bid us give up the ghost as quickly as may be.

"But if this world has no ear for their sorrows, if at each moment fresh tidings overwhelm them, reverberating from Poland like a graveyard bell; if their jailers wish them an early doom and their enemies beckon them from afar like grave-diggers; if even in Heaven they see no hope—then it is no marvel that they loathe men, the world, themselves; that, losing their reason from their long tortures, they spit upon themselves and consume one another.

* * * * * *

"I longed to pass by in my flight, bird of feeble wing—to pass by regions of storm and thunder, and to search out only pleasant shade and fair weather—the days of my childhood, and my home gardens.

* * * * * *

"One happiness remains: when in a grey hour you sit by the fireside with a few of your friends and lock the door against the uproar of Europe, and escape in thought to happier times, and muse and dream of your own land.
[pg xviii]
"But of that blood that was shed so lately, of the tears which have flooded the face of all Poland, of the glory that not yet has ceased resounding: of these to think we had never the heart! For the nation is in such anguish that even Valour, when he turns his gaze on its torture, can do naught but wring the hands.

* * * * * *

"Those generations black with mourning—that air heavy with so many curses—there—thought dared not turn its flight to a sphere dreadful even to the birds of thunder.

* * * * * *

"O Mother Poland! Thou wast so lately laid in the grave. No man has the strength to speak of thee!
* * * * * *

"Ah! whose lips can dare to fancy that to-day they will at last find the magic word that will soften marble-like despair, that will lift the stony lid from men's hearts, and will open eyes heavy with so many tears?

"Some time—when the lions of vengeance shall cease to roar, when the blare of the trumpet shall be stilled, when the ranks shall be broken, when our eagles with a flight like lightning shall settle on the ancient boundaries of Boleslaw the Brave, and, eating their fill of corpses, shall be drenched with blood, and finally fold their wings to rest; when the last enemy shall give forth a cry of pain, become silent, and proclaim liberty to the world: then, crowned with oak leaves, throwing aside their swords, our knights will seat themselves unarmed and deign to hear songs. When the world envies their present fortune they will [pg xix] have leisure to hear of the past! Then they will weep over the fate of their fathers, and then those tears will not soil their cheeks.

"To-day, for us, unbidden guests in the world, in all the past and in all the future—to-day there is but one region in which there is a crumb of happiness for a Pole: the land of his childhood! That land will ever remain holy and pure as first love; undisturbed by the remembrance of errors, not undermined by the deceitfulness of hopes, and unchanged by the stream of events.

* * * * * *

"Gladly would I greet with my thoughts those lands where I rarely wept and never gnashed my teeth; lands of my childhood, where one roamed over the world as through a meadow, and among the flowers knew only those that were lovely and fair, throwing aside the poisonous, and not glancing at the useful.

"That land, happy, poor, and narrow; as the world is God's, so that was our own! How everything there belonged to us, how I remember all that surrounded us, from the linden that with its magnificent crown afforded shade to the children of the whole village, down to every stream and stone; how every cranny of the land was familiar to us, as far as the houses of our neighbours—the boundary line of our realm!

"And if at times a Muscovite made his appearance, he left behind him only the memory of a fair and glittering uniform, for we knew the serpent only by his skin.

"And only the dwellers in those lands have remained true to me until now; some as faithful friends, some as trusty allies! For *who* dwelt there? Mother, brothers, [pg xx] kindred, good neighbours! When one of them passed away, how tenderly did they speak of him! How many memories, what long-continued sorrow, in that land where a servant is more devoted to his master than in other countries a wife to her husband; where a soldier sorrows longer over his weapons than here a son over his father; where they weep longer and more sincerely over a dog than here the people weep for a hero!

"And in those days my friends aided my speech and cast me word after word for my songs; like the fabled cranes on the wild island, which flew in spring over the enchanted palace and heard the loud lament of an enchanted boy: each bird threw the boy a single feather; he made him wings and returned to his own people.

* * * * * *

"O, if some time I might attain this joy—that this book might find shelter beneath roofs of thatch, and that the village girls, as they spin and turn the wheel, humming the while their much-loved verses, of the girl who so loved to make music that while fiddling she lost her geese, or of the orphan, who, fair as the dawn, went to drive home the birds at eventide—if even those village girls might take into their hands this book, simple as their songs!

"So in my own day, along with the village sports, they sometimes read aloud, under the linden tree on the green, the song of Justina,7 or the story of Wieslaw; 8 and the bailiff, dozing at the table, or the steward, or even the master of the farm, did not forbid us to read; [pg xxi] he himself would deign to listen, and would interpret the harder places to the younger folk; he praised the beauties and forgave the faults.

"And the young folk envied the fame of the bards, which in their own land still echoes through the woods and the fields; of bards to whom dearer than the laurel of the Capitol is a wreath plaited by the hands of a village girl, of blue cornflowers and green rue."

1.
Quoted from a letter of Krasinski, by Kallenbach, Adam Mickiewicz (Cracow, 1897), vol. ii. p. 174.

2.
Poland, a Study of the Land, People, and Literature (London and New York, 1903), p. 284.

3.
Vilna on our maps; Wilno is the Polish spelling.

4.
English readers are fortunate in possessing an excellent account of the life and writings of Mickiewicz in the work by Miss Monica M. Gardner, Adam Mickiewicz, the National Poet of Poland (London and New York, 1911).

5.
I am here indebted to Kallenbach (Adam Mickiewicz , Cracow, 1897), and Pilat (Introduction to edition of Pan Tadeusz of Towarzystwo Literackie , Lemberg).

6.
Brückner, Geschichte der polnischen Litteratur (Leipzig, 1901), p. 371.

7.
By Franciszek Karpinski, 1741-1825.

8.
By Kazimierz Brodzinski, 1791-1835.
[pg xxii]

LIST OF THE PRINCIPAL CHARACTERS IN " PAN TADEUSZ " WITH NOTES ON POLISH

PRONUNCIATION

The principal characters in Pan Tadeusz are as follows. The approximate pronunciation of each proper name is indicated in brackets, according to the system used in Webster's New International Dictionary.
Thaddeus (Tadeusz) Soplica [Tadĕ'ōōsh Sŏ-plē'tsä].
Jacek Soplica, his father [Yä'tsĕk],
Judge Soplica, brother of Jacek.
Telimena, a distant relative of the Soplicas and of
the Horeszkos [Tĕ-lĭ-mĕ'nä, Hŏ-rĕsh'kŏ].
Zosia, ward of Telimena [Zŏ'shä],
Hreczecha, the Seneschal [Hrĕ-chĕ'hä].
The Chamberlain.
Protazy Brzechalski, the Apparitor [Prŏ-tä'zĭ Bzhĕ-häl'skĭ].
The Assessor.
Bolesta, the Notary [Bŏ-lĕs'tä].
The Count, a distant relative of the Horeszko
family.
Gerwazy Rembajlo, the Warden, formerly a servant
of the Horeszko family [Gĕr-vä'zĭ Rĕmbaī'wŏ].
Rykov, a Russian captain [Rĭ'kŏf].
Jankiel, a Jew [Yän'kyĕl].
Maciej (Maciek) Dobrzynski [Mä'chä (Mä'chĕk)
Dŏb-zhĭn'skĭ].
[pg xxiii]
Sprinkler (also called Baptist), Bucket, Buzzard,
Razor, Awl, the Prussian: all members of
the Dobrzynski clan.
Henryk Dombrowski [Hĕn'rĭk Dŏmbrŏf'skĭ].
Otton-Karol Kniaziewicz [Ŏt'tŏn-Kä'rŏl Knyä-zhĕ'vĭch].
The following names are frequently mentioned in the poem: Kosciuszko [Kŏ-shchōōsh'kŏ], Rejtan [Rä'tän], Mickiewicz [Mits-kyĕ'vĭch]. Note also the words wojewoda [vŏ-yĕ-vŏ'da] and kontusz [kŏn'tōōsh].

Polish names in this book are generally given in their original spelling, except that the diacritical marks used on many letters in the Polish alphabet are here omitted, and that *on* (or *om*) and *en* (or *em*) are substituted for the nasal vowels indicated in Polish by *a* with a cedilla and *e* with a cedilla. But the English names *Thaddeus, Sophia, Eva, Rosa, Thomas* , and *Joseph* have been substituted for the Polish forms Tadeusz, Zofia, Ewa, Roza, Tomasz, and Jozef . (Yet the Polish title of the poem, Pan Tadeusz, has been left unchanged, as it has become widely known through works on Poland, and as a suitable substitute for it is hard to find: *Pan Thaddeus* would be a displeasing hybrid.) The few Russian names that occur are given as though transliterated from the Russian, not in the Polish form: *Suvorov* , not *Suwarow* .

The Polish Pan, Pani , and Panna correspond roughly to the English *Mr., Mrs.* , and *Miss* . But Pani may be used of unmarried women of high social station; it is regularly applied to Telimena, and once, by the reverent Gerwazy, even to little Zosia (page 320).

As an aid to the pronunciation of the minor names the following directions may be of some service:—
[pg xxiv]
Accent all names on the penult, or next to the last syllable.

Pronounce *cz* as *ch, sz* as *sh, rz* as *zh* (azure), *j* as *y* (*aj, ej, oj* as *ī, ā, oi*). W is ordinarily pronounced as *v* , but before surd consonants it has the sound *f* . *Ch* is pronounced as in German, but before vowels it need not be distinguished from the English *h* . The Polish *l* has two values, one of which resembles the English *l* , while the other (the crossed *l*) approximates to the English *w* . S is ordinarily pronounced as in English, but before *i* it has a sound somewhat like *sh* ; *si* before a vowel (as in Zosia) has the same sound, the *i* not being pronounced, but serving as an indication of the "soft" pronunciation of the preceding sibilant. In the same circumstances *z* (and *zi*) are pronounced somewhat like *zh* . The Polish alphabet also contains a dotted *z* (here represented by plain *z*) which is pronounced like *zh* . Dz before *i* (and *dzi* before a vowel) are pronounced somewhat like English *j* in *jet* . C is ordinarily pronounced like *ts* , but *c* before *i* (and *ci* before a vowel) are sounded somewhat like *ch* .

The vowels may be given the familiar "Italian" values; *y* need not be distinguished from *i* . (But on *i* as a diacritical sign, modifying a preceding sibilant, see the preceding paragraph.) Furthermore, *i* following a consonant (not a sibilant) and preceding a vowel, is pronounced like *y* , as in Jankiel (Yän'kyĕl).

These rules, it must be said, are incomplete and inexact to a degree that will shock any person with a scientific knowledge of Polish pronunciation. In the present instance brevity seemed of more importance than strict accuracy.
[pg 1]
PAN TADEUSZ
OR
THE LAST FORAY IN LITHUANIA 1

BOOK I.—THE FARM

ARGUMENT

Return of the young master—A first meeting in the chamber, a second at table—The Judge's weighty lecture on courtesy—The Chamberlain's political remarks on fashions—Beginning of the quarrel over Bobtail and Falcon—Lamentations of the Seneschal—The last Apparitor—Glance at the political conditions of Lithuania and Europe at this period.

Lithuania , my country, thou art like health; how much thou shouldst be prized only he can learn who has lost thee. To-day thy beauty in all its splendour I see and describe, for I yearn for thee.

Holy Virgin, who protectest bright Czenstochowa and shinest above the Ostra Gate in Wilno! 2 Thou who dost shelter the castle of Nowogrodek with its faithful folk! As by miracle thou didst restore me to health in my childhood—when, offered by my weeping mother to thy protection, I raised my dead eyelids, and could straightway walk to the threshold of thy shrine to thank God for the life returned me—so by miracle thou wilt return us to the bosom of our country. Meanwhile bear my grief-stricken soul to those wooded hills, to those green meadows stretched far and wide along the blue Niemen; to those fields painted with various [pg 2] grain, gilded with wheat, silvered with rye; where grows the amber mustard, the buckwheat white as snow, where the clover glows with a maiden's blush, where all is girdled as with a ribbon by a strip of green turf on which here and there rest quiet pear-trees.

Amid such fields years ago, by the border of a brook, on a low hill, in a grove of birches, stood a gentleman's 3 mansion, of wood, but with a stone foundation; the white walls shone from afar, the whiter since they were relieved against the dark green of the poplars that sheltered it against the winds of autumn. The dwelling-house was not large, but it was spotlessly neat, and it had a mighty barn, and near it were three stacks of hay that could not be contained beneath the roof; one could see that the neighbourhood was rich and fertile. And one could see from the number of sheaves that up and down the meadows shone thick as stars—one could see from the number of ploughs turning up early the immense tracts of black fallow land that evidently belonged to the mansion, and were tilled well like garden beds, that in that house dwelt plenty and order. The gate wide-open proclaimed to passers-by that it was hospitable, and invited all to enter as guests.

A young gentleman had just entered in a two-horse carriage, and, after making a turn about the yard, he stopped before the porch and descended; his horses, left to themselves, slowly moved towards the gate, nibbling the grass. The mansion was deserted, for the porch doors were barred and the bar fastened with a pin. The traveller did not run to make inquiries at the farmhouse but opened the door and ran into the mansion, for he was eager to greet it. It was long since he had seen the house, for he had been studying in a distant [pg 3] city and had at last finished his course. He ran in and gazed with eager emotion upon the ancient walls, his old friends. He sees the same furniture, the same hangings with which he had loved to amuse himself from babyhood, but they seemed less beautiful and not so large as of old. And the same portraits hung upon the walls. Here Kosciuszko, 4 in his Cracow coat, 5 with his eyes raised to heaven, held his two-handed sword; such was he when on the steps of the altar he swore that with this sword he would drive the three powers from Poland or himself would fall upon it. Farther on sat Rejtan, 6 in Polish costume, mourning the loss of liberty; in his hands he held a knife with the point turned against his breast, and before him lay Phaedo and The Life of Cato . Still farther on Jasinski, 7 a fair and melancholy youth, and his faithful comrade Korsak 8 stand side by side on the entrenchments of Praga, on heaps of Muscovites, hewing down the enemies of their country—but around them Praga is already burning.

He recognised even the tall old musical clock in its wooden case near the chamber door, and with childish joy he pulled at the string, in order to hear Dombrowski's old mazurka. 71

He ran about the whole house and searched for the room that had been his own when he was a child, ten years before. He entered, drew back, and surveyed the walls with astonished eyes: could this room be a woman's lodgings? Who could live here? His old uncle was unmarried, and his aunt had dwelt for years in St. Petersburg. Could that be the housekeeper's chamber? A piano? On it music and books; all abandoned in careless confusion: sweet disorder!
[pg 4]
Not old could the hands have been that had so abandoned them! There too, a white gown, freshly taken from the hook to put on, was spread upon the arm of a chair. In the windows were pots of fragrant flowers: geraniums, asters, gillyflowers, and violets. The traveller stepped to one of the windows—a new marvel was before him. On the bank of the brook, in a spot once overgrown with nettles, was a tiny garden intersected by paths, full of clumps of English grass and of mint. The slender wooden fence, fashioned into a monogram, shone with ribbons of gay daisies. Evi-

dently the beds had but just been sprinkled; there stood the tin watering-pot full of water, but the fair gardener could nowhere be seen. She had only now departed; the little gate, freshly touched, was still trembling; near the gate could be seen on the sand the print of a small foot that had been without shoe or stocking—on the fine dry sand, white as snow; the print was clear but light; you guessed that it was left in quick running by the tiny feet of some one who scarce touched the ground.

The traveller stood long in the window gazing and musing, breathing in the fragrance of the flowers. He bent down his face to the violet plants; he followed the paths with his curious eyes and again gazed on the tiny footprints; he kept thinking of them and trying to guess whose they were. By chance he raised his eyes, and there on the wall stood a young girl—her white garment hid her slender form only to the breast, leaving bare her shoulders and her swan's neck. Such attire a Lithuanian maiden is wont to wear only early in the day; in such she is never seen by men. So, though there was no witness near, she had folded her arms on [pg 5] her breast, in order to add a veil to her low garment. Her hair, not spread out in loose ringlets but twisted in little knots and wrapped in small white curl-papers, marvellously adorned her head, for in the sunlight it shone like a crown on the image of a saint. Her face could not be seen, for she had turned towards the meadow, and with her eyes was seeking some one far off, below her. She caught sight of him, laughed, and clapped her hands; like a white bird she flew from the wall to the turf, and flashed through the garden, over stiles and flowers, and over a board supported on the wall of the chamber; before the young man was aware, she had flown in through the window, glittering, swift, and light as a moonbeam. Humming to herself, she seized the gown and ran to the mirror; suddenly she saw the youth, and the gown fell from her hands and her face grew pale with fright and wonder. The face of the traveller flamed with a rosy blush, as a cloud when it is touched with the morning glow; the modest youth half closed his eyes and hid them with his hand; he wished to speak and ask for pardon, but only bowed and stepped back. The maiden uttered a pitiful, indistinct cry, like a child frightened in its sleep; the traveller looked up in alarm, but she was there no longer; he departed in confusion and felt the loud beating of his heart; he knew not whether this strange meeting should cause him amusement or shame or joy.

Meanwhile in the farmhouse they had not failed to notice that some new guest had driven up before the porch. They had already taken the horses to the stable and already, as befits an honourable house, had given them generously of oats and hay, for the Judge 9 was never willing to adopt the new fashion of sending a guest's [pg 6] horse to a Jew's inn. The servants had not come out to welcome the traveller, but do not think that in the Judge's mansion service was careless; the servants were waiting until the Seneschal 10 should attire him, who now behind the mansion was arranging for the supper. He took the place of the master, and in his absence was wont himself to welcome and entertain guests, being a distant relative of the master and a friend of the house. Seeing the guest, he stealthily made his way to the farmhouse, for he could not come out to greet the stranger in a homespun dressing-gown; there he put on as quickly as he might his Sunday garment, made ready since early morning, for since morning he had known that at supper he should sit with a multitude of guests.

The Seneschal recognised the traveller from afar, spread out his arms, and with a cry embraced and kissed him. Then began a hurried, confused discourse, in which they were eager to tell the events of many years in a few brief words, mingled, as the tale went forward, with queries, exclamations, and new greetings. When the Seneschal had asked his fill of questions, at the very last he told the story of that day.

"It is good, my Thaddeus," —for so they called the young man, whose first name had been given him in honour of Kosciuszko, as a token that he was born at the time of the war 11 — "it is good, my Thaddeus, that you have returned home this day, just when we have with us so many fair young ladies. Your uncle is thinking of soon celebrating your marriage. You have a wide choice: at our house a numerous company has for days been gathering for the session of the territorial court, to conclude our ancient quarrel with the Count. [pg 7] The Count himself is to arrive to-morrow; the Chamberlain 12 is already here with his wife and daughters. The young men have gone to the wood to amuse themselves shooting, and the old men and the women are looking at the harvest near the wood, where they are doubtless awaiting the young men. Come on, if you wish, and soon we shall meet your dear uncle, the Chamberlain, and the honoured ladies."

The Seneschal and Thaddeus walked along the road towards the wood and could not say enough to each other. The sun was approaching the end of his course in the sky and shone less strongly but more broadly than by day, all reddened, as the healthy face of a husbandman, when, after finishing his work in the fields, he returns to rest: already the gleaming circle was descending on the summit of the grove, and already the misty twilight, filling the tips and the branches of the trees, bound and, as it were, fused the whole forest into one mass, and the grove showed black like an immense building, and the sun red above it like a fire on the roof; then the sun sank; it still shone through the branches, as a candle through the chinks of window shutters; then it was extinguished. And suddenly the scythes that were ringing far and wide among the grain, and the rakes that were being drawn over the meadow, became quiet and still; such were the orders of the Judge, on whose farm work closed with the day. "The Lord of the world knows how long we should toil; when the sun, his workman, descends from heaven, it is time for the husbandman to withdraw from the field." So the Judge was wont to speak, and the will of the Judge was sacred to the honest Steward; for even the waggons on which they had already begun to load the [pg 8] sheaves of grain, went unfilled to the stable; the oxen rejoiced in the unaccustomed lightness of their load.

The whole company was just returning from the grove, gaily, but in order; first the little children with their tutor, then the Judge with the wife of the Chamberlain; beside them the Chamberlain, surrounded by his family; after the older people came the young ladies, with the young men beside them; the young ladies walked a half-step before the young men: so decorum bids. No one there had arranged the order, no one had so placed the gentlemen and the ladies, but each without conscious thought kept the order: for the Judge in his household observed the ancient customs, and never allowed that respect should be neglected for age, birth, intelligence, or office: "By such breeding," said he, "houses and nations win fame, and with its fall, houses and nations go to ruin." So the household and the servants grew accustomed to order; and a passing guest, whether kinsman or stranger, when he visited the Judge, as soon as he had been there a short time, accepted the established ways of which all about him breathed.

Short were the greetings that the Judge bestowed upon his nephew. With dignity he offered him his hand to salute, and kissing him on the temple he gave him a hearty welcome; though out of regard for the guests he talked little with him, one could see from the tears that he quickly wiped away with the sleeve of his kontusz, 13 how he loved young Thaddeus.

After the master all, both men and beasts, were returning home together from the harvest fields and from the grove, from the meadows and from the pastures. Here a flock of bleating sheep squeezed into the [pg 9] lane and raised a cloud of dust; behind them slowly stepped a herd of Tyrolese heifers with brazen bells; there the horses neighing rushed home from the freshly mown meadow. All ran to the well, of which the wooden sweep ceaselessly creaked and filled the trough.

The Judge, though wearied, and though surrounded by guests, did not neglect the weighty duties of his farm, but himself went to the well: at evening a farmer can best see how his stable prospers, and never entrusts that care to servants—for the Judge knew that the master's eye fattens the horse.

The Seneschal and Protazy the Apparitor 14 were standing in the hall, lanterns in hand, and were arguing with some warmth, for in the Seneschal's absence the Apparitor had secretly ordered the supper tables to be carried out from the mansion and to be set up hastily in the old castle of which the remains could be seen near the wood. Why this transfer? The Seneschal made wry faces and begged the Judge's pardon; the Judge was amazed, but the thing had been done; it was already late and difficult to correct it; he preferred to make excuses to his guests and to lead them to the ruins. On the way the Apparitor kept explaining to the Judge why he had altered his master's arrangements: on the farm no room was spacious enough for so many guests—and guests of such high station; in the castle the great hall was still well preserved, the vaulted roof was whole—to be sure one wall was cracked and the windows were without panes, but in summer that would do no harm; the nearness of the cellars was convenient for the servants. So speaking, he winked at the Judge; it was evident from his mien that he had other, more important reasons, but concealed them.
[pg 10]
The castle stood two thousand paces from the mansion, of stately architecture, and of imposing bulk, the ancestral home of the ancient house of the Horeszkos. The owner had perished at the time of the disorders in the country; 15 the domain had been entirely ruined by the sequestrations of the government, by the carelessness of the guardians, and by the verdicts of the courts; part had fallen to distant relatives on the female side, the rest had been divided among the creditors. No one wished to take the castle, for a simple gentleman could hardly afford the cost of maintaining it; but the Count, a rich young noble and a distant relative of the Horeszkos, when he became of age and returned home from his travels to live near by, took a fancy to the walls, explaining that they were of Gothic architecture, though the Judge from documents tried to convince him that the architect was from Wilno and not a Goth. At all events the Count wished to have the castle, and suddenly the same desire seized the Judge, no one could tell why. They began a suit in the district court, then in the court of appeal, before the Senate, again in the district court and before the governor's council; finally after great expense of money, and numerous decrees, the case returned again to the court of domains.

The Apparitor said rightly that in the hall of the castle there was room both for the gentlemen of the bar and for the invited guests. This hall was as large as a refectory, and it had a vaulted roof supported on pillars, and a stone flooring; the walls were unadorned, but clean. Upon them were fastened the horns of stags and roes, with inscriptions telling where and when these trophies had been obtained; there too were engraved the armorial bearings of the hunters, with the name of [pg 11] each written out in full; on the ceiling gleamed the Half-Goat, the arms of the Horeszkos.

The guests entered in order and stood about the table. The Chamberlain took his place at the head; this honour befitted him from his age and his office; advancing to it he bowed to the ladies, the old men, and the young men. By him took his station a Bernardine monk, a collector of alms for his order, and next the Bernardine was the Judge. The Bernardine pronounced a short grace in Latin, brandy was passed to the gentlemen; then all sat down, and silently and with relish they ate the cold Lithuanian salad of beet leaves. 16

Thaddeus, though a young man, by virtue of being a guest, had a seat at the head of the table, with the ladies, beside His Honour the Chamberlain; between him and his uncle there remained one empty place, which seemed to be awaiting some one. The uncle often glanced at this place and then at the door, as though he were assured of some one's coming and desired it; and Thaddeus followed his uncle's glance to the door, and with him fixed his eyes on the empty seat. Marvellous to relate, the places round about were occupied by maidens on whom a prince might have gazed without shame, all of them high born, and every one young and pretty; but Thaddeus kept looking at that spot where no one was sitting. That place was a riddle; young people love riddles. Distraught, to his fair neighbour the Chamberlain's daughter he said only a few scattering words; he did not change her plate or fill her glass, and he did not entertain the young ladies with polite discourse such as would have shown his city breeding. That one empty place allured him and dazzled him; it was no longer empty, for he had filled it with his [pg 12] thoughts. Over that place ran a thousand guesses, as after a rain, little toads hop hither and thither over a lonely meadow; among them one form was queen, like a water lily on a fair day raising its white brow above the surface of a lake.

The third course was being served. The Chamberlain, pouring a drop of wine into Panna Rosa's glass and passing a plate of cucumbers to his younger daughter, said: "I must wait on you myself, my dear daughters, though I am old and clumsy." Thereat several young men started up from the table and served the young ladies. The Judge, throwing a sidelong glance at Thaddeus and adjusting somewhat the sleeves of his kontusz, poured out some Hungarian wine and spoke thus:—

"To-day, as the new fashion bids us, we send our young men to the capital to study, and I do not deny that our sons and grandsons have more book learning than their elders; but each day I perceive how our young men suffer because there are no schools that teach how to conduct oneself in polite society. Of old, the young gentry went to the courts of the lords; I myself was for ten years a member of the household of the Wojewoda,26 the father of His Honour the Chamberlain." (As he said this he pressed the Chamberlain's knees.) "By his counsels he fitted me for the public service, and did not dismiss me from his care until he had made a man of me. In my home his memory will ever be dear; each day do I pray God for his soul. If at his court I profited less than others, and since my return have been ploughing the fields at home, while others, more worthy of the regard of the Wojewoda, have since attained the highest offices in the land, at least this [pg 13] much I profited, that in my home no one will ever reproach me for failing to show respect or courtesy to all—and boldly do I say it, courtesy is not an easy science, nor one of slight account. Not easy, for it is not confined to moving one's legs gracefully in bowing or to greeting with a smile each man one meets; for such fashionable courtesy seems to me that of a merchant, not that of old Poland, nor that of a true gentleman. Courtesy should be extended to all, but for each it is different; for not without courtesy is the love of children for their parents, or the regard paid by a husband to his wife in society, or that of a master for his servants, and yet each sort of courtesy has its distinctive mark. One must study long in order without mistake to pay to each his due respect. And our elders did study: in noble mansions the discourse furnished the listener a living history of his land, and the talk among the gentry formed the household annals of the county. Thereby a brother gentleman was made to feel that all knew of him and did not esteem him lightly; so a gentleman kept a watch upon his own habits. But to-day you must ask no man who he is or of what parents, with whom he has lived or what he has done. Every man enters where he will, so long as he be not a government spy or a beggar. As Vespasian did not smell of money, 17 and cared not to know whence it came, from what hands or lands, so now they care not to know a man's family or habits. It suffices that he be of full weight and that the stamp be seen upon him; thus men value friends as Jews value money."

While speaking thus, the Judge surveyed his guests in order; for though he always spoke fluently and with discretion, he knew that the youth of to-day are impatient, [pg 14] that they are bored by long speeches, even by the most eloquent. But all were listening in deep silence; the Judge with his eye seemed to take counsel of the Chamberlain; the Chamberlain did not interrupt the speech by praise, but with a frequent nodding of his head he assented to it. The Judge ceased speaking, the other with a nod begged him to continue. So the Judge filled the Chamberlain's beaker and his own cup, and spoke further:—

"Courtesy is no slight thing: when a man learns to respect as is fitting the age, birth, virtues, and ways of others, at the same time he comes to recognise also his own dignity; as in weighing with scales, in order to learn our own weight, we must put some one in the opposite pan. And worthy of your especial attention is the courtesy that young men owe to the fair sex, above all when the distinction of family, and the generosity of fortune heighten inborn charms and talents. Through courtesy is the path to the affections, and by it houses are joined in splendid union—thus thought our elders. And therefore——"

Here the Judge with a sudden turn of his head nodded at Thaddeus and bestowed on him a stern glance; it was evident that he had now reached the climax of his speech.

Thereupon the Chamberlain tapped his golden snuffbox and said:—

"My dear Judge, in former times it was still worse. At present I know not whether the fashion changes even us old men, or whether the young men are better than before, but I see less cause of scandal. Ah, I remember the times when on our fatherland there first descended the fashion of imitating the French; when [pg 15] suddenly brisk young gentlemen from foreign lands swarmed in upon us in a horde worse than the Nogai Tatars, abusing here, in our country, God, the faith of our fathers, our law and customs, and even our ancient garments. Pitiable was it to behold the yellow-faced puppies, talking through their noses—and often without noses—stuffed with brochures and newspapers of various sorts, and proclaiming new faiths, laws, and toilets. That rabble had a mighty power over minds, for when the Lord God sends punishment on a nation he first deprives its citizens of reason. And so the wiser heads dared not resist the fops, and the whole nation feared them as some pestilence, for within itself it already felt the germs of disease. They cried out against the dandies but took pattern by them; they changed faith, speech, laws, and costumes. That was a masquerade, the licence of the Carnival season, after which was soon to follow the Lent of slavery.

"I remember,—though then I was but a little child,—when the Cup-Bearer's son came to visit my father in the district of Oszmiana, in a French carriage; he was the first man in Lithuania who wore French clothes. Everybody ran after him as after a buzzard;18 they envied the house before the threshold of which the Cup-Bearer's son halted his two-wheeled chaise, which passed by the French name of cabriolet. Within it sat two dogs instead of footmen, and on the box a German, lean as a board; his long legs, thin as hop-poles, were clad in stockings, and shoes with silver buckles; the tail of his wig was tied up in a sack. The old men burst out laughing at that equipage, but the country boors crossed themselves, saying that a Venetian devil was travelling abroad in a German carriage. To describe the [pg 16] son of the Cup-Bearer himself would be a long story; suffice it to say that he seemed to us an ape or a parrot in a great peruke, which he liked to compare to the Golden Fleece, and we to elf-locks. 19 At that time even if any one felt that the Polish costume was more comely than this aping of a foreign fashion, he kept silent, for the young men would have cried out that he was hindering culture, that he was checking progress, that he was a traitor. Such at that time was the power of prejudice!

"The Cup-Bearer's son announced that he was going to reform us and introduce order and civilisation; he proclaimed to us that some eloquent Frenchmen had made a discovery, that all men are equal—though this was written long ago in Holy Writ and every parish priest prates of it from the pulpit. The doctrine was ancient, the question was of its application. But at that time such general blindness prevailed that they did not believe the oldest things in the world if they did not read of them in a French newspaper. The Cup-Bearer's son, despite equality, had taken the title of marquis. It is well known that titles come from Paris, and at that time the title of marquis was in fashion there; however, when in the course of years the fashion changed, this same marquis took the title of democrat; finally, with the changing fashion, under Napoleon, the democrat arrived from Paris as a baron; if he had lived longer, perhaps he would have shifted again, and instead of a baron would have called himself once more a democrat. For Paris boasts of frequent changes of fashion, and whatever a Frenchman invents is dear to a Pole.

"Thank God, that now if our young men go abroad, [pg 17] it is no longer for clothes, nor to seek new laws in wretched printing shops, nor to study eloquence in the cafes of Paris. For now Napoleon, a clever man and a swift, gives us no time to prate or to search for new fashions. Now there is the thunder of arms, and the hearts of us old men exult that the renown of the Poles is spreading so widely throughout the world; glory is ours already, and so we shall soon again have our Republic. From laurels always springs the tree of liberty. Only it is sad that for us the years drag on so long in idleness, and they are always so far away. It is so long to wait!, and even news is so scarce. Father Robak," 20 he said in a lower voice to the Bernardine, "I have heard that you have received tidings from beyond the Niemen; perhaps you know something of our army?"

"Not a thing," answered Robak with indifference; it was evident that he had not enjoyed listening to the talk. "Politics bore me; if I have a letter from Warsaw, it is on business of our Order. That is the affair of us Bernardines; why should we talk of that at supper? Here there are laymen, whom such things do not concern."

So speaking, he looked askance at a Muscovite guest who was sitting among the banqueters; this was Captain Rykov, an old soldier who was quartered in a village hard by, and whom the Judge for courtesy's sake had invited to the supper. Rykov ate with a relish, and had been mixing little in the conversation, but at the mention of Warsaw he raised his head and said, with a Russian accent, and with a few slips of expression:—

"Chamberlain! Ah, sir, you are always curious about [pg 18] Bonaparte, and are always eager to hear from Warsaw. Ah, Fatherland! I am no spy, but I understand Polish.—Fatherland! I feel it all, I understand! You are Poles, I am Russian; just now we are not fighting—there is an armistice, so we are eating and drinking together. Often at the outposts our fellows will be chatting with the French and drinking brandy; when they cry 'Hurrah,' then comes the cannonading. There's a Russian proverb: 'I love the man I fight with; clasp your sweetheart to your heart, but beat her like a fur cloak.' I say we shall have war. An adjutant of the staff came to Major Plut 21 the day before yesterday: 'Get ready for the march!' We shall move either against the Turks or the French. O, that Bonaparte is a rare bird! Now that Suvorov is gone maybe he will give us a drubbing. In our regiment we used to say, when we were marching against the French, that Bonaparte was a wizard 22 —well, so was Suvorov a wizard too, so there were tricks against tricks. Once in battle, where did he disappear? To look for Bonaparte! But he changed himself into a fox, so Suvorov became a hound; so Bonaparte changed again into a cat; they started to claw each other, but Suvorov became a pony. Now notice what happened with Bonaparte finally——"

Here Rykov broke off and began to eat. At that moment the servant came in with the fourth course, and suddenly the side doors were opened.

A new guest, young and fair, came in; her sudden appearance, her beauty and her carriage, her toilet, all attracted the eye. Everybody greeted her; evidently all except Thaddeus were acquainted with her. Her figure was fine and elegant, her bosom charming; her gown was of pink silk, low cut, and with short sleeves, [pg 19] the collar of lace. In her hands she twirled a fan for mere pastime, for it was not hot; the gilded fan as it waved spread around it a dense shower of sparks. Her head was like a milliner's model; the hair was frizzled and curled and intertwined with pink ribbons; amid them a diamond, half hidden from sight, shone like a star in the tail of a comet. In a word it was a holiday toilet; several whispered that it was too elaborate for the country and for every day. Though her skirt was short, the eye could not see her feet, for she ran very swiftly, or rather she glided, like the puppets that on the Festival of the Three Kings boys hidden in booths slide to and fro. She ran in and, greeting all with a slight bow, was about to seat herself in the place reserved for her. That was difficult, for there were no chairs for the guests, who were sitting in four rows on four benches; either a whole row must move or she must climb over the bench. Skilfully she managed to squeeze in between two benches, and then between the table and the line of those seated at it she rolled on like a billiard ball. In her course she brushed past our young man, and, catching a flounce on some one's knee, slipped a little, and in her distraction supported herself on the shoulder of Thaddeus. Politely begging his pardon, she took her seat between him and his uncle, but she ate nothing; she only fanned herself, or twirled the handle of her fan, or adjusted her lace collar, or with a light touch of her hand smoothed her ringlets and the knots of bright ribbon among them.

This interruption of the conversation had lasted some four minutes. Meanwhile there had begun at the end of the table first gentle murmurs and then conversation in a subdued voice; the men were discussing their day's [pg 20] hunting. Between the Assessor 23 and the Notary 24 there had arisen a stubborn and more and more noisy dispute over a bobtailed hound, in the ownership of which the Notary took pride, maintaining that this dog had caught the hare; while the Assessor was demonstrating, despite the arguments of the Notary, that that honour belonged to his own hound Falcon. They asked the opinion of the others; so all in turn took sides either for Bobtail or for Falcon, some as experts, others as eyewitnesses. At the opposite end of the table the Judge was saying in a low voice to his new neighbour: "I beg your pardon, we had to sit down, it was impossible to put off supper till later; the guests were hungry, for they had had a long walk over the fields; and I thought that to-day you would not join us at table." After these words he talked quietly with the Chamberlain over a full winecup about political affairs.

Since both ends of the table were thus occupied, Thaddeus gazed intently at the unknown lady. He remembered that when he had first glanced at the place he had at once guessed for whom it was destined. He blushed, and his heart beat faster than its wont. So he now beheld, the solution of the mystery upon which he had pondered. So it had been ordained that by his side should sit that beauty whom he had seen in the twilight; to be sure she now seemed of taller stature, for she was in full dress, and costume may make one seem larger or smaller. But the hair of the first had seemed short and of a bright golden colour, while this lady had long, curling, raven tresses. The colour must have come from the sun's rays, which at evenfall shed a glow over everything. At that time he had not noticed the girl's face—she had vanished too quickly. But thought is [pg 21] wont to guess a lovely face; he had imagined that surely she must have black eyes, a fair complexion, and lips as red as twin cherries; in his neighbour he found such a face, such eyes, and such lips. In age perhaps there was the greatest difference; the little gardener had seemed to him a young girl, this lady was already of ripe years. But youth never asks beauty for its baptismal certificate; to a young man every woman is young, to a lad every beauty seems of his own age, and to an innocent boy every sweetheart seems a maiden.

Thaddeus, though he was now almost twenty years of age, and from childhood had dwelt in Wilno, a large city, had been under the charge of a priest, who looked after him and brought him up in the rules of strict old-fashioned virtue. Therefore Thaddeus brought home to his native heath a pure soul, a lively imagination, and an innocent heart, but at the same time no small desire to sow his wild oats. He had some time ago resolved that he would permit himself to enjoy in the country his long forbidden liberty; he knew that he was handsome, he felt himself young and vigorous; and as an inheritance from his parents he had received health and good spirits. His name was Soplica; all the Soplicas, as is well known, are large, strong, powerful men, apt at the soldier's trade, but less diligent over their books.

Thaddeus had not degenerated from his forebears; he rode well on horseback and walked well; he was not dull, but he had made little progress in his studies, though his uncle had spared nothing on his education. He liked better to shoot, or to practise with a sabre; he knew that they had intended to fit him for the army, that his father in his will had expressed this desire; while sitting in school he yearned constantly for the [pg 22] sound of the drum. But his uncle had suddenly changed his first intentions, and had sent him word to come home and to marry and take over the farming; he had promised to give him at first a little village, and later the whole estate.

All these virtues and good qualities of Thaddeus had attracted the gaze of his neighbour, an observant woman. She had measured his tall and shapely form, his strong shoulders, his broad chest, and she looked into his face, on which a blush rose as often as the young man met her eyes. For he had already entirely recovered from his first timidity, and looked on her with a bold glance, in which fire blazed; even so did she gaze on him, and their four pupils glowed opposite one another as do candles at the Advent mass.

She started a conversation with him in French. Thaddeus had returned from town, from school: so she asked his opinions about new books and authors, and from his answers derived new questions; she went so far as to speak of painting, of music, of dancing—even of sculpture! She proved herself equally familiar with the pencil, with tunes, and with books, until Thaddeus was petrified by so much learning, and feared that he might become the butt of ridicule, and stammered like a little lad before his teacher. Luckily the teacher was beautiful and lenient; his neighbour guessed the cause of his perturbation, and shifted the talk to less deep and difficult subjects, to the cares and troubles of existence in the country, and how one must amuse oneself, and how divide the time in order to make village life gay and pleasant. Thaddeus answered more boldly, and things went better; in a half-hour they were already fast friends, they even started jests and small [pg 23] quarrels. Finally she placed before him three little balls of bread, three persons to select from; he chose the nearest. The two daughters of the Chamberlain frowned at this; his neighbour laughed, but she did not tell him whom that happy ball was meant to signify.

At the other end of the table they were amusing themselves quite differently, for there the adherents of Falcon, suddenly gathering strength, descended pitilessly on the party of Bobtail. Mighty was the strife; they had not yet eaten the last courses; standing up and drinking, the two factions wrangled. But most terribly was the Notary ruffled—just like a blackcock; when he had once begun, he poured forth his speech without a pause, and adorned it most effectively by his gestures. (The Notary, Pan Bolesta, had once been a lawyer; they called him the preacher, because he was over fond of gestures.) Now he had placed his hands on his sides, extending his elbows backward, and from under his armpits he was thrusting forward his fingers and long nails, thereby representing two leashes of hounds. He was just concluding his speech:—

"Hurrah! The Assessor and I let them go at once, at the very same time, as if the two triggers on a double-barrelled gun had been pressed by one finger. Hurrah! They started, and the hare like an arrow shot into the field; the dogs after him——" (Here as he spoke he ran his hands over the table and with his fingers marvellously imitated the movement of the dogs) "the dogs after him, and they headed him off a bit from the wood. Falcon rushed forward, a fleet dog, but with a poor head; he got the start of Bobtail by so much, a finger's breadth; I knew that he would miss. The hare was no common rogue; he made as if straight for the [pg 24] field, and after him the pack of hounds. The rogue of a hare I Once he knew that the dogs were in a bunch, pst! he went to the right, with a somersault, and after him the stupid hounds; but again, zip! to the left, in just two jumps. The dogs after him, zip! to the left, and my Bobtail, whack!"

Shouting thus the Notary leaned over the table and ran his fingers clear to the other side, and screamed "whack" just over the ear of Thaddeus. Thaddeus and his neighbour, suddenly startled right in the middle of a conversation by this outburst, involuntarily withdrew their heads from each other, like treetops tied together, when the storm parts them; their hands, which had been lying close together under the table, quickly drew apart, and their two faces were clothed with a single blush.

"It is true, my dear Notary," said Thaddeus, in order not to betray his embarrassment, "it is true, without doubt; Bobtail is a finely built hound—if he is equally good at seizing the game."

"Good at seizing!" cried the Notary, "my favourite dog; the idea of his not being good at seizing!"

So Thaddeus once more expressed his pleasure that so handsome a dog had no fault; regretted that he had seen him only as he was returning from the wood, and that he had not had time to appreciate all his good points.

At this the Assessor trembled, dropped his wine-glass from his hand, and levelled at Thaddeus the glance of a basilisk. The Assessor was less noisy and less given to gestures than the Notary, thinner and shorter; but he was terrible at masquerade, ball, or village diet, for they said of him that he had a sting in his tongue. He [pg 25] could make up such witty jests that you might have had them printed in the almanac; they were all so malicious and pointed. He had formerly been a man of property, but he had entirely squandered his inheritance from his father, and his brother's estate as well, through cutting a figure in high society; now he had entered the service of the government, in order to be of some importance in the district. He was very fond of hunting, both for the sport of it and because the peal of the horn and the sight of the circle of beaters recalled to him the days of his youth, when he had kept many hunters and many famous hounds. Of his whole kennel but two dogs remained, and now they wanted to belittle the glory of one of these! So he approached, and, slowly stroking his side whiskers, said with a laugh—but it was a laugh full of poison:—

"A hound without a tail is like a gentleman without an office. A tail is likewise a great help to a hound in running. And do you, sir, regard the lack of one as a proof of excellence? However, we may refer the matter to the judgment of your aunt. Though Pani Telimena has been living in the capital, and has only recently been visiting our neighbourhood, yet she knows more about hunting than do young sportsmen: for knowledge comes of itself with years."

Thaddeus, upon whom this thunderstorm had unexpectedly descended, arose in confusion, and for some moments said nothing, but looked upon his rival more and more terribly and sternly; at that moment by great good luck the Chamberlain sneezed twice. "Vivat!" cried everybody; he bowed to the company, and slowly tapped his snuff-box with his fingers. The snuffbox was of gold, set with diamonds, and in the middle of it was [pg 26] a portrait of King Stanislaw. 25 The king himself had given it to the father of the Chamberlain; after his father the Chamberlain bore it worthily; whenever he tapped upon it, it was a sign that he wished to have the floor for a speech. All became silent, no one dared open his lips. He spoke:—

"Honoured gentlemen, my beloved brothers, the woods and meadows alone are the hunter's forum, therefore such matters I will not pass upon within doors, but I will dissolve our sitting until to-morrow, and will not permit further argument from either faction today. Apparitor, call the case for to-morrow in the field! To-morrow the Count too will be here with all his hunting train, and you, my neighbour Judge, will ride out with us, and Pani Telimena, and the young ladies and gentlemen; in a word we will form a great official hunting party, and the Seneschal, too, will not deny us his companionship."

So saying he offered his snuffbox to the old man.

The Seneschal had been sitting at the corner among the hunters; he had been listening with closed eyes, but had said not a word, although the young men had often inquired his opinion, for no one understood hunting better than he. He kept silent, weighed in his fingers the pinch of snuff that he had taken from the box, and meditated long before he finally used it; he sneezed until the whole room echoed, and shaking his head, he said with a bitter smile:—

"O how this saddens and amazes me in my old age! What would the hunters of old times say of this, if they should see that amid so many gentlemen, in so large a gathering, disputes over a hound's tail had to be debated? What would old Rejtan say of this were he to [pg 27] come to life again? He would go back to Lachowicze and lay himself in his grave. What would the old wojewoda Niesiolowski 26 say, a man who still has the finest kennel in the world, and maintains in lordly wise two hundred hunters, and who has a hundred waggon-loads of nets in his castle of Woroncza, and yet for so many years has been abiding like a monk within his house? No one can persuade him to accept an invitation to hunt; he refused even Bialopiotrowicz 27 himself! For what would he capture at your hunts? It would be fine glory, if such a gentleman, in accordance with the present fashion, should ride out against rabbits! In my time, sir, in hunter's language, the boar, the bear, the elk, the wolf were known as noble beasts, but beasts without tusks, horns, or claws were left for hired servants or farm labourers. No gentleman would ever consent to take in hand a musket that had been put to shame by having small shot sprinkled in it! To be sure they kept hounds, for when they were returning from a hunt it might happen that some wretched hare would start up from beneath a steed; then they let loose the pack at it for sport, and the little lads chased it on ponies before the eyes of their parents, who hardly deigned to look on such a chase, much less to quarrel over it! So I beg that Your Honour the Chamberlain will deign to recall your commands, and will forgive me that I cannot ride to such a hunting party, and never will set foot in one! My name is Hreczecha, and since the days of King Lech 28 no Hreczecha has ever ridden out after hares."

Here the laughter of the young men drowned the speech of the Seneschal. They rose from the table; the Chamberlain moved first; this honour befitted him from his [pg 28] age and his office; as he advanced he bowed to the ladies, the old men, and the young men. After him went the Collector of Alms, and the Judge alongside the Bernardine; at the threshold the Judge offered his arm to the Chamberlain's wife, Thaddeus to Telimena, the Assessor to the Carver's daughter, and finally the Notary to Panna Hreczecha, the daughter of the Seneschal.

Thaddeus went to the stable with several of the guests, and felt disturbed, glum, and morose; he thought over all the events of the day, the meeting and the supper by the side of his fair neighbour—and in particular the word "aunt" buzzed continually in his ear like an importunate fly. He would have liked to learn more about Pani Telimena from the Apparitor, but he could not catch him; nor did he see the Seneschal, for immediately after supper all had followed the guests out, as befits serving men, and had gone to prepare the rooms for rest. The older people and the ladies slept in the mansion; the young men Thaddeus, as the host's representative, had been directed to take to the stable, where they were to sleep on the hay.

Within a half-hour it was as quiet on the whole estate as in a cloister after the bell for prayer; the silence was interrupted only by the voice of the night watchman. All were asleep. The Judge alone did not close his eyes; as the head of the estate, he was thinking over a walking party, and the coming entertainment within the house. He gave orders to the stewards, the overseers, and the grain-wardens; to the scribes, the housekeeper, the huntsmen, and the grooms; and he had to look through all the day's accounts; finally he told the Apparitor that he wished to undress. The [pg 29] Apparitor undid his belt, a belt from Sluck, 29 a massive belt, on which glittered tassels thick as helmet-plumes; on one side it was gold brocade with purple flowers, on the reverse black silk with silver cross-stripes. Such a belt may be worn equally well on either side, golden for a holiday, and black for mourning. The Apparitor alone knew how to undo and fold up this belt; he took this trouble upon himself and ended with the following speech:—

"Where was the harm that I moved the tables to the old castle? No one has lost thereby, and you, sir, will perhaps gain, for the suit now before the court concerns the ownership of that castle. From this day we have acquired a right to the castle, and notwithstanding all the fury of the opposite side I will prove that we have taken the castle into our possession. For whoever invites guests to supper in a castle proves that he holds possession there—or takes it; we will even summon the opposite side as witnesses: I remember such happenings in my time."

The Judge was already asleep. So the Apparitor quietly went out into the hall, seated himself by a candle, and took from his pocket a little book that always served him as a Prayer Book, 30 and from which he never was parted, either at home or on a journey. It was the Court Calendar; 31 there in order were written down cases which years ago the Apparitor had proclaimed with his own voice, before the authorities, or of which he had managed to learn later. To common men the Calendar seems a mere list of names, but to the Apparitor it was a succession of magnificent pictures. So he read and mused: Oginski and Wizgird, the Dominicans and Rymsza, Rymsza and Wysogierd, Radziwill and [pg 30] Wereszczaka, Giedrojc and Rodultowski, Obuchowicz and the Jewish commune, Juraha and Piotrowski, Maleski and Mickiewicz, and finally Count Horeszko and Soplica; and, as he read, he called forth from these names the memory of mighty cases, and all the events of the trial; and before his eyes stand the court, plaintiff, defendant, and witnesses; and he beholds himself, how in a white smock and dark blue kontusz he stands before the tribunal, with one hand on his sabre and the other on the table, summoning the two parties. "Silence!" he calls. Thus dreaming and finishing his evening prayer, gradually the last court apparitor in Lithuania fell asleep.

Such were the amusements and disputes of those days in the quiet Lithuanian village, while the rest of the world was swimming in tears and blood, and while that man, the god of war, surrounded by a cloud of regiments, armed with a thousand cannon, harnessing to his chariot golden eagles beside those of silver, 32 was flying from the deserts of Libya to the lofty Alps, casting thunderbolt on thunderbolt, at the Pyramids, at Tabor, Marengo, Ulm, and Austerlitz. Victory and Conquest ran before and after him. The glory of so many exploits, heavy with the names of heroes, went roaring from the Nile to the North, until at the shores of the Niemen it was beaten back as from crags by the Muscovite lines that defended Lithuania as with walls of iron against tidings terrible for Russia as the plague.

And yet now and then, like a stone from the sky, news came even to Lithuania; now and then an old man, lacking a hand or a foot, who was begging his bread, would stand and cast cautious eyes around, when he had received alms. If he saw no Russian soldiers in the yard, [pg 31] or Jewish caps, or red collars, then he would confess who he was: he was a member of the Polish legions, and was bringing back his old bones to that fatherland which he could no longer defend. Then how all the family—how even the servants embraced him, choking with tears! He would seat himself at the board and tell of history more strange than fable; he would relate how General Dombrowski 33 was making efforts to penetrate from the Italian land into Poland, how he was gathering his countrymen on the plains of Lombardy; how Kniaziewicz 34 was issuing commands from the Roman Capitol, and how, as a victor, he had cast in the eyes of the French an hundred bloody standards torn from the descendants of the Cæsars; how Jablonowski 35 had reached the land where the pepper grows and where sugar is produced, and where in eternal spring bloom fragrant woods: with the legion of the Danube there the Polish general smites the negroes, but sighs for his native soil.

The words of the old man would spread secretly through the village; the lad who heard them would vanish suddenly from home, would steal mysteriously through the forests and swamps, pursued by the Muscovites, would leap to hiding in the Niemen, and beneath its flood swim to the shore of the Grand Duchy of Warsaw, where he would hear sweet words of greeting, "Welcome, comrade!" But before he departed, he would climb a stony hill and call to the Muscovites across the Niemen: "Until we meet again!" Thus there had stolen away Gorecki, Pac, and Obuchowicz; Piotrowski, Obolewski, Rozycki, Janowicz, the Mirzejewskis, Brochocki and the brothers Bernatowicz, Kupsc, Gedymin, and others whom I will not enumerate; [pg 32] they had abandoned their kinsmen and their beloved land, and their estates, which were seized for the Tsar's treasury.

Sometimes there came to Lithuania a collector of alms from a foreign convent, and after he became more closely acquainted with the lords of an estate, he would show them a gazette, which he cut out from his scapulary. In it would be set forth the number of soldiers and the names of all the leaders in every legion; with an account of the victory of each or of his doom. After many years, a family would have news for the first time of the life, the glory, or the death of a son; the house would put on mourning, but dared not tell for whom they mourned. The neighbours merely guessed the news, and only the quiet grief of the gentry, or their quiet joy, was the gazette of the peasants.

Robak was probably just such a mysterious collector of alms; he often conversed apart with the Judge, and always after these talks tidings of some sort spread abroad in the neighbourhood. The bearing of the Bernardine betrayed the fact that this monk had not always worn a cowl, and had not grown old within cloister walls. Over his right ear, somewhat above his temple, he had a scar as broad as one's palm, where the skin had been sheared off; and on his chin was the recent trace of a lance or bullet; these wounds he had surely not received while reading the missal. But not merely his grim glance and his scars, even his movements and his voice had something soldierlike about them.

At the Mass, when with uplifted arms he turned from the altar to the people, in order to pronounce, "The Lord be with you," he often turned as skilfully—with a [pg 33] single movement—as if he were executing a right-about-face at the command of his captain; and he pronounced the words of the liturgy to the people in the same tone as an officer standing before a squadron: the boys who served him at the mass remarked this. Robak was also better versed in political affairs than in the lives of the saints; and when he was riding about gathering alms he often tarried in the district town. He had a multitude of interests: now he received letters, which he never opened in the presence of strangers; now he sent off messengers, but whither and for what he did not say; often he stole out by night to the squires' mansions, and continually whispered with the gentry; he trudged through all the neighbouring villages, and in the taverns talked not a little with the village boors, and always of what was going on in foreign lands. Now he came to arouse the Judge, who had already been an hour asleep; surely he had some tidings.

[pg 34]

BOOK II.—THE CASTLE

ARGUMENT

Hunting the hare with hounds—A guest in the castle—The last of the retainers tells the story of the last of the Horeszkos—A glance into the garden—The girl among the cucumbers—Breakfast—Pani Telimena's St. Petersburg story—New outbreak of the quarrel over Bobtail and Falcon—The intervention of Robak—The Seneschal's speech—The wager—Off for mushrooms.

Who among us does not remember the years when, as a young lad, with his gun on his shoulder, he went whistling into the fields, where no rampart, no fence blocked his path; where, when you overstepped a boundary strip, you did not recognise it as belonging to another! For in Lithuania a hunter is like a ship upon the sea; wherever he will, and by whatever path he will, he roams far and wide! Like a prophet he gazes on the sky, where in the clouds there are many signs that the hunter's eye can see; or like an enchanter he talks with the earth, which, though deaf to city-dwellers, whispers into his ear with a multitude of voices.

There a land rail calls from the meadow—it is vain to seek it, for it flees away through the grass like a pike in the Niemen; there above your head sounds the bell of early spring, the lark, hidden as deeply in the sky; there an eagle rustles with its broad wings through the airy heights, spreading terror among sparrows as a comet among stars; or a hawk, hanging beneath the [pg 35] clear blue vault, flutters its wings like a butterfly impaled on a pin, until, catching sight in the meadow of a bird or a hare, it swoops upon it from on high like a falling star.

When will the Lord God permit us to return from our wanderings, and again to dwell upon our ancestral fields, and to serve in the cavalry that makes war on rabbits, or in the infantry that bears arms against birds; to know no other weapons than the scythe and the sickle, and no other gazettes than the household accounts!

Over Soplicowo arose the sun, and it already fell on the thatched roofs, and through the chinks stole into the stable; and over the fresh, dark-green, fragrant hay of which the young men had made them a bed there streamed twinkling, golden bands from the openings of the black thatch, like ribbons from a braid of hair; and the sun teased the faces of the sleepers with its morning beams, like a village girl awakening her sweetheart with an ear of wheat. Already the sparrows had begun to hop and twitter beneath the thatch, already the gander had cackled thrice, and after it, as an echo, the ducks and turkeys resounded in chorus, and one could hear the bellowing of the kine on their way to the fields.

The young men had arisen; Thaddeus still lay dozing, for he had gone to sleep last of all. From the supper of the day before he had come back so disquieted that at cockcrow he had not yet closed his eyes, and on his couch he tossed about so violently that he sank into the hay as into water; at last he fell sound asleep. Finally a cool breeze blew in his eyes, when the creaking doors of the stable were opened with a crash; and the Bernardine, Father Robak, came in with his belt of [pg 36] knotted cord, calling out, "Surge, puer!" and plying jocosely over his shoulders his knotted belt.

Already in the yard could be heard the cries of the hunters; horses were being led forth, waggons were coming up; hardly could the yard contain such a throng. The horns sounded, they opened the kennels. The pack of hounds rushing out whined joyfully; seeing the chargers of the huntsmen and the leashes of their keepers, the dogs as if mad scampered about the enclosure, then ran and put their necks in the collars. All this foreboded a very fine hunt; at last the Chamberlain gave the order to proceed.

The hunters started slowly, one after another, but beyond the gate they spread out in a long line; in the middle of it rode side by side the Assessor and the Notary, and though they occasionally cast a malicious glance at each other, they conversed in friendly fashion, like men of honour, who were on their way to settle a mortal quarrel; no one from their words could have remarked their mutual hatred: the Notary led Bobtail, the Assessor Falcon. The ladies in carriages brought up the rear; the young men, galloping alongside near the wheels, talked with the ladies.

Father Robak walked with slow steps about the yard, finishing his morning prayers, but he glanced at Thaddeus, frowned, smiled, and finally motioned to him with his finger. When Thaddeus rode up, Robak with his finger on his nose made him a threatening sign; but despite the requests and entreaties of Thaddeus that he would explain to him clearly what he meant, the Bernardine did not deign to answer or even to look at him again; he merely pulled his cowl over his face and finished his prayer: so Thaddeus rode off and joined the guests.

[pg 37]

Just at that instant the hunters were holding their leashes and all were standing motionless in their places; each gave a sign to the other to be silent, and all had turned their eyes to a stone near which the Judge had halted: he had caught sight of the game, and was waving his arms in order to make his orders known. All understood him and stopped, and slowly across the field trotted the Assessor and the Notary; Thaddeus, being nearer, arrived before them, paused beside the Judge, and gazed at the spot to which he was pointing. It was long since he, had been in the field; on the grey expanse it was hard to distinguish the grey rabbit, especially amid the stones. The Judge pointed him out; the poor hare was crouched cowering beneath a stone, pricking up its ears; with a crimson eye it met the gaze of the hunters; as if bewitched, and conscious of its destiny, for very terror it could not turn its eye away from theirs, but beneath the rock crouched dead as a rock. Meanwhile the dust in the field came nearer and nearer, Bobtail was running in his leash and after him the fleet Falcon; then the Assessor and the Notary shouted at once behind them, "At him," and vanished with the dogs in clouds of dust.

While they were thus pursuing the hare, the Count made his appearance near the castle wood. All the neighbours knew that this gentleman could never present himself at the appointed time; to-day also he had overslept, and was therefore in a scolding humour with his servants. Seeing the hunters in the field, he galloped towards them, with the skirts of his long white coat, of English cut, trailing in the wind. Behind him were mounted servants, wearing little black shiny caps like mushrooms, short jackets, striped boots, and white [pg 38] pantaloons; the servants whom the Count thus costumed, in his mansion were called *jockeys*.

The galloping train was rushing towards the meadows, when the Count caught sight of the castle and checked his horse. It was the first time that he had seen the castle so early, and he could not believe that these were the same walls, so wonderful a freshness and beauty had the early morning imparted to the outlines of the building. The Count marvelled at so new a sight. The tower seemed to him twice as high, for it rose up above the early mist; the tin roof was gilded by the sun, and beneath it shone in the sashes fragments of the broken panes, breaking the eastern beams into many-coloured rainbows; the lower stories were wrapped in a mantle of mist that hid from the eye the cracks and huge nicks. The cries of the distant hunters, borne on the winds, echoed several times against the castle walls; you would have sworn that the cry came from the castle, that under the curtain of fog the walls had been restored and were again inhabited.

The Count liked new and unwonted sights, and called them romantic; he used to say that he had a romantic head, but truth to say he was an out-and-out crank. Sometimes when chasing a fox or a hare he would suddenly stop and gaze mournfully at the sky, like a cat when it sees a sparrow on a tall pine; often he wandered through the wood without dog or gun, like a run-away recruit; often he sat by a brook motionless, inclining his head over a stream, like a heron that wants to consume all the fish with its eye. Such were the queer habits of the Count; everybody said that there was some screw loose in him. Yet they respected him, for he was a gentleman of ancient lineage, rich, kind to his [pg 39] peasants, and affable and friendly with his neighbours, even with the Jews.

The Count's horse, which he had turned off the road, trotted straight across the field to the threshold of the castle. The Count, left solitary, sighed, looked at the walls, took out paper and pencil, and began to draw. Thereupon, looking to one side, he saw a dozen steps away a man who seemed likewise a lover of the picturesque; with his head thrown back and his hands in his pockets he seemed to be counting the stones with his eyes. The Count recognised him at once, but he had to call several times before Gerwazy heard his voice. He was a man of gentle birth, a servitor of the ancient lords of the castle, the last that remained of the Horeszkos' retainers; a tall grey-haired old man with a hale and rugged countenance, ploughed by wrinkles, gloomy and stern. Of old he had been famous among the gentry for his jollity; but since the battle in which the owner of the castle had perished, Gerwazy had changed, and now for many years he had not gone to any fair or merry-making; since then no one had heard his witty jests or seen a smile upon his face. He always wore the ancient livery of the Horeszkos, a long yellow coat with skirts, trimmed with lace that now was yellow, but once had doubtless been gilt; around its edge was embroidered in silk their coat of arms, the Half-Goat, and thence all the neighbours had given the title of Half-Goat to the old gentleman. Sometimes also, from a phrase that he incessantly repeated, they called him My-boy, sometimes Notchy, for his whole bald head was notched with scars. His real name was Rembajlo, but no one knew his coat of arms; he called himself the Warden, because years ago he had held that office in the castle. And he [pg 40] still wore a great bunch of keys at his girdle, on a band with a silver tassel, though he had nothing to open with them, for the gates of the castle stood gaping wide. However he had found two folding doors, which he had repaired and set up at his own expense, and he amused himself daily with unlocking these doors. In one of the empty rooms he had chosen a habitation for himself; though he might have lived at the Count's mansion on alms, he refused, for he pined away everywhere else, and felt out of sorts unless he was breathing the air of the castle.

As soon as he caught sight of the Count, he snatched the cap from his head, and honoured with a bow the kinsman of his lords, inclining a great bald pate that shone from afar and was slashed with many a sabre, like a chopping-block. He stroked it with his hand, came up, and, once more bending low, said mournfully:—

"My boy, young master—pardon me, that I speak thus to Your Excellency the Count; such is merely my custom, and it betokens no lack of respect. All the Horeszkos used to say 'My boy'; the last Pantler, my lord, was fond of the phrase. Is it true, my boy, that you grudge a penny for a lawsuit, and are yielding this castle to the Soplicas? I would not believe it, yet so they say all through the district."

Here he gazed at the castle and sighed incessantly.

"What is there strange in that?" said the Count. "The cost is great and the bother greater yet; I want to finish up, but the stupid old gentleman is obstinate; he foresaw that he could tire me out. Indeed I cannot hold out longer, and to-day I shall lay down arms and accept such conditions of agreement as the court may offer me."

[pg 41]

"Of agreement?" cried Gerwazy, "of agreement with the Soplicas? with the Soplicas, my boy?" (So speaking he contorted his lips as though he were amazed at his own words.) "Agreement with the Soplicas! My boy, young master, you are jesting, aren't you? The castle, the abode of the Horeszkos, pass into the hands of the Soplicas! Only deign to dismount from the steed; let us go into the castle; just look it over a bit! You do not know yourself what you are doing; do not refuse; dismount!" And he held the stirrup for him to dismount.

They entered the castle; Gerwazy stopped at the threshold of the hall:—

"Here," he said, "the ancient lords, surrounded by their retinue, used often to sit in their chairs, after they had dined. The lord settled the disputes of the peasants, or good humouredly told various curious stories to his guests, or found amusement in their tales and jests. But in the courtyard the young men fought with staves or broke in the master's Turkish ponies."

They entered the hall.— "In this immense paved hall," said Gerwazy, "you cannot find as many stones as tuns of wine have been broached here in the good old times. The gentry, when invited to a diet, a district assembly, a family holiday, or a hunting party, would pull the casks from the wine cellar on their girdles. During the banquet an orchestra was stationed in that gallery and played the organ36 and various other instruments; and when they proposed a health the trumpets thundered in chorus; the vivats followed in orderly succession, the first to the health of His Majesty the King, then to the Primate, 37 then to Her Majesty the Queen, then to the Gentry and the whole Republic. [pg 42]

But finally, after the fifth glass had been drunk, they always proposed, 'Let us love one another!' a toast unceasing, which, proclaimed while daylight still lingered, thundered on till dawn, when horses and waggons stood ready to carry each guest to his lodging."

They passed through several rooms; Gerwazy in silence now fixed his gaze on the wall and now on the vaulted ceiling, recalling now a sad and now a pleasant memory; sometimes, as though he would say, "All is over," he bowed his head in sorrow; sometimes he waved his hand—evidently even recollection was a torture to him and he wished to drive it off. Finally they paused, in a large room on the upper story, once set with mirrors; to-day the mirrors had been removed and the frames stood empty; the sashes lacked their panes; directly opposite the door was a balcony. Going out on it, the old man bowed his head in thought, and buried his face in his hands; when he uncovered it it wore an expression of great sadness and despair. The Count, though he did not know what all this meant, when he looked at the face of the old man felt a certain emotion, and pressed his hand. The silence lasted for a moment; then the old man broke it, shaking his uplifted right hand:—

"There can be no agreement, my boy, between the Soplica and the blood of the Horeszkos; in you flows the blood of the Horeszkos; you are a kinsman of the Pantler by your mother the Mistress of the Hunt, whose mother was the child of the second daughter of the Castellan,38 who was, as is well known, the maternal uncle of my lord. Now listen to a story of your own family, which took place in this very room and no other.

"My late lord the Pantler, the first gentleman of the [pg 43] district, a rich man and of noted family, had but one child, a daughter beautiful as an angel; so not a few of the gentry and the young notables paid their court to the Pantler's daughter. Among the gentry there was one great roistering blade, a fighting bully, Jacek Soplica, who was called in jest the Wojewoda; in truth he was of great influence in the wojewodeship, for he had absolute authority over the whole family of the Soplicas and controlled their three hundred votes according to his will, although he himself possessed nothing except a little plot of ground, a sabre, and great mustaches that stretched from ear to ear. So the Pantler often invited this ruffian to his place and entertained him there, especially at the time of the district diets, in order to make himself popular among the fellow's kinsmen and partisans. The mustachioed champion was so much elated by his courteous reception that he took it into his head that he might become his host's son-in-law. He came to the castle more and more frequently, even when uninvited, and finally settled down among us as if in his own home, and it seemed that he was on the point of declaring himself; but they remarked this, and served him at the table with black soup. 39 It may very well be that the Pantler's daughter had taken a fancy to the Soplica, but that she kept it a deep secret from her parents.

"Those were the times of Kosciuszko; my lord supported the Constitution of the Third of May,40 and was already gathering the gentry in order to go to the aid of the Confederates, when suddenly the Muscovites encircled the castle by night; there was barely time to fire an alarm signal from the mortar, and to close the gates below and fasten them with a bar. There was no one in the whole castle except the Pantler, myself, and [pg 44] the lady; the cook and two turnspits, all three drunk; the parish priest, a servingman, and four footmen, all bold fellows. So to arms and to the windows! Here a throng of Muscovites came streaming across the terrace to the door, shouting 'Hurrah!' But we met them with bullets from ten guns, 'Back with you!' Nothing could be seen; the servants shot without cessation from the lower stories, and my lord and I from the balcony. All went finely, although amid such great alarm. Twenty guns lay here on this floor; we shot one and they handed us another; the parish priest attended diligently to this task, and the lady and her daughter, and the serving maids: there were but three marksmen, yet the fire was unceasing. The Muscovite boors showered on us a hail of bullets from below; we replied from above sparsely, but with better aim. Three times that rabble pressed up to the door, but each time three of them bit the dust: so they fled behind the storehouse. It was already early dawn; with a cheerful face the Pantler came out on the balcony with his gun, and whenever a Muscovite thrust forth his brow from behind the storehouse he at once fired—and he never missed; each time a black helmet fell on the grass; so that at length scarcely a man crept out from behind the wall. The Pantler, seeing his enemies in confusion, thought of making a sally; he seized his sabre, and, shouting from the balcony, gave orders to the servants; turning to me he said: 'Follow me, Gerwazy!' At that instant there was a shot from behind the gate; the Pantler's speech faltered, he turned red, turned pale, tried to speak, spat blood. Then I perceived that he had received the bullet full in the breast; my lord, tottering, pointed towards the gate. I recognised that villain Soplica, I [pg 45] recognised him! by his stature and by his mustaches I By his shot the Pantler had perished; I saw it! The villain still held his gun raised aloft; smoke still came from the barrel! I sighted at him; the brigand stood as if petrified! Twice I fired, and both shots missed; whether from hatred or from grief, I aimed ill. I heard the shrieks of women; I looked around—my lord was no longer living."

Here Gerwazy paused and burst into a flood of tears; then he concluded:—

"The Muscovites had already broken down the door, for after the death of the Pantler I stood helpless and did not know what was going on around me. Luckily to our help came Parafianowicz, bringing from Horbatowicze two hundred of the Mickiewiczes, who are a numerous and a valiant family of gentry, every man of them, and nourish an immemorial hatred of the Soplicas.

"Thus perished a powerful, pious, and just lord, whose ancestors had held seats in the Senate, worn badges of honour, and carried the hetman's staff of office; a father to his peasants, a brother to the gentry—and he had no son left after him to vow vengeance on his grave! But he had faithful servants; with the blood of his wound I wet my broadsword, called the penknife—you have surely heard of my penknife, famous at every diet, market, and village assembly—and swore to notch it on the shoulders of the Soplicas. I pursued them at diets, forays, and fairs; two I hewed down in a brawl, two others in a duel; one I burnt in a wooden building, when with Rymsza we sacked Korelicze—he was baked like a mudfish; but those whose ears I have cut off I cannot count. One only is left who has not yet received a reminder from me! He is the own dear [pg 46] brother of that mustachioed bully; he still lives, and boasts of his wealth; the edge of his field borders on the Horeszkos' castle; he is respected in the district, he has an office, he is a judge! And you will yield the castle to him? Shall his base feet wipe the blood of my lord from this floor? No! While Gerwazy has but a pennyworth of spirit, and enough strength to move even with one little finger his penknife, which still hangs on the wall, never shall a Soplica get this castle!"

"O!" cried the Count, raising his hands on high, "I had a fair foreboding that I loved these walls, though I knew not that they contained such treasures, so many dramatic memories, and so many tales! When once I seize from the Soplicas the castle of my ancestors, I will establish you within its walls as my burgrave: your tale, Gerwazy, has mightily affected me. I regret that you did not lead me here at the hour of midnight; draped in my cloak I should have sat upon the ruins and you would have told me of bloody deeds. I regret that you have no great gift of narration! Often have I heard and often do I read such traditions; in England and Scotland every lord's castle, in Germany every count's mansion was the theatre of murders! In every ancient, noble, powerful family there is a report of some bloody or treacherous deed, after which vengeance descends as an inheritance to the heirs: in Poland for the first time do I hear of such an incident. I feel that in me flows the blood of the manly Horeszkos, I know what I owe to glory and to my family. So be it I I must break off all negotiations with the Soplica, even though it should come to pistols or to the sword! Honour bids me!"

He spoke, and moved on with solemn steps, and [pg 47] Gerwazy followed in deep silence. Before the gate the Count stopped, mumbling to himself; gazing at the castle he quickly mounted his horse, and thus in distraction he concluded his monologue:—

"I regret that this old Soplica has no wife, or fair daughter whose charms I might adore! If I loved her and could not obtain her hand a new complication would arise in the tale; here the heart, there duty! here vengeance, there love!"

So whispering he applied the spurs, and the horse flew towards the Judge's mansion, just as the hunters came riding out of the wood from the other direction. The Count was fond of hunting: hardly had he perceived the riders, when, forgetting everything, he galloped straight towards them, passing by the yard gate, the orchard, and the fences; but at a turn of the path he looked around and checked his horse near the fence—it was the kitchen garden. Fruit trees planted in rows shaded a broad field; beneath them were the vegetable beds. Here sat a cabbage, which bowed its venerable bald head, and seemed to meditate on the fate of vegetables; there, intertwining its pods with the green tresses of a carrot, a slender bean turned upon it a thousand eyes; here the maize lifted its golden tassels; here and there could be seen the belly of a fat watermelon that had rolled far from its parent stalk into a distant land, as a guest among the crimson beets.

The beds were intersected by furrows; in each trench there stood, as if on guard, ranks of hemp stalks, the cypresses of the vegetable garden, calm, straight, and green; their leaves and their scent served to defend the beds, for through their leaves no serpent dares to press, and their scent kills insects and caterpillars. [pg 48] Farther away towered up the whitish stalks of poppies; on them you might think a flock of butterflies had perched, fluttering their wings, on which flashed, with all the colours of the rainbow, the gleam of precious stones; with so many different, living tints did the poppies allure the eye. Amid the flowers, like the full moon amid the stars, a round sunflower, with a great, glowing face, turned after the sun from the east to the west.

Beside the fence stretched long, narrow, rounded hillocks, free from trees, bushes, and flowers: this was the cucumber patch. They had grown finely; with their great, spreading leaves they covered the beds as with a wrinkled carpet. Amid them walked a girl, dressed in white, sinking up to her knees in the May greenery; stepping down from the beds into the furrows, she seemed not to walk but to swim over the leaves and to bathe in their bright colour. Her head was shaded with a straw hat, from her brow there waved two pink ribbons and some tresses of bright, loose hair; in her hands she held a basket, and her eyes were lowered; her right hand was raised as if to pluck something: as a little girl when bathing tries to catch the fishes that sport with her tiny feet, so she at every instant bent down with her hands and her basket to gather the cucumbers against which she brushed with her foot, or of which her eye caught sight.

The Count, struck with so marvellous a sight, stood still. Hearing from afar the trampling of his comrades, he motioned to them with his hand to stop their horses: they halted. He gazed with outstretched neck, like a long-billed crane that stands apart from the flock, on one leg, keeping guard with watchful eyes, and [pg 49] holding a stone in the other foot, in order not to fall asleep.

The Count was awakened by a pattering on his shoulders and brow; it was the Bernardine, Father Robak, who held aloft in his hand the knotted cords of his belt.

"Will you have cucumbers?" he cried; "Here they are!" [So saying he showed him the knots on his belt, which were shaped like cucumbers. 41] "Look out for danger, in this garden patch there is no fruit for you; nothing will come of it!"

Then he threatened him with his finger, adjusted his cowl, and departed; the Count tarried on the spot a moment more, cursing and yet laughing at this sudden hindrance. He glanced at die garden, but she was no longer in the garden; only her pink ribbon and her white gown flashed through the window. On the garden bed one could see the path by which she had flown, for the green leaves, spurned by her foot in her flight, raised themselves and trembled an instant before they became quiet, like water cut by the wings of a bird. Only on the place where she had been standing, her abandoned willow basket, empty and overturned, was still poised upon the leaves and tossing amid the green waves.

An instant later all was silent and deserted; the Count fixed his eyes on the house and strained his ears; still he mused, and still the huntsmen stood motionless behind him.—Then in the quiet deserted house arose first a murmur, then an uproar and merry cries, as in an empty hive when bees fly back into it: that was a sign that the guests had returned from hunting, and that the servants were busying themselves with breakfast.
[pg 50]
Through all the rooms there reigned a mighty bustle; they were carrying about platters, plates of food and bottles; the men, just as they had come in, in their green suits, walked about the rooms with plates and glasses, and ate and drank; or, leaning against the window casements, they talked of guns, hounds, and hares. The Chamberlain and his family and the Judge were seated at the table; in a corner the young ladies whispered together; there was no such order as is observed at dinners and suppers. In this old-fashioned Polish household this was a new custom; at breakfasts the Judge, though loth, permitted such disorder, but he did not commend it.

There were likewise different dishes for the ladies and for the gentlemen. Here they carried around trays with an entire coffee service, immense trays, charmingly painted with flowers, and on them fragrant, smoking tin pots, and golden cups of Dresden china, and with each cup a tiny little jug of cream. In no other country is there such coffee as in Poland. In Poland, in a respectable household, a special woman is, by ancient custom, charged with the preparation of coffee. She is called the coffee-maker; she brings from the city, or gets from the river barges, 42 berries of the finest sort, and she knows secret ways of preparing the drink, which is black as coal, transparent as amber, fragrant as mocha, and thick as honey. Everybody knows how necessary for coffee is good cream: in the country this is not hard to get; for the coffee-maker, early in the day, after setting her pots on the fire, visits the dairy, and with her own hands lightly skims the fresh flower of the milk into a separate little jug for each cup, that each of them may be dressed in its separate little cap.
[pg 51]
The older ladies had risen earlier and had already drunk their coffee; now they had had made for them a second dish, of warm beer, whitened with cream, in which swam curds cut into little bits.

The gentlemen had their choice of smoked meats; fat half-geese, hams, and slices of tongue—all choice, all cured in home fashion in the chimney with juniper smoke. Finally they brought in stewed beef with gravy 43 as the last course: such was breakfast in the Judge's house.

In adjoining rooms two separate companies had gathered. The older people, grouped about a small table, talked of new ways of farming, and of the new imperial edicts, which were growing more and more severe. The Chamberlain discussed the current rumours of war and based on them conclusions as to politics. The Seneschal's daughter, putting on blue spectacles, amused the Chamberlain's wife by telling fortunes with cards. In the other room the younger men talked over the hunt in a more calm and quiet fashion than was usually the case; for the Assessor and the Notary, both mighty orators, the foremost experts on the chase and the best huntsmen, sat opposite each other glum and angry. Both had set on their hounds well, both had felt certain of victory, when in the middle of the field there turned up a patch of unreaped spring corn belonging to a peasant. Into this the hare fled; Bobtail and Falcon were each about to seize it, when the Judge checked the horsemen at the border of the field; they had to obey, although in great wrath. The dogs returned without their prey, and no one knew for sure whether the beast had escaped or had been caught; no one could guess whether it had fallen into the clutches of [pg 52] Bobtail, or of Falcon, or of both at once. The two sides held different opinions, and the settlement of the quarrel was postponed to the future.

The old Seneschal passed from room to room, glancing absentmindedly about him; he mixed neither in the talk of the hunters nor in that of the old men, and evidently had something else on his mind. He carried a leather flapper; sometimes he would stop, meditate long, and—kill a fly on the wall.

Thaddeus and Telimena, standing on the threshold in the doorway between the rooms, were talking together; no great distance divided them from hearers, so they whispered. Thaddeus now learned that Aunt Telimena was a rich lady, that they were not so near of kin as to be separated by the canons of the Church; that it was not even certain that Aunt Telimena was any blood relation of her nephew, although his uncle called her sister, because their common kindred had once so styled them despite the difference of their years; that later, during her long residence in the capital, she had rendered inestimable services to the Judge; for which reason the Judge greatly respected her, and in society liked, perhaps as a mere whim, to call himself her brother, which Telimena, for friendship's sake, did not forbid him. These confessions lightened the heart of Thaddeus. They also informed each other of other things; and all this happened in one short, brief moment.

But in the room to the right, tempting the Assessor, the Notary casually remarked:—

"I said yesterday that our hunting party could not succeed; it is still too early, the grain is still in the ear, and there are many strips of unreaped spring corn, belonging to the peasants. For this reason the Count [pg 53] did not come, despite our invitation. The Count has an excellent knowledge of the chase; he has often discoursed of the proper time and places for hunting. The Count from childhood up has dwelt in foreign parts, and he says that it is a mark of barbarism to hunt, as we do, with no regard to laws, ordinances, and government regulations; to ride over another man's estate without the knowledge of the owner, without respecting any man's landmarks or boundaries; to course the fields and woods in spring as well as in summer; sometimes to kill a fox just when it is moulting, or to allow the hounds to run down a pregnant hare in the winter corn, or rather to torture it, with great damage to the game. Hence the Count admits with regret that civilisation is on a higher plane among the Muscovites, for there they have ukases of the Tsar on hunting, and police supervision, and punishment for offenders."

"As I love my mother," said Telimena, turning to the left-hand room and fanning her shoulders with a small batiste handkerchief; "the Count is not mistaken; I know Russia well. You people would not believe me when I used to tell you in how many respects the watchfulness and strictness of that government are worthy of praise, I have been in St. Petersburg more than once or twice! Tender memories I charming images of the past! What a city! Have none of you been in St. Petersburg? Perhaps you would like to see a map of it; I have a map of the city in my desk. In summer St. Petersburg society usually lives in dachas , that is, in rural palaces (dacha means cottage). I lived in a little palace, just above the river Neva, not too near the city, and not too far from it, on a small artificial hill. Ah, what a cottage that was! I still have the plan [pg 54] in my desk. Now to my misfortune a certain petty official, who was serving on an inquest, hired a house near by. He kept several hounds; what torture, when a petty official and a kennel live close by! Whenever I went out into the garden with a book to enjoy the light of the moon and the coolness of the evening, immediately a dog would rush up and wag its tail and prick up its ears as if it were mad. I was often terrified. My heart foreboded some misfortune from those dogs, and so it came to pass: for when I went into the garden on a certain morning, a hound throttled at my feet my beloved little King Charles spaniel! Ah, he was a lovely little dog; Prince Sukin 44 gave him to me as a present to remember him by—clever, and lively as a squirrel; I have his portrait, only I don't want to go to my desk now. Seeing it strangled, owing to my great distress I had a fainting spell, spasms, palpitation of the heart; perhaps my health might have suffered even more severely. Luckily, just then there rode up on a visit Kirilo Gavrilich Kozodusin, 45 the Master of the Hunt of the Court, who inquired the cause of so serious an attack. He had the police sergeant pulled in by the ears; the man stood there pale, trembling, and scarcely alive. 'How dare you,' shouted Kirilo with a voice of thunder, 'course in spring a pregnant doe, here under the nose of the Tsar?' The amazed sergeant in vain swore that he had not yet begun his hunting, and that with the august permission of the Master of the Hunt, the beast coursed seemed to him to be a dog and not a doe. 'What!' shouted Kirilo, 'do you dare, you scoundrel, to say that you have more knowledge of hunting and the varieties of beasts than I, Kozodusin, the Tsar's Jagermeister? The Chief of Police shall at once pass [pg 55] judgment between us,' They summoned the Chief of Police and told him to take down the evidence. 'I,' said Kozodusin, 'hereby testify that this is a doe; he impudently alleges that it is a domestic dog. Judge between us, which of us better understands beasts and hunting.' The Chief of Police understood the duties of his office, and was greatly amazed at the insolence of the sergeant; taking him aside he gave him brotherly advice to plead guilty and thereby atone for his offence. The Master of the Hunt was mollified and promised that he would intercede with the Emperor and somewhat mitigate the sentence. The matter ended by the dogs being sent to be strangled, and the sergeant to prison for four weeks. This trifle amused us the whole evening; the next day the story spread abroad that the Master of the Hunt had taken up the case of my little dog, and I even know for a fact that the Emperor himself laughed over it."

Laughter arose in both rooms. The Judge and the Bernardine were playing at marriage; spades were trumps, and the Judge was just about to make an important play. The Monk could hardly breathe for excitement, when the Judge caught the beginning of the story, and was so interested in it that with head thrown back and card uplifted, ready to take the trick, he sat quiet and only alarmed the Bernardine, until, when the story was ended, he played his knave, and said with a laugh:—

"Let whoever will praise the civilisation of the Germans, or the strict discipline of the Muscovites; let the men of Great Poland46 learn from the Suabians to go to law over a fox, and summon constables to arrest a hound that has ventured into another man's grove; in Lithuania, thank the Lord, we keep up the old ways: [pg 56] we have enough game for ourselves and for our neighbours, and shall never complain to the police about it; and we have enough grain, so that the dogs will not famish us by running through the spring wheat or the rye; on the peasants' fields alone do I forbid hunting."

"It is no wonder, sir," called the Steward from the room at the left, "since you pay dear for such game. The peasants are glad of the chance; when a dog runs into their wheat, if he shakes out ten ears, then you repay three score and are not content even with that; often the boors get a thaler into the bargain. Believe me, sir, that the peasants will grow very insolent, if——"

The rest of the Steward's argument the Judge could not hear, for between the two discourses there had begun a dozen conversations, jests, stories, and even disputes.

Thaddeus and Telimena had been forgotten by all the rest of the company, and were absorbed in each other.—The lady was glad that her wit had amused Thaddeus so greatly; in return, the young man showered compliments on her. Telimena spoke more and more slowly and softly, and Thaddeus pretended that he could not hear her in the buzz of voices; so, whispering, he drew so near her that he felt on his face the pleasant warmth of her brow; holding his breath, he caught her sighs with his lips, and with his eye he followed every sparkle of her glance.

Then between them there suddenly darted first a fly and after it the Seneschal's flapper.

In Lithuania there are swarms of flies. Among them there is a special variety, called "gentry flies"; in colour and form they are quite like others, but they have a broader breast, a larger belly than the common sort; as they fly they hum loudly and buzz beyond all endurance, [pg 57] and they are so strong that they will break right through a spider's web; or if one is caught, it will buzz there for three days, for it can contend with the spider in single combat. All this the Seneschal had carefully observed, and he argued further that these gentry flies produce the smaller folk, corresponding among flies to the queen bee in a swarm, and that with their destruction the remnant of those insects would perish. To be sure, neither the housekeeper nor the parish priest had ever believed these deductions of the Seneschal, but held quite different views as to the nature of flies; the Seneschal, however, did not waver from his ancient habit; whenever he caught sight of such a fly he immediately pursued it. Just at that moment a "gentleman" trumpeted above his ear; twice the Seneschal swung at it, and to his amazement missed; a third time he swung at it, and almost knocked out a window. At last the fly, bewildered by such an uproar, seeing on the threshold two people that barred his retreat, threw itself in desperation between their faces. Even there the right hand of the Seneschal darted in pursuit of it; the blow was so violent that the two heads sprang apart like the two halves of a tree torn asunder by a thunderbolt; both bumped against the doorposts so violently that they got black and blue spots.

Luckily no one noticed this, for the conversation, which hitherto had been lively and animated, but fairly orderly, ended in a sudden clamorous outburst. As, when foxhunters are entering a wood, one hears from time to time the crackling of trees, scattered shots, and the baying of the pack; but then the master of the hounds unexpectedly starts the game; he gives the signal, and a hubbub arises in the throng of huntsmen [pg 58] and dogs, as if every tree of the thicket had found a voice: such is the case with conversation—it moves on slowly, until it happens on a weighty topic, as dogs on the game. The game of the hunters' talk was that furious dispute of the Notary and the Assessor over their famous hounds. It lasted only a short time, but they accomplished much in a single instant, for in one breath they hurled so many words and insults that they exhausted the usual three-fourths of a dispute—taunts, anger, and challenge—and were already getting ready to use their fists.

So all rushed towards them from the other room, and, pouring through the doorway like a swift wave, carried away the young couple who were standing on the threshold like Janus, the two-headed god.

Before Thaddeus and Telimena could smooth the hair on their heads, the threatening shouts had died away; a murmur mixed with laughter was spreading through the throng, a truce had come to the brawl; the Monk had appeased it—an old man, but strong and with very broad shoulders. Just as the Assessor had run up to the Jurist, and when the combatants were already making threatening gestures at each other, he suddenly seized them both by the collar from behind, and twice knocking their two heads violently together like Easter eggs, he spread out his arms like a signpost, and tossed them at the same moment into opposite corners of the room; for a moment he stood still with outstretched arms, and cried, "Pax, pax, pax vobiscum ; peace be with you!"

Both factions were amazed and even began to laugh. Because of the respect due to a cleric they did not dare to revile the Monk, and after such a test no one had any desire to start a quarrel with him. And Father Robak [pg 59] soon calmed the assembly; it was evident that he had not sought any triumph; he did not further threaten the two brawlers or scold them; he only adjusted his cowl, and, tucking his hands into his belt, quietly left the room.

Meanwhile the Chamberlain and the Judge had taken a stand between the two factions. The Seneschal, as if aroused from deep thought, stepped into their midst and ran his fiery eye over the assembly; wherever he still heard a murmur, there he waved soothingly his leather flapper, as a priest his sprinkler; finally, raising impressively the handle of it on high, like a marshal's staff, he imposed silence.

"Hold your peace!" he repeated, "and bear in mind, you who are the foremost hunters in the district, what will come of a scandalous brawl. Are you aware? These young men, in whom is the hope of our country, who are to bring fame to our groves and forests, who, alas! even now neglect the chase, may receive thereby a new impulse to despise it, if they see that those who should give examples to others, bring back from the chase only wrangling and quarrels. Have also due regard for my grey hairs, for I have known greater sportsmen than you, and I have often judged between them as an arbitrator. In the Lithuanian forests who has been equal to Rejtan, either in stationing a line of beaters, or in himself encountering the beast? Who can compare himself with Jerzy Bialopiotrowicz? Where is there such a marksman to-day as Zegota, who with a pistol shot could hit a rabbit on the run? I knew Terajewicz, who, when he went out for wild boars, took no other arms than a pike, and Budrewicz, who used to fight singly against a bear! Such men did our forests once behold! If it came to a dispute, how did they settle [pg 60] the dispute. Why, they chose judges and set up stakes. Oginski lost three thousand acres of woodland over a wolf, and a badger cost Niesiolowski several villages! Now do you gentlemen follow the example of your elders, and settle your dispute in this way, even though you may set up a smaller stake. Words are wind; to wordy disputes there is no end; it is a shame to tire our ears longer with a brawl over a rabbit: so do you first choose arbitrators; and, whatever their verdict may be, conscientiously abide by it. I will beg the Judge not to forbid the master of the hounds to lead the chase even across the wheat, and I hope that I shall obtain this favour from my lord."

So saying, he embraced the knees of the Judge.

"A horse!" shouted the Notary, "I will stake a horse with his caparison; and I will further covenant before the local court, that I deposit this ring as a reward for our arbitrator, the Judge."

"I," said the Assessor, "will stake my golden dog-collars, covered with lizard-skin, with rings of gold, and my leash of woven silk, the workmanship of which is as marvellous as the jewel that glitters upon it. That outfit I wished to leave as an inheritance to my children, if I should marry; that outfit was given me by Prince Dominik Radziwill,47 when once I hunted with him and with Prince Marshal Sanguszko and General Mejen, 48 and when I challenged them all to course their hounds with me. There—something unexampled in the history of the chase—I captured six hares with a single bitch. We were then hunting on the meadow of Kupisko; Prince Radziwill could not keep his seat upon his horse, but, dismounting, embraced my famous hound Kania, 49 and thrice kissed her on the head. And then, thrice [pg 61] patting her on the muzzle, he said, 'I dub thee hence-forward Princess of Kupisko.' Thus does Napoleon give principalities to his generals, from the places at which they have gained great victories."

Telimena, wearied with the prolonged wrangling, wanted to go out into the fresh air, but sought a partner. She took a little basket from the peg. "Gentlemen, I see that you wish to remain within doors," she said, wrapping around her head a red cashmere shawl, "but I am going for mushrooms: follow me who will!" Under one arm she took the little daughter of the Chamberlain, with the other she raised her skirt up to her ankles. Thaddeus silently hastened after her—to seek mushrooms!

The plan of a walking party was very welcome to the Judge, who saw in it a means of settling a noisy dispute; so he called out:—

"Gentlemen, to the woods for mushrooms! The one who brings the finest to the table I will seat beside the prettiest girl; I will pick her out myself. If a lady finds it, she shall choose for herself the handsomest young man." [pg 62]

BOOK III.— FLIRTATION

ARGUMENT

The Count's expedition to the garden—A mysterious nymph feeding geese—The resemblance of mushroom-gathering to the wanderings of the shades in the Elysian Fields—Varieties of mushrooms—Telimena in the Temple of Meditation—Consultation in regard to the settlement of Thaddeus—The Count as a landscape painter—Thaddeus's artistic observations on trees and clouds—The Count's thoughts on art—The bell—The love note—A bear, sir!

The Count returned home, but he kept checking his horse, turning back his head, and gazing at the garden; and once it seemed to him that a mysterious, snow-white gown again flashed from the window; and that again something light fell from on high, and flitting across the garden in the twinkling of an eye, glittered among the green cucumbers, like a sunbeam that steals out from a cloud and falls on a slab of flint in a ploughed field, or on a small sheet of water in a green meadow.

The Count dismounted and sent his

servants to the house, but himself set out secretly for the garden; soon he reached the fence, found an opening in it, and slunk in quietly, as a wolf into a sheepfold; unluckily he jostled some dry gooseberry bushes. The little gardener glanced around as though frightened by the rustling, but perceived nothing; however, she ran to the other side of the garden. But along the edge, among the great sorrel plants and amid the leaves of burdock, the Count, leaping like a frog over the grass, quietly crawled near on his hands and knees; he put out his head, and beheld a marvellous sight.

[pg 63]
In that part of the garden grew scattered cherry trees; among them grain and vegetables, purposely of mixed varieties: wheat, maize, beans, bearded barley, millet, peas, and even bushes and flowers. The housekeeper had devised such a garden for the poultry; she was famous for her skill—her name was Mrs. Hennibiddy, born Miss Turkee. Her invention made an epoch in poultry-raising: to-day it is universally known, but in those times it was still passed about as a novelty and received under the seal of secrecy by only a few persons, until at last the almanac published it under the heading, A cure for hawks and kites, or a new method of raising poultry — that meant this garden patch.

As soon as the cock that keeps watch stands still, and, throwing back and holding motionless his bill, and inclining to one side his head with its red comb, that he may the more easily aim at the heavens with his eye, perceives a hawk hanging beneath the clouds, he calls the alarm: at once the hens take refuge in this garden—even the geese and peacocks, and the doves in their sudden fright, if they have not time to hide beneath the roof.

Now no enemy was to be seen in the sky, but the summer sun was burning fiercely; from it the birds had taken refuge in the grove of grain: some were lying on the turf, others bathing in the sand.

Amid the birds' heads rose little human heads, uncovered, with short hair, white as flax, their necks bare to the shoulders; in their midst was a girl, a head higher than they, with longer hair. Just behind the children sat a peacock, and spread out wide the circle of its tail into a many-coloured rainbow, against the deep blue of which the little white heads were relieved [pg 64] as on the background of a picture; they gathered radiance, being surrounded by the gleaming eyes of the tail as by a wreath of stars, and they shone amid the grain as in the transparent ether, between the golden stalks of the maize, the English grass with its silvery stripes, the coral mercury, and the green mallow, the forms and colours of which were mingled together like a lattice plaited of silver and gold, and waving in the air like a light veil.

Above the mass of many-coloured ears and stalks hung like a canopy a bright cloud of butterflies, 50 whose four-parted wings were light as a spider's web and transparent as glass; when they hover in the air they are hardly visible, and, though they hum, you fancy that they are motionless.

The girl waved in her uplifted hand a grey tassel, like a bunch of ostrich plumes, and seemed to be protecting with it the heads of the children from the golden rain of the butterflies—in her other hand shone something horn-like and gilded, apparently an instrument for feeding children, for she approached it to each child in turn; it was formed like the golden horn of Amalthea.

Even though thus engaged she turned her head towards the gooseberry bushes, mindful of the rustling she had heard among them, and not knowing that her assailant had already drawn near from the opposite direction, crawling like a serpent over the borders. Suddenly he jumped out from the burdock; she looked—he was standing near at hand, four beds away from her, and was bowing low. She had already turned away her head and lifted her arms, and was hurrying to fly away like a frightened lark, and already her light steps [pg 65] were brushing over the leaves, when the children, frightened by the entrance of the stranger, and the flight of the girl, began to wail piteously. She heard them, and felt that it was unseemly to desert little children in their fright; she went back, hesitating, but she must needs go back, like an unwilling spirit, summoned by the incantations of a diviner. She ran up to divert the child that was shrieking the loudest, sat down by him on the ground, and clasped him to her bosom; the others she soothed with her hand and with tender words until they became calm, hugging her knees with their little arms and snuggling their heads, like chickens beneath their mother's wing. "Is it nice to cry so?" she said, "is it polite? This gentleman will be afraid of you; he did not come to frighten you, he is not an ugly old beggar; he is a guest, a kind gentleman, just see how pretty he is."

She looked herself; the Count smiled pleasantly, and was evidently grateful to her for so many praises. She noticed this, and stopped, lowered her eyes, and blushed all over like a rosebud.

He was really a handsome gentleman; of tall stature, with an oval face, fair and with rosy cheeks; he had mild blue eyes and long blonde hair. The leaves and tufts of grass in the Count's hair, which he had torn off in crawling over the borders, showed green like a disordered wreath.

"O thou!" he said, "by whatever name I must honour thee, whether thou art a goddess or a nymph, a spirit or a phantom, speak! Doth thine own will call thee to earth, or doth another's power bind thee in this vale? Ah! I comprehend—surely some disdained lover, some powerful lord or envious guardian imprisons [pg 66] thee in this castle park as if under enchantment! Thou art worthy that knights should fight for thee in arms, and that thou shouldst be the heroine of mournful ballads! Unfold to me, fair one, the secret of thy dreadful fate! Thou shalt find a deliverer—henceforth, as thou rulest my heart by thy nod, so rule my arm."

He stretched forth his arms.—She listened to him with a maiden's blush, but with a face once more cheerful. As a child likes to look at gay pictures and finds amusement in glittering counters before he learns their true worth, so her ears were soothed by the sounding words of which she did not understand the meaning. Finally she asked: "Where do you come from, sir, and what are you looking for here in the garden?"

The Count opened his eyes, confused and amazed, and did not reply. Finally, lowering the tone of his discourse, he said:—

"Pardon me, my little lady; I see that I have spoiled your fun! O pardon me, I was just hurrying to breakfast; it is late and I wanted to get there on time. You know that by the road one has to make a circuit; through the garden it seems to me there is a short cut to the house."

"There is your way, sir," said the girl; "only you must not spoil the vegetable beds; there is the path between the strips of grass."

"To the left?" asked the Count, "or to the right?"

The little gardener, filled with curiosity, raised her blue eyes and seemed to scrutinise him, for a thousand steps away the house was in plain sight, and the Count was asking the way! But the Count needs must say something to her, and was seeking an excuse for conversation.

[pg 67]

"Do you live here? near the garden? or in the village? How happens it that I have not seen you at the mansion? Have you come recently? Perhaps you are a visitor?"

The girl shook her head.

"Pardon me, my little lady, but is not that your room, where we see the window?"

"If she is not a heroine of romance," he was thinking to himself, "she is a young and fresh and very pretty girl. Very often a great soul, a great thought, hidden in solitude, blooms like the rose in the midst of the forest; it will be sufficient to bring it forth to the light, and put it before the sun, to have it amaze by a thousand bright colours those who gaze upon it!"

The little gardener meanwhile remained silent. She merely lifted up one child, who was hanging on her arm, took another by the hand, and, driving several of them before her like geese, moved on through the garden.

"Can you not," she said turning around, "drive my stray birds back into the grain?"

"I drive birds!" cried the Count in amazement.

Meanwhile she had vanished behind the shade of the trees. Only for a moment there shone from behind the hedgerow, through the dense greenery, something like two blue eyes.

The deserted Count long remained standing in the garden; his soul, like the earth after sunset, gradually grew cool, and took on dark colours. He began to muse, but he had very unpleasant dreams; he awoke, not knowing himself with whom he was angry. Alas, he had found little, and had had too great expectations! For, when he was crawling over the field towards that [pg 68] shepherdess, his head had burned and his heart leapt high; so many charms had he seen in the mysterious nymph, so wondrously had he decked her out, so many conjectures had he made! He had found everything quite different; to be sure, she had a pretty face, and a slender figure—but how lacking in elegance! And that tender face and lively blush, which painted excessive, vulgar happiness! Evidently her mind was still slumbering and her heart inactive. And those replies, so village-like, so common!

"Why should I deceive myself?" he exclaimed; "I guess the secret, too late! My mysterious nymph is simply feeding geese!"

With the disappearance of the nymph, all the magic glory had suffered a change; those bright bands, that charming network of gold and silver, alas! was that all merely straw?

The Count, wringing his hands, gazed on a bunch of cornflowers tied round with grasses, which he had taken for a tuft of ostrich plumes in the maiden's hand. He did not forget the instrument: that gilded vessel, that horn of Amalthea, was a carrot! He had seen it being greedily consumed in the mouth of one of the children. So good-bye to the spell, the enchantment, the marvel!

So a boy, when he sees chickory flowers enticing the hand with soft, light, blue petals, wishes to stroke them and draws near—he blows—and with the puff the whole flower flies away like down on the wind, and in his hands the too curious inquirer sees only a naked stalk of grey-green grass.

The Count pulled his hat over his eyes and returned whence he came, but shortened the way by striding [pg 69] over the vegetables, the flowers, and the gooseberry bushes, until, vaulting the fence, he at last breathed freely! He remembered that he had spoken to the girl of breakfast: so perhaps everybody was already informed of his meeting with her in the garden, near the house; perhaps they would send to look for him. Had they noticed his flight? Who knows what they would think? So he had to go back. Bending down near the fence, along the boundary strip, and through the weeds, after a thousand turns he was glad to come out finally on the highway, which led straight to the yard of the mansion. He walked along the fence and turned away his head from the garden as a thief from a corn house, in order to give no sign that he thought of visiting it, or had already done so. Thus careful was the Count, though no one was following him; he looked in the opposite direction from the garden, to the right.

Here was an open grove, with a floor of turf; over this green carpet, among the white trunks of the birches, under the canopy of luxuriant drooping boughs, roamed a multitude of forms, whose strange dance-like motions and strange costumes made one think them ghosts, wandering by the light of the moon. Some were in tight black garments, others in long, flowing robes, bright as snow; one wore a hat broad as a hoop, another was bare-headed; some, as if they had been wrapt in a cloud, in walking spread out on the breeze veils that trailed behind their heads as the tail behind a comet. Each had a different posture: one had grown into the earth, and only turned about his downcast eyes; another, looking straight before him, as if in a dream, seemed to be walking along a line, turning neither to the right nor to the left. But all continually bent down to the ground in [pg 70] various directions, as if making deep bows. If they approached one another, or met, they did not speak or exchange greetings, being in deep meditation, absorbed in themselves. In them the Count saw an image of the shades in the Elysian Fields, who, not subject to disease or care, wander calm and quiet, but gloomy.

Who would have guessed that these people, so far from lively and so silent, were our friends, the Judge's comrades? From the noisy breakfast they had gone out to the solemn ceremony of mushroom-gathering; being discreet people, they knew how to moderate their speech and their movements, in order under all circumstances to adapt them to the place and time. Therefore, before they followed the Judge to the wood, they had assumed a different bearing, and put on different attire, linen dusters suitable for a stroll, with which they covered and protected their kontuszes; and on their heads they wore straw hats, so that they looked white as spirits in Purgatory. The young people had also changed their clothes, except Telimena and a few who wore French attire.—This scene the Count had not understood, being unfamiliar with village customs; hence, amazed beyond measure, he ran full speed to the wood.

Of mushrooms 51 there were plenty: the lads gathered the fair-cheeked fox-mushrooms, so famous in the Lithuanian songs as the emblem of maidenhood, for the worms do not eat them, and, marvellous to say, no insect alights on them; the young ladies hunted for the slender *pine-lover*, which the song calls the colonel of the mushrooms. 52 All were eager for the *orange-agaric;* this, though of more modest stature and less famous in song, is still the most delicious, whether fresh or salted, [pg 71] whether in autumn or in winter. But the Seneschal gathered the toadstool *fly-bane*.

The remainder of the mushroom family are despised because they are injurious or of poor flavour, but they are not useless; they give food to beasts and shelter to insects, and are an ornament to the groves. On the green cloth of the meadows they rise up like lines of table dishes: here are the *leaf-mushrooms* with their rounded borders, silver, yellow, and red, like little glasses filled with various sorts of wine; the *kozlak*, like the bulging bottom of an upturned cup; the *funnels*, like slender champagne glasses; the round, white, broad, flat *whities*, like china coffee-cups filled with milk; and the round *puff-ball*, filled with a blackish dust, like a pepper-shaker. The names of the others are known only in the language of hares or wolves; by men they have not been christened, but they are innumerable. No one deigns to touch the wolf or hare varieties; but whenever a person bends down to them, he straightway perceives his mistake, grows angry and breaks the mushroom or kicks it with his foot: in thus defiling the grass he acts with great indiscretion.

Telimena gathered neither the mushrooms of wolves nor those of humankind; distracted and bored, she gazed around with her head high in air. So the Notary angrily said of her that she was looking for mushrooms on the trees; the Assessor more maliciously compared her to a female looking about for a nesting-place.

She seemed in search of quiet and solitude; slowly she withdrew from her companions and went through the wood to a gently sloping hillock, well shaded by the trees that grew thickly upon it. In the midst of it was a grey rock; from under the rock a stream gurgled and [pg 72] spouted, and at once, as if it sought the shade, took refuge amid the tall, thick greenery, which, watered by it, grew luxuriantly on all sides. There that swift rogue, swaddled in grasses and bedded upon leaves, motionless and noiseless, whispered unseen and almost inaudibly, like a tired child laid in a cradle, when its mother ties above it the bright green curtains, and sprinkles poppy leaves beneath its head. It was a lovely and quiet spot; here Telimena often took refuge, calling it the Temple of Meditation.

Standing above the stream, she threw on the greensward, from her shoulders, her waving shawl, red as carnelian; and, like a swimmer who bends down to the wintry bath before she ventures to plunge in, she knelt and slowly inclined on her side; finally, as if drawn down by the stream of coral, she fell upon it and stretched out at full length: she rested her elbow on the grass, her temple on her palm, with her head bent down; beneath her head glittered the vellum paper of a French book; over the alabaster pages of the book there wound her black ringlets and pink ribbons.

Amid the emerald of the luxuriant grass, on the carnelian shawl, in her long gown, as though in a wrapper of coral, against which her hair was relieved at one end and her black shoes at the other, while along the sides glittered her snowy stockings, her handkerchief, and the whiteness of her hands and face, she showed from afar like a many-coloured caterpillar, crawling upon a green maple leaf.

Alas! all the charms and graces of this picture vainly awaited experts to appreciate them; no one heeded them, so deeply were all engrossed in the gathering of mushrooms. But Thaddeus heeded them and kept [pg 73] glancing sideways; and, not daring to go straight on, edged along obliquely. As a huntsman, when, seated between two wheels beneath a moving canopy of boughs, he advances on bustards; or, when approaching plover, he hides himself behind his horse, putting his gun on the saddle or beneath the horse's neck, as if he were dragging a harrow or riding along a boundary strip, but continually draws near to the place where the birds are standing: even so did Thaddeus steal forward.

The Judge foiled his plan; and, cutting him off, hurried to the spring. In the wind fluttered the white skirts of his dressing-gown and a large handkerchief, of which the end was fastened in his girdle; his straw hat, tied beneath his chin, flapped in the wind from his swift motion like a burdock leaf, falling now on his shoulders and now again over his eyes; in his hand was an immense staff:

thus strode on the Judge. Bending down and washing his hands in the stream, he sat down on the great rock in front of Telimena, and, leaning with both hands on the ivory knob of his enormous cane, he thus began his discourse:—

"You see, my dear, that ever since our Thaddeus has been our guest, I have been not a little disquieted. I am childless and old; this good lad, who is really my only comfort in the world, is the future heir of my fortune. By the grace of heaven I shall leave him no bad portion of gentleman's bread; it is time too that we think over his future and his settlement. But now, my dear, pray observe my distress! You know that Jacek, my brother, Thaddeus's father, is a strange man, whose intentions are hard to penetrate. He refuses to return home; God knows where he is hiding; he will not even let us inform his son that he is alive, and yet he continually gives us [pg 74] directions in regard to him. At first he wanted to send him to the legions; I was fearfully distressed. Later, however, he agreed that he might remain at home and marry. He would easily find a wife; I have a match in mind for him. None of our citizens compares in name or connections with the Chamberlain; his elder daughter Anna is of marriageable age, a fair and well-dowered young lady. I wanted to begin negotiations."

At this Telimena grew pale, closed her book, rose a bit, and sat up.

"As I love my mother," she said, "is there any sense in this, my dear brother? Are you a God-fearing man? So you think that you will really be doing a good turn to Thaddeus if you make a sower of buckwheat out of the young man! You will close the world to him! Believe me, some time he will curse you! To think of burying such talent in the woods and the garden! Believe me, judging from my knowledge of him, he is a capable boy, worthy of acquiring polish in the great world. You will do well, brother, if you send him to the capital, for instance, to Warsaw; or, if you wish to know my real opinion, to St. Petersburg. I shall surely be going there this winter on business; we will consider together what to do with Thaddeus. I know many people there and have influence; that is the best means of making a man. Through my aid he will gain access to the leading houses, and when he is known to important people he will get an office and a decoration; then let him abandon the service if he wishes and return home, being by that time of some importance and well known in society. What do you think about that, brother?"

"In his early years," said the Judge, "it is not bad for a young man to gain social experience, to see the [pg 75] world, and acquire polish among men. I myself, when young, covered no small ground; I have been in Piotrkow and in Dubno, now following the court as a lawyer, now attending to my own affairs; I have even visited Warsaw. Not a little did I profit by this. I should like to send out my nephew also among men, simply as a traveller, as an apprentice who is finishing his term, in order that he might acquire some little knowledge of the world. Not for the sake of office-holding or decorations! I beg your most humble pardon; a rank in the Muscovite hierarchy, a decoration, what sort of distinction are they? What man among our ancient notables—nay, even among those of this present day—what man of any prominence among the district gentry cares for such trifles? And yet these men are esteemed among us, for we respect in them their family, their good name, or their office—but a local office, conferred by the votes of their fellow-citizens, and not by the influence of any one set in authority."

"If that is your opinion, brother," interrupted Telimena, "so much the better; send him out as a traveller."

"You see, sister," said the Judge, mournfully scratching his head, "I should like to do so very much, but what if I have new perplexities! Brother Jacek has not abandoned the oversight of his son, and has just sent down upon me that Bernardine Robak, who has arrived from across the Vistula, a friend of my brother, who knows all his plans. And so the fates have already uttered their decree as to Thaddeus, and will have him marry, but marry Zosia, your ward; the young couple will receive, besides my own fortune, a dowry in ready money by the generosity of Jacek. You know that he is [pg 76] rich, and that through his favour I possess almost all my own estate; thus he has the right to give directions. Pray think this over, in order that it may be accomplished with the least possible trouble; we must make them acquainted. To be sure, they are very young, especially little Zosia, but that is no matter; it is time at last to release Zosia from confinement, for at all events she is growing up and is no longer a child."

Telimena, amazed and almost panic-stricken, raised herself gradually and knelt on the shawl; at first she listened with attention, then with a gesture she opposed him, waving her hand vigorously over her ear, as if she were driving off the unpleasant words like gnats, back into the mouth of the speaker.

"Ha! ha! that is a new idea! Whether that is good or bad for Thaddeus," she said angrily, "you may judge for yourself, my dear sir. I don't care anything about Thaddeus, plan for him yourselves; make him a steward, or put him in a tavern; let him be a bar-tender, or bring game for your table from the woods; do with him whatever you wish! But as for Zosia! What have you men to do with Zosia? I control her hand; I alone. That Jacek provided money for Zosia's education, and that he has assigned her a small yearly allowance, and has deigned to promise more, does not mean that he has bought her. Besides you both know, and it is pretty generally known too, that your generosity for us is not without its reasons; the Soplicas owe something to the family of the Horeszkos."

To this part of her speech the Judge listened with indescribable confusion and grief and with evident repugnance. As though fearing what she might say [pg 77] further, he bowed his head, made a gesture of assent, and flushed deeply.

Telimena concluded by saying:—

"I have had the care of her; I am of her kin, Zosia's only guardian. No one but me shall ever plan her happiness!"

"But what if she finds happiness in this marriage?" said the Judge, raising his eyes; "what if she likes young Thaddeus?"

"What if she likes him? That's a pear on a willow tree! Like him or not—much I care for that! To be sure Zosia will not be a wealthy match, but yet she is not a common village girl, a simple gentleman's daughter; her ancestors were called, 'Your Grace' ; she is the child of a wojewoda; her mother was a Horeszko: she will get a husband! I have taken such pains with her education—if only she has not degenerated into savagery here!"

The Judge listened with attention, looking her in the eye; he was apparently mollified, for he said cheerfully enough:—

"Well, what's to be done? God knows that I have sincerely wished to do the right thing. Only do not be angry, sister; if you do not agree, sister, you are quite within your rights. It is a sad business, but there is no use being angry. I gave the advice, for my brother bade me; no one here is using compulsion. If you refuse Thaddeus, sister, I will reply to Jacek that through no fault of mine the betrothal of Thaddeus and Zosia cannot come to pass. Now I will take my own counsel; perhaps I can open negotiations with the Chamberlain and arrange the whole matter."

In the meantime Telimena's wrath had cooled down:—
[pg 78]
"I do not refuse him, my dear brother; not at all! You said yourself that it is rather early, that they are too young. Let us think it over and wait; that will do no harm. Let us make the young people acquainted; we will observe them—we must not thus expose to chance the happiness of others. Only I caution you betimes, brother, do not prompt Thaddeus, and do not urge him to fall in love with Zosia, for the heart is not a servant, and acknowledges no master, and will not let itself be forcibly put in chains."
54

Thereat the Judge, arising, walked away in deep thought. Thaddeus approached from the opposite side, pretending that the search for mushrooms had enticed him there; the Count slowly moved on in the same direction.

During the dispute between the Judge and Telimena the Count had been standing behind the trees, mightily affected by the scene. He took from his pocket paper and pencil, implements that he had always with him, and, leaning on a stump and spreading out the sheet before him, he was evidently drawing a picture, and saying to himself: "They might have been grouped thus intentionally, he on the rock, she on the grass, a picturesque group! What characteristic heads! and what contrasting faces!"

He approached, checked himself, wiped his lorgnette, brushed his eyes with his handkerchief, and continued to gaze:—

"Is this marvellous, this charming prospect destined to perish or to be transformed when I approach near it? Will that velvet grass prove only poppies and beets? In that nymph shall I discover only a mere housekeeper?"

Although before this the Count had often seen [pg 79] Telimena at the Judge's house, where he had been a frequent visitor, he had paid little heed to her; he was now amazed to find her the model of his picture. The beauty of the spot, the charm of her posture, and the taste of her attire had so changed her that she was hardly recognisable. Her eyes shone with her recent anger, which was not yet extinct; her face, animated by the fresh breath of the breeze, by her dispute with the Judge, and by the sudden arrival of the young men, had assumed a deep flush, of unwonted liveliness.

"Madam," said the Count, "deign to pardon my boldness; I come both to crave forgiveness and to express my gratitude. To crave forgiveness, since I have stealthily followed your steps; and to express gratitude, since I have been the witness of your meditations. Much have I injured you, and much do I owe to you! I have interrupted a moment of meditation; to you I owe moments of inspiration! blessed moments! Condemn the man; but the artist awaits your forgiveness. Much have I dared, and more will I dare! Judge!"

Here he knelt and offered her his landscape.

Telimena passed judgment on his sketch with the tone of a courteous lady, but of one conversant with art; of praise she was chary, but she did not spare encouragement.

"Bravo, I congratulate you," she said, "you have no small talent. Only do not neglect it; above all you need to search out a beautiful environment! O happy skies of the Italian lands! rose gardens of the Caesars! ye classic cascades of Tibur, and dread craggy paths of Posilipo! That, Count, is the land of painters! On us may God have pity! A child of the Muses, put out to nurse in Soplicowo, would surely die. My dear Count, [pg 80] I will have this framed, or I will put it in my album, in my collection of drawings, which I have gathered from every source: I have numbers of them in my desk."

So they began to converse of the blue of the skies, of the murmur of waves and of fragrant breezes, and of the summits of crags, mingling here and there, after the fashion of travellers, laughter and mockery at the land of their fathers. And yet around them stretched the forests of Lithuania, so majestic and so full of beauty! The black currant, intertwined with a wreath of wild hop; the service tree, with the fresh blush of a shepherdess; the hazel, like a mænad, with green thyrsuses, decked with the pearls of its nuts as with clusters of grapes; and beneath them the children of the forest, the hawthorn in the embrace of the elder, the blackberry pressing its black lips upon the raspberry. The trees and bushes joined hands with their leaves, like young men and maidens standing ready for a dance around a married pair. In the midst of the company stood the pair, distinguished from all the rest of the forest throng by gracefulness of form and charm of colour; the white birch, the beloved, with her husband the hornbeam. But farther off, like grave elders sitting in silence and gazing on their children and grandchildren, stood on this side hoary beeches, and on that matronly poplars; and an oak, bearded with moss, and bearing on its humped back the weight of five centuries, supported itself—as on the broken pillars of sepulchres—on the petrified corpses of other oaks, its ancestors.

Thaddeus writhed, being not a little wearied by the long conversation in which he could not take part. But when they began to glorify the forests of foreign [pg 81] lands, and to enumerate in turn every variety of their trees—oranges, cypresses, olive trees, almonds, cactuses, aloes, mahogany, sandalwood, lemons, ivy, walnuts, even fig trees—praising extravagantly their forms, flowers, and bark, then Thaddeus constantly sniffed and grimaced, and finally could no longer restrain his wrath.

He was a simple lad, but he could feel the charm of nature, and, gazing on his ancestral forest, he said full of inspiration:—

"In the botanical garden at Wilno I have seen those vaunted trees that grow in the east and the south, in that fair Italian land—which of them can be compared to our trees? The aloe with its long stalk like a lightning rod? Or the dwarfish lemon tree with its golden balls and lacquered leaves, short and dumpy, like a woman who is small and ugly, but rich? Or the much-praised cypress, long, thin, and lean, which seems the tree, not of grief, but of boredom? They say that it looks very sad upon a grave; but it is like a German flunkey in court mourning, who does not dare to lift his arms or turn his head, for fear that he may somehow offend against etiquette.

"Is not our honest birch tree fairer, which is like a village woman weeping for her son, or a widow for her husband, who wrings her hands and lets fall over her shoulders to the ground the stream of her loose tresses? Mute with grief, how eloquently she sobs with her form! Count, if you are in love with painting, why do you not paint our own trees, among which you are sitting? Really, the neighbours will laugh at you, since, though you live in the fertile plain of Lithuania, you paint only crags and deserts."
[pg 82]
"Friend," said the Count, "beautiful nature is the form, the ground, the material, but the soul is inspiration, which rises on the wings of imagination, is polished by taste, and is supported by rules. Nature is not enough, enthusiasm is not enough; the artist must fly away into the spheres of the ideal! Not everything that is beautiful can be painted! You will learn all this from books in the course of time. As for painting: for a picture one requires viewpoints, grouping, ensemble—and sky, the Italian sky! Hence in landscape art Italy was, is, and will be the country of painters. Hence also, except for Breughel—not Van der Helle, but the landscapist, for there are two Breughels55 —and except for Ruysdael, in the whole north where has there been a landscape artist of the first rank? The sky, the sky is necessary."

"Our painter Orlowski," 56 interrupted Telimena, "had a Soplica's taste. (You must know that this is the malady of the Soplicas, not to like anything except their own country.) Orlowski, who spent his life in St. Petersburg, a famous painter (I have some of his sketches in my desk), dwelt close by the Emperor, in his court, as in paradise; and, Count, you cannot believe how homesick he was, he loved constantly to call to mind the days of his youth; he glorified everything in Poland, land, sky, forests. "

"And he was right," cried Thaddeus warmly; "that Italian sky of yours, so far as I have heard of it, is blue and clear, but yet is like frozen water: are not wind and storm a hundred times more beautiful? In our land, if you merely raise your head, how many sights meet your eye! how many scenes and pictures from the very play of the clouds! For each cloud is different; for [pg 83] instance, in spring they crawl like lazy tortoises, heavy with showers, and send down from the sky to the earth long streamers like loose tresses: those are the streams of rain. The hail cloud flies swiftly on the wind like a balloon; it is round and dark-blue, with a glint of yellow in the centre; around it may be heard a mighty uproar. Even these white cloudlets of every day, just see how rapidly they change! At first they are like a flock of wild geese or swans; and from behind, the wind, like a falcon, drives them into a dense throng; they crowd together, grow and increase; new marvels! They gain curved necks, send forth manes, shoot out rows of legs, and over the vault of the skies they fly like a herd of chargers across the steppe. All are white as silver; they have fallen into confusion; suddenly masts grow from their necks, and from their manes broad sails; the herd changes into a ship, and majestically floats slowly and quietly across the blue plain of the skies!"

The Count and Telimena looked up; Thaddeus with one hand pointed out a cloud to them, while with the other he squeezed Telimena's dainty fingers. The quiet scene lasted for several minutes; the Count spread a sheet of paper on his hat and took out his pencil; then, unwelcome to their ears, the house bell resounded, and straightway the quiet wood was full of cries and uproar.

The Count, nodding his head, said in an impressive tone:—

"Thus fate is wont to end all in this world by the sound of a bell. The calculations of mighty minds, the plans of imagination, the sports of innocence, the joys of friendship, the outpourings of feeling hearts! when [pg 84] the bronze roars from afar all is confused, shattered, perturbed—and vanishes!"

Then, turning a feeling glance on Telimena, he added, "What remains?" and she said to him, "Remembrance" ; and, desiring somewhat to relieve the Count's sadness, she gave him a forget-me-not that she had plucked. The Count kissed it and pinned it on his bosom. Thaddeus on the other side separated the branches of a shrub, seeing that through the greenery something white was stealing towards him. This was a little hand white as a lily; he seized it, kissed it, and silently buried his lips in it as a bee in the cup of a lily. On his lips he felt something cold; he found a key and a bit of white paper curled up in the hole of it; this was a little note. He seized it and hid it in his pocket; he did not know what the key meant, but that little white note would explain.

The bell still pealed, and, as an echo, from the depths of the quiet woods there resounded a thousand cries and shouts; this was the uproar of people searching for one another and calling, the signal that the mushroom-gathering was over for the day: the uproar was not at all gloomy or funereal, as it had seemed to the Count, but a dinner uproar. 57 Every noon this bell, calling from the gable, invited the guests and servants home to dinner; such had been the custom on many old estates, and in the Judge's house it had been preserved. So from the wood there came a throng carrying boxes, and baskets, and handkerchiefs with their ends tied up—all full of mushrooms; each young lady carried in one hand, like a folded fan, a large *pine-lover* ; in the other *tree-fungi* tied together in a bunch, like field flowers, and *leaf-mushrooms* of various colours. The Seneschal [pg 85] had his *fly-bane* . With empty hands came Telimena, and after her the young gentlemen.

The guests entered in order and stood about the table. The Chamberlain took his place at the head; this honour befitted him from his age and his office; advancing to it he bowed to the ladies, the old men, and the young men. By him the Monk took his station, and next the Bernardine was the Judge. The Bernardine pronounced a short grace in Latin, brandy was passed around; thereupon all sat down, and in silence and with relish they ate the cold Lithuanian salad of beet leaves.

The dinner was more quiet than usual; no one talked, despite the host's entreaties. The factions involved in the mighty strife over the dogs were thinking of the morrow's contest and the wager; great thought is wont to constrain the lips to silence. Telimena, though she talked constantly with Thaddeus, was forced to turn now and then to the Count, and even now and then to glance at the Assessor; thus a hunter gazes at the same time at the net into which he is coaxing goldfinches, and at the snare for sparrows. Thaddeus and the Count were both content with themselves, both happy, both full of hopes, and therefore not inclined to chatter. The Count would cast a proud look at the flower, and Thaddeus would stealthily gaze into his pocket, to see whether that little key had not run away; he would even reach in his hand and finger the note which he had not yet read. The Judge, pouring out Hungarian wine and champagne for the Chamberlain, served him diligently, and often pressed his knees; but he had no zest for conversation with him, and it was evident that he felt certain secret cares.

They changed the plates and the viands in silence; [pg 86] at last the tiresome routine of the dinner was interrupted by an unexpected guest. A forester, rushing in, did not even observe that it was dinner time, but ran up to his master; from his bearing and his expression it was clear that he was the bringer of important and unwonted tidings. On him the whole company turned their gaze; recovering his breath somewhat, he said: "A bear, sir!" All guessed the rest, that the beast had come out from the jungle , 58 that it was slipping through to the wilderness beyond the Niemen; all immediately recognised that it must be pursued at once, although they had not consulted together or thought the matter over. The common thought was evident from the clipped words, the lively gestures, the various orders that were issued, which, though they came tumultuously and at one time from so many lips, still all tended to a like aim.

"To the village!" shouted the Judge, "on horseback, for the headman of the peasants! To-morrow at daybreak let the beaters be ready, but volunteers! Whoever comes with a pike I will release from two days' work on the roads and five days' field-service for myself."

"Hurry," cried the Chamberlain, "saddle my grey, and gallop full speed to my house; get quickly my two bull-dogs,59 which are famous all over the district; the male is named Sprawnik, and the bitch Strapczyna. 60 Gag them, tie them in a sack, and to save time bring them here on horseback."

"Vanka," cried the Assessor in Russian to his boy, "draw my Sanguszko hunting knife over the whetstone; you know, the knife that the prince presented to me; and look to my belt, to see whether there is a bullet in every cartridge."

[pg 87]

"Get the guns ready!" shouted everybody.

The Assessor kept calling: "Lead, lead! I have a bullet mould in my game bag."

"Tell the parish priest," added the Judge, "to serve mass early to-morrow in the forest chapel; a very short offertory for hunters, the usual mass of St. Hubert."

After the orders had been given a silence followed. All were deep in thought and cast their eyes around as if looking for some one; slowly the Seneschal's venerable face attracted and united all eyes. This was a sign that they were seeking a leader for their future expedition and that they offered the staff of office to the Seneschal. The Seneschal rose, understood the will of his comrades, and, rapping impressively on the table, he drew from his bosom a golden chain, on which hung a watch large as a pear.

"To-morrow," he said, "at half past four, the gentlemen hunters and the beaters will present themselves at the forest chapel."

He spoke, and moved from the table; after him went the Forester. These two had to plan and arrange the chase.

Even so act generals, when they ordain a battle for the morrow—the soldiers throughout the camp clean their arms and eat, or sleep on cloaks or saddles, free from care, but the generals consult within the quiet tent.

Dinner was interrupted, the day passed in the shoeing of horses, the feeding of dogs, the gathering and cleaning of arms; at supper hardly any one came to the table. Even the faction of Bobtail ceased to be agitated by its long and weighty quarrel with the party of Falcon; the Notary and the Assessor went arm in arm to look for [pg 88] lead. The rest, wearied with toil, went early to sleep, in order to rise in good season.

[To-day Thaddeus had been given a room in an out-building. Going in, he closed the door and hid the candle in the fireplace, pretending that he had already gone to sleep—but he did not close his eyes. He evidently awaited the night, and to him the time seemed long. He stood by the window and through the opening cut in the shutter observed the doings of the watchman, who was continually walking about the yard. When he saw him far away, at one bound he leapt out, closed the window, and bending to the ground crept along like a pointer. His further steps the autumn night shrouded in thick darkness. 61] [pg 89]

BOOK IV— DIPLOMACY AND THE CHASE

ARGUMENT

A vision in curl papers awakes Thaddeus—Belated discovery of a mistake—The tavern—The emissary—The skilful use of a snuffbox turns discussion into the proper channel—The jungle—The bear—Danger of Thaddeus and the Count—Three shots—The dispute of the Sagalas musket with the Sanguszko musket settled in favour of the single-barrelled Horeszko carbine—Bigos—The Seneschal's tale of the duel of Dowejko and Domejko, interrupted by hunting the hare—End of the tale of Dowejko and Domejko.

Ye comrades of the Grand Dukes of Lithuania, trees of Bialowieza, Switez, Ponary, and Kuszelewo! whose shade once fell upon the crowned heads of the dread Witenes and the great Mindowe, and of Giedymin, when on the height of Ponary, by the huntsmen's fire, he lay on a bear skin, listening to the song of the wise Lizdejko; and, lulled by the sight of the Wilia and the murmur of the Wilejko, he dreamed of the iron wolf; 62 and awakened, by the clear command of the gods, he built the city of Wilno, which sits among the forests as a wolf amid bison, wild boars, and bears.

From this city of Wilno, as from the she-wolf of Rome, went forth Kiejstut and Olgierd and his sons, 63 as mighty hunters as they were famous knights, in pursuit now of their enemies and now of wild beasts. A hunter's dream disclosed to us the secrets of the future, that Lithuania ever needs iron and wooded lands.

Ye forests! the last to come hunting among you was [pg 90] the last king who wore the cap of Witold, 64 the last fortunate warrior of the Jagiellos, and the last huntsman among the rulers of Lithuania. Trees of my Fatherland! if Heaven grants that I return to behold you, old friends, shall I find you still? Do ye still live? Ye, among whom I once crept as a child—does great Baublis 65 still live, in whose bulk, hollowed by ages, as in a goodly house, twelve could sup at table? Does the grove of Mendog 66 still bloom by the village church? And there in the Ukraine, does there still rise on the banks of the Ros, before the mansion of the Holowinskis, that linden tree so far-spreading that beneath its shade a hundred youths and a hundred maidens were wont to join as partners in the dance?

Monuments of our fathers! how many of you each year are destroyed by the axes of the merchants, or of the Muscovite government! These vandals leave no refuge either for the forest warblers or for the bards, to whom your shade was as dear as to the birds. Yet the linden of Czarnolas, responsive to the voice of Jan Kochanowski, inspired in him so many rimes! 67 Yet that prattling oak still sings of so many marvels to the Cossack bard! 68

How much do I owe to you, trees of my Homeland! A wretched huntsman, fleeing from the mockery of my comrades, in exchange for the game that I missed how many fancies did I capture beneath your calm, when in the wild thicket, forgetful of the chase, I sat me down amid a clump of trees! Around me here the greybearded moss showed silver, streaked with the blue of dark, crushed berries; there heathery hillocks shone red, decked with cowberries as with rosaries of coral.—All about was darkness: over me the branches hung like low, thick, green clouds; somewhere above the [pg 91] motionless vault the wind played with a wailing, roaring, howling, crashing thunder; a strange, deafening uproar! It seemed to me that there above my head rolled a hanging sea.

Below, the crumbling remains of cities meet the eye. Here an overthrown oak protrudes from the ground, like an immense ruin; on it seem to rest fragments of walls and columns; on this side are branching stumps, on that half-rotted beams, enclosed with a hedge of grass. Within the barricade it is terrible to look: there dwell the lords of the forest, wild boars, bears, and wolves; at the gate lie the half-gnawed bones of some unwary guests. Sometimes there rise up through the green of the grass, like two jets of water, a pair of stag's antlers; and a beast flits between the trees like a yellow streak, as when a sunbeam falls between the forest trees and dies.

And again there is quiet below. A woodpecker on a fir tree raps lightly and flies farther on and vanishes; it has hidden, but does not cease to tap with its beak, like a child when it has hidden and wishes to be sought for. Nearer sits a squirrel, holding a nut in its paws and gnawing it; its tail hangs over its eyes like the plume over a cuirassier's helmet: even though thus protected, it keeps glancing about; perceiving the guest, this dancer of the woods skips from tree to tree and flashes like lightning; finally it slips into an invisible opening of a stump, like a Dryad returning to her native tree. Again all is quiet.

Now a branch shakes from the touch of some one's hand, and between the parted clusters of the service berries shines a face more fair than they. It is a maiden gathering berries or nuts; in a basket of simple bark [pg 92] she offers you freshly gathered cowberries, rosy as her lips. By her side walks a youth who bends down the branches of the hazel tree; the girl catches the nuts as they flash by her.

Now they have heard the peal of the horns and the baying of the hounds;

they guess that a hunt is drawing near them; and between the dense mass of boughs, full of alarm, they vanish suddenly from the eye, like deities of the forest.

In Soplicowo there was a great commotion; but neither the barking of the dogs, nor the neighing of the horses and the creaking of the carts, nor the blare of the horns that gave the signal for the hunt could stir Thaddeus from his bed; falling fully dressed on his couch, he had slept like a marmot in its burrow. None of the young men thought of looking for him in the yard; every one was occupied with his own affairs and was hurrying to his appointed place; they entirely forgot their sleeping comrade.

He was snoring. Through the heart-shaped opening that was cut in the shutter the sun poured into the darkened room like a fiery column, straight on the brow of the sleeping lad. He wanted to doze longer and twisted about, trying to avoid the light; suddenly he heard a knocking and awoke; cheerful was his awakening. He felt blithe as a bird and breathed freely and lightly; he felt himself happy and smiled to himself. Thinking of all that had happened to him the day before, he blushed and sighed, and his heart beat fast.

He looked at the window. Marvellous to say, in the sunlit aperture, within that heart, there shone two bright eyes, opened wide, as is wont to be the case when [pg 93] one gazes from daylight into darkness; he saw also a little hand, raised like a fan on the side towards the sun, to shield the gaze; the tiny fingers, turned towards the rosy light, reddened clear through, as if made of rubies; he beheld curious lips, slightly parted, and little teeth that shone like pearls among corals; and the face, though it was protected from the sun by a rosy palm, itself glowed all over like the rose.

Thaddeus was sleeping beneath the window; himself hidden in the shade, lying on his back, he wondered at the marvellous apparition, which was directly above him, almost touching his face. He did not know whether he was awake, or whether he was imagining one of those dear, bright childish faces that we remember to have seen in the dreams of our innocent years. The little face bent down: he beheld, trembling with fear and joy, alas! he beheld most clearly—he recalled and recognised now that short, bright golden hair done up in tiny curl papers white as snow, like silvery pods, which in the gleam of the sun shone like a crown on the image of a saint.

He started up, and the vision straightway vanished, frightened by the noise; he waited, but it did not return! He only heard again a thrice-repeated knocking and the words: "Get up, sir; it is time for hunting, you have overslept." He jumped from his couch, and with both hands pushed back the shutters, so that their hinges rattled, and flying open they knocked against the wall on either side. He rushed out and looked around, amazed and confused, but he saw nothing, nor did he perceive traces of any one. Not far from the window was the garden fence; on it the hop leaves and the flowery garlands were trembling; had some light hands [pg 94] touched them or had the wind stirred them? Thaddeus gazed long on them, but did not dare enter the enclosure; he only leaned on the fence, raised his eyes, and, with his finger pressed on his lips, bade himself be silent, in order not to break the stillness by a hasty word. Then he rapped his forehead, as though he were tapping for some ancient memories that had been lulled to sleep within him; finally, gnawing his fingers, he drew blood, and shouted at the top of his voice: "It serves me right, it does."

In the yard, where a few moments before there had been so many cries, now everything was desolate and silent as in a graveyard; all had gone afield. Thaddeus pricked up his ears, and put his hands to them like trumpets; he listened till the wind that blew from the forest brought to him the sound of horns and the shouts of the hunting throng.

Thaddeus's horse was waiting saddled in the stable. So, musket in hand, he vaulted upon it, and like a madman galloped towards the inns that stood near the forest chapel, where the beaters were to have gathered at early dawn.

The two taverns bent forward from either side of the road, threatening each other with their windows like enemies. The old one rightfully belonged to the owner of the castle; the new one Judge Soplica had built to spite the castle. In the former, as in his own inheritance, Gerwazy ruled supreme; in the latter Protazy occupied the highest place at the table.

The new tavern was not peculiar in its appearance. The old one was built according to an ancient model, which was invented by Tyrian carpenters, and later spread abroad over the world by the Jews; a style of [pg 95] architecture completely unknown to foreign builders: we inherit it from the Jews.

The tavern was in front like an ark, behind like a temple; the ark was Noah's genuine oblong chest, known to-day under the simple name of stable; in it there were various beasts, horses, cows, oxen, bearded goats; and above flocks of birds; and a pair each of various sorts of reptiles—and likewise insects. The rear portion, formed like a marvellous temple, reminded one by its appearance of that edifice of Solomon that Hiram's carpenters, the first skilled in the art of building, erected on Zion. The Jews imitate it to this day in their schools, and the design of the schools may be traced in their taverns and stables. The roof of lath and straw was peaked, turned-up, and crooked as a Jew's torn cap. From the gable protruded the edges of a balcony, supported on a row of close-set wooden columns; the columns, which were a great architectural marvel, were solid, though half decayed, and were put up crooked, as in the tower of Pisa; they did not conform to Greek models, for they lacked bases and capitals. On the columns rested semicircular arches, also of wood, in imitation of Gothic art. Above were artistic ornaments, crooked as the arms of Sabbath candlesticks, 69 executed not with the graver or chisel, but with skilful blows of the carpenter's hatchet; at their ends hung balls, somewhat resembling the buttons that the Jews hang on their foreheads when they pray, and which, in their own, tongue, they call cyces. In a word, from a distance the tottering, crooked tavern was like a Jew, when he nods his head in prayer; the roof is his cap, the disordered thatch his beard, the smoky, dirty walls his black frock, and in front the carving juts out like the cyces on his brow.

[pg 96]

In the centre of the tavern was a partition like that in a Jewish school; one portion, divided into long and narrow rooms, was reserved exclusively for ladies and gentlemen who were travelling; the other formed one immense hall. Along each wall stretched a many-footed narrow, wooden table; by it were benches, which, though lower, were as like the table as children are like their father. On these benches around the room sat peasants, both men and women, and likewise some of the minor gentry, all in rows; only the Steward sat by himself. After early Mass they had come from the chapel to Jankiel's, since it was Sunday, to have a drink and to amuse themselves. By each a cup of greyish brandy was already frothing, the hostess was running about with the bottle, serving every one. In the centre of the room stood the host, Jankiel, in a long gown that reached to the floor, and was fastened with silver clasps; one hand he had tucked into his black silk girdle, with the other he stroked in dignified fashion his grey beard. Casting his eye about, he issued orders, greeted the guests who came in, went up to those that were seated, and started conversation, reconciled persons quarrelling, but served no one—he only walked to and fro. The Jew was old, and famed everywhere for his probity; for many years he had been keeping the tavern, and no one either of the peasants or of the gentry had ever made complaint against him to his landlord. Of what should they complain? He had good drinks to choose from; he kept his accounts strictly, but without any knavery; he did not forbid merriment, but would not endure drunkenness. He was a great lover of entertainments; at his tavern marriages and christenings were celebrated; every Sunday he had musicians come from the village, including a bass viol and bagpipes.

[pg 97]

He was familiar with music and was himself famous for his musical talent; with the dulcimer, his national instrument, he had once wandered from estate to estate and amazed his hearers by his playing and his songs, for he sang well and with a trained voice. Though a Jew, he had a fairly good Polish pronunciation, and was particularly fond of the national songs, of which he had brought back a multitude from each trip over the Niemen, kolomyjkas 70 from Halicz and mazurkas from Warsaw. A report, I do not know how well founded, was current throughout the district, that he was the first to bring from abroad and make popular in that time and place the song which is to-day famous all over the world, and which was first played in the Ausonian land to Italians by the trumpets of the Polish legions. 71 The talent of song pays well in Lithuania; it gains people's affection and makes one famous and rich. Jankiel had made a fortune; sated with gain and glory, he had hung his nine-stringed dulcimer upon the wall, and settling down with his children in the tavern he had taken up liquor-selling. Besides this he was the under-rabbi in the neighbouring town, and always a welcome guest in every quarter, and a household counsellor: he had a good knowledge of the grain trade on the river barges; 72 such knowledge is needful in a village. He had also the reputation of being a patriotic Pole. 73

He was the first to bring to an end the quarrels between the two taverns, which had often led even to bloodshed, by leasing them both. He was equally respected by the old partisans of the Horeszkos and by the servants of Judge Soplica. He alone knew how to keep an ascendancy over the terrible Warden of the Horeszkos and the quarrelsome Apparitor; in Jankiel's [pg 98] presence both Gerwazy terrible of hand and Protazy terrible of tongue stifled their ancient wrongs.

Gerwazy was not there; he had gone to join the beaters, not wishing that the Count, young and inexperienced, should undertake alone so important and difficult an expedition. So he had gone with him for counsel, and likewise for defence.

To-day Gerwazy's place, the farthest from the threshold, between two benches, in the very corner of the tavern (called pokucie 74), was occupied by the Monk, Father Robak, the alms-gatherer. Jankiel had seated him there; he evidently highly respected the Bernardine, for whenever he noticed that his glass was empty he immediately ran up and told them to pour out for him July mead. 75 They said that the Bernardine and he had been acquainted when young, somewhere off in foreign lands. Robak often came by night to the tavern, and consulted secretly with the Jew about important matters; they said that the Monk was smuggling goods, but this was a slander unworthy of belief.

Leaning on the table, Robak was discoursing in a low voice; a throng of gentry surrounded him and pricked up their ears, and bent down their noses to the Monk's snuffbox. Each took a pinch, and the gentlemen sneezed like mortars.

"Reverendissime," said Skoluba with a sneeze, "that is fine tobacco, it goes way up to your topknot. Never since I have worn a nose"—here he stroked his long nose—"have I met its like"—here he sneezed a second time. "It is real Bernardine, doubtless made in Kowno, a city famous throughout the world for tobacco and mead. I was there in——"

"To the health of you all, my noble gentlemen!"

[pg 99]

Robak interrupted him. "As for the tobacco—hm—it comes from farther off than my friend Skoluba thinks; it comes from Jasna Gora, the Bright Mountain; the Paulist Brethren prepare such tobacco in the city of Czenstochowa,76 where stands the image, famed for so many miracles, of Our Lady the Virgin, Queen of the Crown of Poland: she is likewise still called Duchess of Lithuania! She still watches over her royal crown, but in the Duchy of Lithuania the schism 77 is now established!"

"From Czenstochowa?" said Wilbik. "I confessed myself there when I went on a pilgrimage thirty years ago. Is it true that the French are now visiting the city, and that they are going to tear down the church and seize the treasury—for this is all printed in the Lithuanian Courier?"

"No, it is not true," said the Bernardine. "His Majesty the Emperor Napoleon is a most exemplary Catholic; the Pope himself anointed him, and they live in harmony, and spread the faith among the French people, which has become a trifle corrupted. To be sure they have contributed much silver from Czenstochowa to the national treasury, for the Fatherland, for Poland, as the Lord God himself bids; his altars are always the treasury of the Fatherland. Why, in the Duchy of Warsaw we have a Polish army of a hundred thousand, perhaps soon there will be more. And who will pay that army? Will it be you Lithuanians? You are now giving your pennies only for the Muscovite coffers."

"The devil we are!" cried Wilbik; "they take them from us by force."

"O, my dear sir," a peasant spoke up humbly, bowing [pg 100] to the Monk and scratching his head, "for the gentry it is only half bad, but they skin *us* like linden bark."

"You stupid son of Ham!" 78 cried Skoluba, "it is easier for you; you peasants are as used to skinning as eels; but for us *men of birth*, us gentlemen accustomed to golden liberty! Ah, brothers! Why, in old times a gentleman on his garden patch——"

"Yes, yes," they all cried, "was a wojewoda's match." 79

"To-day they even deny our gentle birth; they bid us hunt up papers and prove it by documents."

"That's nothing for such as you!" shouted Juraha. "Your precious ancestors were peasants who obtained nobility, but I am of princes' blood! To ask me for a patent, showing when I became a nobleman! Only God remembers that! Let the Muscovite go to the forest and ask the oak grove who gave it a patent to grow above all the shrubs!"

"Prince!" said Zagiel. "Go tell that to some one else! You will find no end of princes' coronets in this district."

"You have a cross in your coat of arms," shouted Podhajski; "that is a covert allusion to the fact that a baptised Jew was a member of your line."

"That is false!" interrupted Birbarz; "now I spring from the blood of Tatar counts, and yet my coat bears crosses above a ship."

"The white rose of five petals," cried Mickiewicz, "with a cap in a golden field: it is a princely coat; Stryjkowski writes frequently of it." 80

After this a mighty hubbub arose all over the room. The Bernardine had recourse to his snuffbox; he offered a pinch to each of the orators in turn, and the wrangling [pg 101] immediately subsided: each accepted for courtesy's sake, and sneezed several times. The Bernardine, taking advantage of the intermission, continued:—

"Ah! this tobacco has made great men sneeze! Will you believe me that four times General Dombrowski has taken a pinch from this snuffbox?"

"Dombrowski!" they shouted.

"Yes, yes, he, the general. I was in the camp when he was recapturing Dantzic from the Germans.81 He had something to write; and, fearing that he might go to sleep, he took a pinch, sneezed, and twice patted me on the back. 'Father Robak,' he said, 'Father Bernardine, perhaps we shall see each other in Lithuania before the year is over. Tell the Lithuanians to receive me with Czenstochowa tobacco; I take none but that.'"

The Monk's speech aroused such amazement and such joy that the whole noisy assembly was silent for a moment; then they repeated under their breath the words, "Tobacco from Poland? Czenstochowa? Dombrowski? from the Italian land?" until finally all at once, as if thought had fused with thought and word with word, all cried with one voice, as if a signal had been given: "Dombrowski!" All shouted together, all embraced one another; the peasant and the Tatar count, the prince's hat and the cross, the white rose, the griffin, and the ship; they forgot everything, even the Bernardine; they only sang and shouted: "Brandy, mead, wine!"

Father Robak listened to the song for a long time; finally he wanted to cut it short. So he took in both hands his snuffbox, broke up the melody with a sneeze; and, before they got together again, he hastened to speak thus:—
[pg 102]
"You praise my tobacco, my good friends; now see what is going on inside the snuffbox."

Here, wiping with his handkerchief the soiled base of the box, he showed them a little painted army, like a swarm of flies: in the middle sat a man on a charger, the size of a beetle, evidently the leader of the troop; he had made his horse rear, as though he wanted to leap into the skies; one hand he held on the bridle, the other up to his nose.

"Gaze," said Robak, "at that threatening form, and guess whose it is."

All looked with curiosity.

"That is a great man, an emperor, but not of the Muscovites; their tsars have never used tobacco."

"A great man," cried Cydzik, "and in a long grey coat? I thought that great men wore gold, for among the Muscovites any sort of a general, sir, fairly shines with gold, like a pike in saffron."

"Bah!" interrupted Rymsza; "why, in my youth I saw Kosciuszko, the chief of our nation: he was a great man, but he wore a Cracow peasant's coat, that is to say, a czamara."

"Much he wore a czamara!" retorted Wilbik. "They used to call it a taratatka." 82

"But the taratatka has fringe," shouted Mickiewicz, "and the other is entirely plain."

Thereupon there arose disputes over the various forms of the taratatka and the czamara.

The ingenious Robak, seeing that the conversation was thus becoming scattered, undertook again to gather it to a focus—to his snuffbox: he treated them, they sneezed and wished one another good health; he continued his speech:—
[pg 103]
"When the Emperor Napoleon in an engagement takes snuff time after time, it is a sure sign that he is winning the battle. For example, at

Austerlitz: the French just stood beside their cannon, and on them charged a host of Muscovites. The Emperor gazed and held his peace; whenever the French shot, the Muscovites were simply mowed down by regiments like grass. Regiment after regiment galloped on and fell from the saddle; whenever a regiment fell, the Emperor took a pinch of snuff, until finally Alexander with his little brother Constantine and the German Emperor Francis fled from the field. So the Emperor, seeing that the fight was over, gazed at them, laughed, and dusted his fingers. And now if any of you gentlemen who are present here ever serves in the army of the Emperor, let him remember this."

"Ah! my dear Monk!" cried Skoluba, "when will that be? Why, on every holiday set down in the calendar they prophesy to us that the French are coming, A man looks and looks until his eyes are weary, but the Muscovite keeps on holding us by the neck as he always has. I fear that before the sun rises the dew will ruin our eyes."

"Sir, it is womanish to complain," said the Bernardine, "and a Jewish trick to wait with folded hands until some one rides up to the tavern and knocks on the door. With Napoleon it is not so hard to beat the Muscovites; he has already three times thrashed the hide of the Suabians, he has trodden down the nasty Prussians, and has cast back the English straight across the sea: surely he will be equal to the Muscovites. But, my dear sir, do you know what will be the result? The gentry of Lithuania will mount their steeds and seize [pg 104] their sabres, but not until there is no longer any enemy with whom to fight. Napoleon, after crushing everybody alone, will finally say: 'I can get along without you: who are you?' So it is not enough to await a guest, not enough even to invite him in; one needs to gather the servants and set up the tables; and before the banquet one must clean the house of dirt; clean the house, I repeat; clean the house, my boys!"

A silence followed, and then voices in the throng:—

"How clean our house? What do you mean by that? We will do everything for you, we are ready for anything; only, my dear Father, pray explain yourself more clearly."

The Monk glanced out of the window, interrupting the conversation; he noticed something peculiar, and put his head out of the window. In a moment he said, rising:—

"To-day we have no time, later we will talk together more at length. To-morrow I shall be in the district town on business, and on the way I will call on you gentlemen to gather alms."

"Then call at Niehrymow to spend the night," said the Steward; "the Ensign will be glad to see you, sir. An old Lithuanian proverb says: 'As lucky a man as an alms-gatherer in Niehrymow.'"

"And be good enough to visit us," said Zubkowski. "You will get a half-piece of linen, a firkin of butter, a sheep or a cow. Remember these words, sir: 'A man is lucky if he strikes it as rich as a monk in Zubkow.'"

"And on us," said Skoluba; "and on us," added Terajewicz; "no Bernardine ever departed hungry from Pucewicze."

Thus all the gentry said good-bye to the Monk with [pg 105] prayers and promises; he was already the other side of the door.

Through the window he had caught sight of Thaddeus flying along the highway, at full gallop, without his hat, with head bent forward, and with a pale, gloomy face, continually whipping and spurring on his horse. This sight greatly disturbed the Bernardine; so he hastened with quick steps after the young man, towards the great forest, which, as far as the eye could reach, showed black along the entire horizon.

Who has explored the deep abysses of the Lithuanian forests up to the very centre, the kernel of the thicket? A fisherman is scarcely acquainted with the bottom of the sea close to the shore; a huntsman skirts around the bed of the Lithuanian forests; he knows them barely on the surface, their form and face, but the inner secrets of their heart are a mystery to him; only rumour or fable knows what goes on within them. For, when you have passed the woods and the dense, tangled thickets, in the depths you come upon a great rampart of stumps, logs, and roots, defended by a quagmire, a thousand streams, and a net of overgrown weeds and ant-hills, nests of wasps and hornets, and coils of serpents. If by some superhuman valour you surmount even these barriers, farther on you will meet with still greater danger. At each step there lie in wait for you, like the dens of wolves, little lakes, half overgrown with grass, so deep that men cannot find their bottom; in them it is very probable that devils dwell. The water of these wells is iridescent, spotted with a bloody rust, and from within continually rises a steam that breathes forth a nasty odour, from which the trees around lose [pg 106] their bark and leaves; bald, dwarfed, wormlike, and sick, hanging their branches knotted together with moss, and with humped trunks bearded with filthy fungi, they sit around the water, like a group of witches warming themselves around a kettle in which they are boiling a corpse.

Beyond these pools it is vain to try to penetrate even with the eye, to say nothing of one's steps, for there all is covered with a misty cloud that rises incessantly from quivering morasses. But finally behind this mist (so runs the common rumour) extends a very fair and fertile region, the main capital of the kingdom of beasts and plants. In it are gathered the seeds of all trees and herbs, from which their varieties spread abroad throughout the world; in it, as in Noah's ark, of all the kinds of beasts there is preserved at least one pair for breeding. In the very centre, we are told, the ancient buffalo and the bison and the bear, the emperors of the forest, hold their court. Around them, on trees, nest the swift lynx and the greedy wolverene, as watchful ministers; but farther on, as subordinate, noble vassals, dwell wild boars, wolves, and horned elks. Above their heads are the falcons and wild eagles, who live from the lords' tables, as court parasites. These chief and patriarchal pairs of beasts, hidden in the kernel of the forest, invisible to the world, send their children beyond the confines of the wood as colonists, but themselves in their capital enjoy repose; they never perish by cut or by shot, but when old die by a natural death. They have likewise their graveyard, where, when near to death, the birds lay their feathers and the quadrupeds their fur. The bear, when with his blunted teeth he cannot chew his food; the decrepit stag, when he can scarcely [pg 107] move his legs; the venerable hare, when his blood already thickens in his veins; the raven, when he grows grey, and the falcon, when he grows blind; the eagle, when his old beak is bent into such a bow that it is shut for ever and provides no nourishment for his throat; 83 all go to the graveyard. Even a lesser beast, when wounded or sick, runs to die in the land of its fathers. Hence in the accessible places, to which man resorts, there are never found the bones of dead animals. 84 It is said that there in the capital the beasts lead a well-ordered life, for they govern themselves; not yet corrupted by human civilisation, they know no rights of property, which embroil our world; they know neither duels nor the art of war. As their fathers lived in paradise, so their descendants live to-day, wild and tame alike, in love and harmony; never does one bite or butt another. Even if a man should enter there, though unarmed, he would pass in peace through the midst of the beasts; they would gaze on him with the same look of amazement with which on that last, sixth day of creation their first fathers, who dwelt in the Garden of Eden, gazed upon Adam, before they quarrelled with him. Happily no man wanders into this enclosure, for Toil and Terror and Death forbid him access.

Only sometimes hounds, furious in pursuit, entering incautiously among these mossy swamps and pits, overwhelmed by the sight of the horrors within them, flee away, whining, with looks of terror; and long after, though petted by their master's hand, they still tremble at his feet, possessed by fright. These ancient hidden places of the forests, unknown to men, are called in hunter's language *jungles* .

[pg 108]
Stupid bear! If thou hadst abode in the jungle, never would the Seneschal have learned of thee; but, whether the fragrance of the honeycomb lured thee, or thou feltest too great a longing for ripe oats, thou earnest out to the edge of the forest, where the trees were less dense, and there at once the forester detected thy presence, and at once sent forth beaters, clever spies, to learn where thou wast feeding and where thou hadst thy lair by night. Now the Seneschal with his beaters, extending his lines between thee and the jungle, cuts off thy retreat.

Thaddeus learned that no short time had already passed since the hounds had entered into the abyss of the forest.

All is quiet—in vain the hunters strain their ears; in vain, as to the most curious discourse, each hearkens to the silence, and waits long in his position without moving; only the music of the forest plays to them from afar. The dogs dive through the forest as loons beneath the sea; but the sportsmen, turning their double-barrelled muskets towards the wood, gaze on the Seneschal. He kneels, and questions the earth with his ear. As in the face of a physician the eyes of friends read the sentence of life or death for one who is dear to them, so the sportsmen, confident in the Seneschal's skill and training, fix upon him glances of hope and terror. "They are on the track!" he said in a low voice, and rose to his feet. He had heard it! They were still listening—finally they too hear; one dog yelps, then two, twenty, all the hounds at once in a scattered pack catch the scent and whine; they have struck the trail and howl and bay. This is not the slow baying of dogs that chase a hare, a fox, or a deer, but a constant, sharp [pg 109] yelp, quick, broken, and furious. So the hounds have struck no distant trail, the beast is before their eyes—suddenly the cry of the pursuit stops, they have reached the beast—again there is yelping and snarling—the beast is defending himself, and is undoubtedly maiming some of them; amid the baying of the hounds one hears more and more often the howl of a dying dog.

The hunters stood still, and each of them, with his gun ready, bent forward like a bow with his head thrust into the forest; they could wait no longer! Already one after another left his station and crowded into the thicket; each wished to be the first to meet the beast; though the Seneschal kept cautioning them, though the Seneschal rode to each station on his horse, crying that whoever should leave his place, be he simple peasant or gentleman's son, should get the lash upon his back. There was no help for it! All, against orders, ran into the wood. three guns sounded at once, then a continual cannonade, until, louder than the reports, the bear roared and filled with echoes all the forest. A dreadful roar, of pain, fury, and despair! After it the yelping of the dogs, the cries of the sportsmen, the horns of the beaters thundered from the centre of the thicket. Some hunters hasten into the forest, others cock their guns, and all rejoice. Only the Seneschal in grief cries that they have missed him. The sportsmen and the beaters had all gone to the same side, between the toils and the forest, to cut off the beast; but the bear, frightened by the throng of dogs and men, turned back into places less carefully guarded, towards the fields, whence the sportsmen set to guard them had departed, where of the many ranks of hunters there remained only the Seneschal, Thaddeus, the Count, and a few beaters.
[pg 110]
Here the wood was thinner; from within could be heard a roaring, and the crackling of breaking boughs, until finally the bear darted from the dense forest like a thunderbolt from the clouds. From all sides the dogs were chasing him, terrifying him, tearing him, until at last he rose on his hind legs and looked around, frightening his enemies with a roar; with his fore paws he tore up now the roots of a tree, now charred stumps, now stones that had grown into the earth, hurling them at dogs and men; finally he broke down a tree, and brandishing it like a club to the right and the left, he rushed straight at the last

guardians of the line of beaters, at the Count and Thaddeus. They stood their ground unafraid, and levelled the barrels of their muskets at the beast, like two lightning-rods at the bosom of a dark cloud; then both at once pulled their triggers (inexperienced lads!) and the guns thundered together: they missed. The bear leapt towards them; they seized with four hands a pike that had been stuck in the earth, and each pulled it towards him; they gazed at the bear till two rows of tusks glittered from a great red mouth, and a paw armed with claws was already descending on their brows. They turned pale, jumped back, and slipped away to where the trees were less dense. The beast reared up behind them, already he was making a slash with his claws; but he missed, ran on, reared up again aloft, and with his black paw aimed at the Count's yellow hair. He would have torn his skull from his brains as a hat from the head, but just then the Assessor and the Notary jumped out from either side, and Gerwazy came running up some hundred paces away in front, and after him Robak, though without a gun—and the three shot together at the same instant. [pg 111] as though at a word of command. The bear leapt into the air. like a hare before the hounds, came down upon his head, and turning a somersault with his four paws, and throwing the bloody weight of his huge body right under the Count, hurled him from his feet to the earth; he still roared, and tried to rise, when the furious Strapczyna and the ferocious Sprawnik descended on him.

Then the Seneschal seized his buffalo horn, which hung by a strap, long, spotted, and crooked as a boa constrictor, and with both hands pressed it to his lips. He blew up his cheeks like a balloon, his eyes became bloodshot, he half-lowered his eyelids, drew his belly into half its size, sending thence into his lungs his entire supply of breath, and began to play. The horn, like a cyclone with a whirling breath, bore the music into the forest and an echo repeated it. The sportsmen became silent, the hunters were amazed by the power, purity, and marvellous harmony of the notes. The old man was once more exhibiting before an audience of huntsmen all that art for which he had once been famous in the forests; straightway he filled and made alive the woods and groves as though he had led into them a whole kennel and had begun the hunt. For in the playing there was a short history of the hunt. First there was a ringing, brisk summons—that was the morning call; then yelp upon yelp whined forth—that was the baying of the dogs; and here and there was a harsher tone like thunder—that was the shooting.

Here he broke off, but he still held the horn. It seemed to all that the Seneschal was still playing on, but that was the echo playing.

He began once more. You might think that the horn [pg 112] was changing its form, and that in the Seneschal's lips it grew now thicker and now thinner, imitating the cries of animals; once, prolonging itself into a wolf's neck, it howled long and piercingly; again, as if broadening into a bear's throat, it roared; then the bellowing of a bison cut the wind.

Here he broke off, but he still held the horn. It seemed to all that the Seneschal was still playing on, but that was the echo playing. Hearing this masterpiece of horn music, the oaks repeated it to the oaks and the beeches to the beeches.

He blew again. In the horn there seemed to be a hundred horns; one could hear mingled outcries of setting on the dogs, wrath and terror of the hunters, the pack, and the beasts: finally the Seneschal raised his horn aloft, and a hymn of triumph smote the clouds.

Here he broke off, but he still held the horn. It seemed to all that the Seneschal was still playing on, but that was the echo playing. In the wood there seemed to be a horn for every tree; one repeated the song to another, as though it spread from choir to choir. And the music went on, ever broader, ever farther, ever more gentle, and ever more pure and perfect, until it died away somewhere far off, somewhere on the threshold of the heavens!

The Seneschal, taking both hands from the horn, spread them out like a cross; the horn fell, and swung on his leather belt. The Seneschal, his face swollen and shining, and his eyes uplifted, stood as if inspired, catching with his ear the last expiring tones. But meanwhile thousands of plaudits thundered forth, thousands of congratulations and shouts of vivat.
[pg 113]
They gradually became quiet, and the eyes of the throng were turned on the huge, fresh corpse of the bear. He lay besprinkled with blood and pierced with bullets; his breast was plunged into the thick, matted grass; his paws were spread out before him like a cross; he still breathed, but he poured forth a stream of blood through his nostrils; his eyes were still open, but he did not move his head. The Chamberlain's bulldogs held him beneath the ears; on the left side hung Strapczyna; on the right Sprawnik, choking his throat, sucked out the black blood.

Thereupon the Seneschal bade place an iron bar between the teeth of the dogs, and thus open their jaws. With the butts of their guns they turned the remains of the beast on its back, and again a triple vivat smote the clouds.

"Well?" cried the Assessor, flourishing the barrel of his musket; "well? how about my little gun? It aims high, does it! Well? how about my little gun? It is not a large birdie,85 but what a showing it made! That is no new thing for it either; it never wastes a charge upon the air. It was a present to me from Prince Sanguszko."

Here he showed a musket which, though small, was of marvellous workmanship, and began to enumerate its virtues.

"I was running," interrupted the Notary, wiping the sweat from his brow, "I was running right after the bear; but the Seneschal called out, 'Stay in your places!' How could I stay there; the bear was making full speed for the fields, like a hare, farther and farther; finally I lost my breath and had no hope of catching up; then I looked to the right: he was standing right there, and [pg

114] the trees were not dense. When I aimed at him, I thought, 'Hold on, Bruin!' and sure enough, there he lies dead. It's a fine gun, a real Sagalas; there is the inscription, Sagalas, London à Balabanowka ." (A famous Polish smith lived there, who made Polish guns, but decorated them in English fashion.)

"How's that?" snorted the Assessor, "in the name of a thousand bears! The idea of your killing it! What rubbish are you talking?"

"Listen," replied the Notary, "this is no court investigation; this is a hunting party; we will summon all as witnesses."

So a furious brawl arose in the company, some taking the side of the Assessor and some that of the Notary. No one remembered about Gerwazy, for all had run in from the sides, and had not noticed what was going on in front. The Seneschal took the floor:—

"Now at all events there is some reason for a quarrel, for this, gentlemen, is no worthless rabbit; this is a bear: here one need have no compunctions about seeking satisfaction, whether it be with the sabre or even with pistols. It is hard to reconcile your dispute, so according to the ancient custom we give you our permission for a duel. I remember that in my time there lived two neighbours, both worthy gentlemen, and of long descent; they dwelt on opposite sides of the river Wilejka; one was named Domejko and the other Dowejko.86 They both shot at the same time at a she-bear; which killed it it was hard to ascertain, and they had a terrible quarrel, and swore to shoot at each other over the hide of the bear: that was in true gentleman's style, almost barrel to barrel. This duel made a great stir, and in those days they sang songs about it. I was their second; [pg 115] how everything came to pass—I will tell you the whole story from the beginning."

Before the Seneschal began to speak, Gerwazy had settled the dispute. He walked attentively around the bear; finally he drew his hanger, cut the snout in two, and in the rear of the head, opening the layers of the brain, he found the bullet. He took it out, wiped it on his coat, measured it with a cartridge, applied it to the barrel of his flintlock, and then said, raising his palm with the bullet resting upon it:—

"Gentlemen, this bullet is not from either of your weapons; it came from this single-barrelled Horeszko carbine." (Here he raised an old flintlock, tied up with strings.) "But I did not shoot it. O, how much daring was needed then! it is terrible to remember it; my eyes grew dark! For both the young gentlemen were running straight towards me, and behind them was the bear—just, just above the head of the Count, the last of the Horeszkos, though in the female line! 'Jesus Maria!' I exclaimed, and the angels of the Lord sent to my aid the Bernardine Monk. He put us all to shame; O, he is a glorious monk! While I trembled, while I dared not touch the trigger, he snatched the musket from my hands, aimed, and fired. To shoot between two heads! at a hundred paces! and not to miss! and in the very centre of his jaw! to knock out his teeth so! Gentlemen, long have I lived, and but one man have I seen who could boast himself such a marksman: that man once famous among us for so many duels, who used to shoot out the heels from under women's shoes, that scoundrel of scoundrels, renowned in memorable times, that Jacek, commonly called Mustachio; his surname I will not mention. But now it is no time for him to be hunting [pg 116] bears; that ruffian is certainly buried in Hell up to his very mustaches. Glory to the Monk, he has saved the lives of two men, and perhaps of three. Gerwazy will not boast, but if the last child of the Horeszkos' blood had fallen into the jaws of the beast, I should no longer be in this world, and perhaps the bear would have gnawed clean my old bones. Come, Father Monk, let us drink your good health!"

In vain they searched for the Monk: all that they could discover was that after the killing of the beast he had appeared for a moment, had leapt towards the Count and Thaddeus, and, seeing that both were safe and sound, had raised his eyes to Heaven, quietly repeated a prayer, and had run quickly into the field, as though some one were chasing him.

Meanwhile at the Seneschal's bidding they had thrown into a heap bundles of heather, dry brushwood, and logs; the fire burst forth, and a grey pine tree of smoke grew up and spread out aloft like a canopy. Over the flame they joined pikes into a tripod; on the spears they hung big-bellied kettles; from the waggons they brought vegetables, meal, roast meats, and bread.

The Judge opened a locked liquor case, in which there could be seen rows of white necks of bottles; from among them he took the largest crystal decanter—this the Judge had received as a gift from the Monk, Robak. It was Dantzic brandy, a drink dear to a Pole. "Long live Dantzic!" cried the Judge, raising the flask on high; "the city once was ours, and it will be ours again!" And he filled each glass with the silvery liquor, until at last it began to drip golden and glitter in the sun. 87

In the kettles they were cooking bigos . 88 In words it is hard to express the wonderful taste and colour of [pg 117] bigos and its marvellous odour; in a description of it one hears only the clinking words and the regular rimes, but no city stomach can understand their content. In order to appreciate Lithuanian songs and dishes, one must have health, must live in the country, and must be returning from a hunting party.

However, even without these sauces, bigos is no ordinary dish, for it is artistically composed of good vegetables. The foundation of it is sliced, sour cabbage, which, as the saying is, goes into the mouth of itself; this, enclosed in a kettle, covers with its moist bosom the best parts of selected meat, and is parboiled, until the fire extracts from it all the living juices, and until the fluid boils over the edge of the pot, and the very air around is fragrant with the aroma.

The bigos was soon ready. The huntsmen with a thrice-repeated vivat, armed with spoons, ran up and assailed the kettle; the copper rang, the vapour burst forth, the bigos evaporated like camphor, it vanished and flew away; only in the jaws of the caldrons the steam still seethed, as in the craters of extinct volcanoes.

When they had eaten and drunk their fill, they put the beast on a waggon, and themselves mounted their steeds. All were gay and talkative, except the Assessor and the Notary, who were more testy than the day before, quarrelling over the merits of that Sanguszko gun and that Sagalas musket from Balabanowka. The Count and Thaddeus also rode on in no merry mood, being ashamed that they had missed and had retreated; for in Lithuania whoever lets a bear get through the circle of beaters must toil long before he repairs his fame.

The Count said that he had reached the pike first, and that Thaddeus had hindered him from encountering [pg 118] the beast; Thaddeus maintained that, being the stronger, and the more skilful in work with a heavy pike, he had wished to relieve the Count of the trouble. Such nipping words they said to each other, now and again, in the midst of the cries and uproar of the train.

The Seneschal was riding in the middle; the worthy old man was merry beyond his wont and very talkative. Wishing to amuse the quarrelsome hunters and to bring them to an agreement, for their benefit he concluded his story of Dowejko and Domejko:—

"Assessor, if I wanted you to fight a duel with the Notary, don't think that I thirst for human blood; God forbid! I wanted to amuse you, I wanted, so to speak, to arrange a comedy for you, to renew a conceit that I invented forty years ago, a splendid one! You are younger men, and do not remember about it, but in my time it was famous from this forest to the woods of Polesie.

"All the animosities of Domejko and Dowejko proceeded, strange to say, from the very unfortunate similarity of their names. For when, at the time of the district diets,89 the friends of Dowejko were recruiting partisans, some one would whisper to a gentleman, 'Give your vote to Dowejko' ; but he, not hearing quite correctly, would give his vote to Domejko. Once when, at a banquet, the Marshal Rupejko proposed a toast, 'Vivat Dowejko,' others shouted 'Domejko' ; and the guests sitting in the middle did not know what to do, especially considering one's indistinct speech at dinner time.

"That was not the worst: once a certain drunken squire had a sword fight in Wilno with Domejko and received two wounds; later that squire, returning home [pg 119] from Wilno, by a strange chance took the same boat as Dowejko. So, when they were journeying along the Wilejka in the same boat, and he asked his neighbour who he was, the reply was 'Dowejko.' Without further ado he drew his blade from under his winter coat; slash, slash, and on Domejko's account he cut off the mustache of Dowejko.

"Finally, as the last straw, it must needs be that on a hunting party things happened thus. The two men of the name were standing near each other, and both shot at the same time at the same she-bear. To be sure, immediately after their shots it did fall lifeless, but before that it had been carrying a dozen bullets in its belly. Many persons had guns of the same calibre. Who killed the bear? Try to find out! How can you tell?

"Here they shouted: 'Enough! We must end this matter once for all. Whether God or the devil united us, we must separate; two of us, like two suns, seem to be too much for one world.' And so they drew their sabres and took their positions. Both were worthy men; the more the other gentry tried to reconcile them, the more furiously they let fly at each other. They changed their arms; from sabres they passed to pistols; they took their positions, we cried that they had put the barriers too near together. They, to spite us, swore to shoot over the skin of the bear, sure death! almost barrel to barrel; both were fine shots. 'Let Hreczecha be our second.' 'All right,' I said, 'let the sexton dig a hole at once, for such a dispute cannot end without results. But fight like gentlemen, and not like butchers. It is well enough to shorten the distance, I see that you are bold fellows; but do you want to shoot with your [pg 120] pistols on each other's bellies? I will not permit it; I agree to pistols, but you shall shoot from a distance neither longer nor shorter than across the bear's hide; with my own hands as second I will stretch the hide of the bear on the ground, and I myself will station you. You shall stand on one side, at the end of the snout, and you at the tail.'— 'Agreed,' they shouted; 'the time?' — 'To-morrow.' — 'The place?' — 'The Usza tavern.' —They parted. But I set to reading Virgil."

Here the Seneschal was interrupted by a cry of "At him!" Right from under the horses a hare had darted out; first Bobtail and then Falcon started after it. They had taken the greyhounds to the hunt, knowing that as they returned through the fields they might very likely happen on a rabbit. They were walking without leashes alongside the horses; when they caught sight of the hare, before the hunters could urge them on they started after it. The Notary and the Assessor wanted to follow on horseback, but the Seneschal checked them, saying; "Hold! stand and watch! I will not permit a person to stir from the spot. From here we can all see well how the hare runs for the field." In very truth, the hare felt behind it the hunters and the pack; it was making for the field; it stretched out behind it its ears like two deer's horns; it showed like a long grey streak extended above the ploughed land; beneath it its legs stuck out like four rods; you would have said that it did not move them, but only tapped the earth on the surface, like a swallow kissing the water. Behind it was dust, behind the dust the dogs; from a distance it seemed that the hare, the dust, and the dogs blended into one body, as though some great serpent were winding over the plain; the hare was the head, the dust in [pg 121] the rear was like a dark blue neck, and the dogs seemed to form a restless double tail.

The Notary and the Assessor gazed with open mouths, and held their breath. Suddenly the Notary grew pale as a handkerchief; the Assessor grew pale too: they saw—something fatal was happening; the farther that serpent went, the longer it became; it was already breaking in half; already that neck of dust had vanished; the head was already near the wood, and the tails somewhere behind! The head disappeared; for one last instant some one seemed to wave a tassel; it was lost in the wood, and near the wood the tail broke up.

The poor dogs ran bewildered along the border; they seemed to offer each other mutual advice and accusations. Finally they came back, slowly bounding over the furrows, with drooping ears and tails between their legs; and, running up, for very shame they did not dare to lift their eyes; and, instead of going to their masters, they stopped on one side.

The Notary drooped his gloomy brow towards his breast; the Assessor glanced around, but in no merry mood. Then they began to explain to the audience how their greyhounds were not used to going without leashes, how the hare had started out suddenly, how it was a poor chase over the ploughed field, where the dogs ought to have had boots, it was all so covered with flints and sharp stones.

They learnedly elucidated the matter, as experienced masters of hounds; from their words the hunters might have profited greatly, but they did not listen attentively; some began to whistle, others to titter; others, remembering the bear, talked about that, being still occupied by the recent hunt. [pg 122]

The Seneschal had hardly once glanced at the hare: seeing that it had escaped, he indifferently turned his head and finished his interrupted discourse:—

"Where did I stop? Aha, at my making them both promise that they would shoot across the bear skin! The gentlemen cried out: 'That is sure death, almost barrel to barrel!' But I laughed to myself, for my friend Maro had taught me that the skin of a beast is no ordinary measure. You know, my friends, how Queen Dido sailed to Libya, and there with great trouble managed to buy a morsel of land, such as could be covered with a bull's hide. 90 On that tiny morsel of land arose Carthage! So I thought that over attentively by night.

"Hardly was day dawning, when from one side came Dowejko in a gig, and from the other Domejko on horseback. They beheld that over the river stretched a shaggy bridge, a girdle of bear skin cut into strips. I stationed Dowejko at the tail of the beast on one side, and Domejko on the other side. 'Now blaze away,' I said, 'for all your lives if you choose, but I won't let you go until you are friends again.' They got furious, but then the gentry present fairly rolled on the ground for laughter; and the priest and I with impressive words set to giving them lessons from the Gospel and from the Statutes. There was no help for it; they laughed and had to be reconciled.

"Their quarrel turned later into a lifelong friendship, and Dowejko married the sister of Domejko; Domejko espoused the sister of his brother-in-law, Panna Dowejko: they divided their property into two equal portions, and on the spot where so strange an occurrence had happened they built a tavern, and called it the Little Bear." [pg 123]

BOOK V.—THE BRAWL

ARGUMENT

Telimena's plans for the chase—The little gardener is prepared for her entry into the great world, and listens to the instructions of her guardian—The hunters' return—Great amazement of Thaddeus—A second meeting in the Temple of Meditation and a reconciliation made easy by the mediation of ants—Conversation at table about the hunt—The Seneschal's tale of Rejtan and the Prince de Nassau interrupted—Preliminaries of peace between the two factions also interrupted—Apparition with a key—The brawl—The Count and Gerwazy hold a council of war.

The Seneschal, after honourably concluding his hunt, was returning from the wood, but Telimena in the depths of the deserted mansion was just beginning her hunting. To be sure she sat without moving, with her arms folded on her breast, but with her thoughts she was pursuing two beasts; she was searching for means to invest and capture them both at once—the Count and Thaddeus. The Count was a young magnate, the heir of a great house, handsome and attractive, and already a trifle in love! Well? He might be fickle! Then, was he sincerely in love? Would he consent to marry? especially a woman some years older than he? and not rich?

With these thoughts Telimena rose from the sofa and stood on tiptoe; you would have said that she had grown tall. She opened slightly her gown over her bosom, leaned sideways, surveyed herself with a diligent eye, and again asked counsel of her mirror; [pg 124] a moment later, she lowered her eyes, sighed, and sat down.

The Count was a grandee! Men of property are changeable in their tastes. The Count was a blond! Blonds are not over passionate. But Thaddeus? a simple lad! an honest boy! almost a child! he was beginning to fall in love for the first time! If well looked to he would not easily break his first ties; besides that, he was already under obligations to Telimena. While they are young, though men are fickle in their thoughts, they are more constant in their feelings than their grandfathers, because they have a conscience. The simple and maidenlike heart of a youth long preserves gratitude for the first sweets of love! It welcomes enjoyment and bids it farewell with gaiety, like a modest meal, which we share with a friend. Only an old drunkard, whose inwards are already burning, loathes the drink in which he drowns himself. All this Telimena knew thoroughly, for she had both sense and large experience.

But what would people say? One could withdraw from their sight, go to another locality, live in retirement, or, what was better, remove entirely from the vicinity, for instance make a little trip to the capital; she might introduce the young lad to the great world, guide his steps, aid him, counsel him, form his heart, have in him a counsellor and brother! Finally, she might enjoy the world herself, while her years permitted.

With these thoughts she walked boldly and gaily several times up and down the chamber—again she lowered her brow.

It might be well also to think about the fate of the Count—could she not manage to interest him in Zosia? [pg 125] She was not rich, but of equal birth to his, of a senatorial family, the daughter of a dignitary. If their marriage should come to pass, Telimena would have a refuge for the future in their home, being kin to Zosia and the one who secured her for the Count; she would be like a mother for the young couple.

After this decisive consultation, held with herself, she called from the window to Zosia, who was playing in the garden.

Zosia was standing bareheaded in her morning gown, holding a sieve aloft in her hands; the barnyard fowls were running to her feet. From one side the rough-feathered hens came rolling like balls of yarn; from the other the crested cocks, shaking the coral helms upon their heads and oaring themselves with their wings over the furrows and through the bushes, stretched out broadly their spurred feet; behind them slowly advanced a puffed-up turkey cock, fretting at the complaints of his garrulous spouse; there the peacocks, like rafts, steered themselves over the meadow with their long tails, and here and there a silver-winged dove would fall from on high like a tassel of snow. In the middle of the circle of greensward extended a noisy, moving circle of birds, girt round with a belt of doves, like a white ribbon, mottled with stars, spots, and stripes. Here amber beaks and there coral crests rose from the thick mass of feathers like fish from the waves. Their necks were thrust forward and with soft movements continually wavered to and fro like water lilies; a thousand eyes like stars glittered upon Zosia.

In the centre, raised high above the birds, white herself, and dressed in a long white gown, she turned about like a fountain playing amid flowers. She took [pg 126] from the sieve and scattered over the wings and heads, with a hand white as pearls, a dense pearly hail of barley grains: it was grain worthy of a lord's table, and was made for thickening the Lithuanian broths; by stealing it from the pantry cupboard for her poultry Zosia did damage to the housekeeping.

She heard the call "Zosia" —that was her aunt's voice! She sprinkled out all at once to the birds the remnant of the dainties, and twirling the sieve as a dancer a tambourine and beating it rhythmically, the playful maiden began to skip over the peacocks, the doves, and the hens. The birds, disturbed, fluttered up in a throng. Zosia, hardly touching the ground with her feet, seemed to tower high above them; before her the white doves, which she startled in her course, flew as before the chariot of the goddess of love.

Zosia with a shout rushed through the window into the chamber, and, out of breath, sat down upon her aunt's lap; Telimena, kissing her and stroking her under the chin, with joy observed the liveliness and charm of the child (for she really loved her ward). But once more she made a solemn face, rose, and walking up and down and across the chamber, and holding her finger on her lips, she spoke thus:—

"My dear Zosia, you are quite forgetful both of your age and of your station in life. Why, to-day you are beginning your fourteenth year; it is time to give up turkeys and hens. Fie! is such fun worthy of a dignitary's daughter? And you have petted long enough those sunburned peasants' children, Zosia! My heart aches to look at you; you have tanned your shoulders dreadfully, like a real little gypsy; and you walk and move like a village girl. From now on I shall see that all this [pg 127] is changed. I shall begin to-day; to-day I shall take you into society, to the drawing-room, to our guests; we have a throng of guests here. See that you do not cause me shame."

Zosia jumped from her place and clapped her hands; and, clasping both arms around her aunt's neck, she wept and laughed by turns for very joy.

"O auntie, it is so long since I have seen any guests! Since I have been living here with the hens and turkeys, the only guest that I have seen was a wild dove. I'm just a little tired of sitting in the chamber; the Judge even says that it is bad for the health."

"The Judge," interrupted her aunt, "has continually been bothering me with requests to take you out into society; has continually been mumbling under his breath that you are already grown up. He doesn't know what he is talking about himself; he is an old fellow who never had any experience in the great world. I know better how much preparation a young lady needs, in order to make an impression when she comes out in society. You see, Zosia, that any one who grows up in the sight of men, even though she may be beautiful and clever, produces no impression, since all have been accustomed to seeing her ever since she was small. But if a well-trained, grown-up young lady suddenly appears glittering before the world from no one knows where, then everybody crowds up to her out of curiosity, observes all her movements, each glance of her eye, attends to her words and repeats them to others; and when a young person gets to be in fashion, every one must praise her, even if he does not like her. I hope that you know how to behave; you grew up in the capital. Though you have been living two years hereabouts, [pg 128] you have not yet completely forgotten St. Petersburg. Well, Zosia, make your toilet; get the things from my desk, you will find ready everything needed for dressing. Hurry up, for at any minute they may come home from hunting."

The chambermaid and a serving girl were summoned; into a silver basin they poured a pitcher of water, and Zosia, fluttering like a sparrow in the sand, washed with the aid of the servant her hands, face, and neck. Telimena opened her St. Petersburg stores and took forth bottles of perfumes, and jars of pomade; she sprinkled Zosia over with choice perfume—the fragrance filled the room—and smeared her hair with ointment. Zosia put on white open-work stockings and white satin shoes from Warsaw. Meanwhile the chambermaid had laced her up, and then thrown a dressing-sack over the young lady's shoulders: after crimping her hair with a hot iron they proceeded to take off the curl-papers; her locks, since they were rather short, they made into two braids, leaving the hair smooth on the brow and temples. Then the chambermaid, weaving into a wreath some freshly gathered cornflowers, gave them to Telimena, who pinned them skilfully on Zosia's head, from the right to the left: the flowers were relieved very beautifully against the light hair, as against ears of grain! They took off the dressing-sack; the toilet was complete. Zosia threw over her head a white gown, and rolled up a little white handkerchief in her hand, and thus, all in white, she looked like a white lily herself.

After adjusting once more both her hair and her apparel, they told her to walk the length and breadth of the room. Telimena observed her with the eyes of [pg 129] an expert; she drilled her niece, grew angry, and grimaced; finally at Zosia's curtsy she cried out in despair:—

"Unhappy me! Zosia, you see what comes of living among geese and shepherds! You stride along like a boy, and turn your eyes to the right and left like a divorced woman! Curtsy! see how awkward you are!"

"O, auntie," said Zosia sadly, "how am I to blame? You have locked me up, auntie; there was nobody to dance with; to pass the time away I liked to feed the birds and to pet the children. But just wait, auntie, till I've lived among other people for a little while; you'll see how I improve."

"Well, of the two evils," said her aunt, "it was better to stay with the birds than with such a rabble as have hitherto been our guests; just recollect who have been our visitors here: the parish priest, who mumbled a prayer or played checkers, and the lawyers with their tobacco pipes! They are noble cavaliers! You would have learned fine manners from them! Now at all events there is some one to show yourself to; we have a well-bred company in the house. Note well, Zosia, we have here a young Count, a gentleman, well educated, a relative of the Wojewoda; see that you are polite to him."

The neighing of horses is heard and the chatter of the hunters; they are at the gate: here they are! Taking Zosia on her arm she ran to the reception room. None of the sportsmen had as yet come in; they had to change their clothes in the chambers, as they did not wish to join the ladies in their hunting coats. The first to enter were the young men, Thaddeus and the Count, who had dressed in great haste.

Telimena discharged the duties of hostess, greeted [pg 130] those who entered, offered them seats, and entertained them with conversation; she presented her niece to each in turn, first of all to Thaddeus, as being his near relative. Zosia curtsied politely; he bowed low, wanted to say something to her, and had already opened his lips; but, when he looked into Zosia's eyes he was so abashed, that, standing dumb before her, he first flushed and then grew pale. What lay upon his heart, he himself could not guess; he felt himself very unhappy—he had recognised Zosia— by her stature and her bright hair and her voice! That form and that little head he had seen as she stood upon the fence; that charming voice had aroused him to-day for the hunt.

The Seneschal extricated Thaddeus from his confusion. Seeing that he was growing pale and that he was tottering on his legs, he advised him to go to his room and rest. Thaddeus took his stand in the corner and leaned on the mantel, without saying a word—his wide-open, wandering eyes he turned now on the aunt and now on the niece. Telimena perceived that his first sight of Zosia had made a great impression on him; she did not guess all, but she seemed rather distracted as she entertained the guests, and did not take her eyes from the young man. Finally, watching her chance, she ran up to him. "Are you well? Why are you so gloomy?" she asked him; she pressed her questions, she hinted about Zosia, and began to jest with him. Thaddeus was unmoved; leaning on his elbow, he kept silent, frowned, and puckered his lips: so much the more did he confuse and amaze Telimena. Suddenly she changed her countenance and the tone of her discourse; she arose in wrath, and with sharp words began to shower on him sarcasms and reproaches. Thaddeus, [pg 131] too, started up, as if stung by a wasp; he looked askance; without saying a word he spat, kicked away his chair, and bolted from the room, slamming the door behind him. Luckily no one of the guests paid attention to this scene except Telimena.

Flying out through the gate, he ran straight into the field. As a pike, when a fisherman's spear pierces through its breast, plunges and dives, thinking to escape, but everywhere drags with it the iron and the line; so Thaddeus bore with him his troubles, as he ploughed through the ditches and vaulted the fences, without aim or path; until, after wandering for no small time, he finally entered the depths of the wood, and, whether on purpose or by chance, happened on the little hill which was the witness of his yesterday's happiness, and where he had received that note, the earnest of love: a place, as we know, called the Temple of Meditation.

When he glanced about, behold! there she was! It was Telimena, solitary, buried in thought, and changed in pose and costume from her of yesterday: dressed all in white, seated upon a stone, and motionless, as if herself carved of stone, she had buried her face in her open hands; though you could not hear her sobs you felt that she was dissolved in tears.

In vain did the heart of Thaddeus defend itself; he took pity, he felt that compassion moved him. He long gazed without speaking, hidden behind a tree; at last he sighed, and said to himself angrily: "Stupid, how is she to blame if I deceived myself?" So he slowly thrust out his head towards her from behind the tree. But suddenly Telimena tore herself from her seat, threw herself to the right and the left, and jumped across the stream; with outstretched arms and dishevelled [pg 132] hair, all pale, she rushed for the wood, leapt into the air, knelt, and fell down; and, not being able to get up again, she writhed on the turf. One could see by her motions from what dreadful torture she was suffering; she seized herself by the breast, the neck, the soles of her feet, her knees. Thaddeus sprang towards her, thinking that she had gone mad or was having an epileptic fit. But these movements proceeded from a different cause.

By a neighbouring birch tree was a great ant-hill; the frugal insects were wont to crawl around over the grass, mobile and black. Whether from necessity or from pleasure one cannot tell, they were especially fond of visiting the Temple of Meditation; from the hillock, their capital, to the shores of the spring they had trodden a path, by which they led their troops. Unfortunately Telimena was sitting in the middle of the pathway; the ants, allured by the sheen of the snow-white stocking, crawled up on it, and in swarms began to tickle and bite. Telimena was forced to run away and shake herself, finally to sit down on the grass and catch the insects.

Thaddeus could not refuse her his aid; brushing her gown he bent down to her feet; by chance he approached his lips to Telimena's temples—in so tender a posture, though they said nothing of their recent quarrels, nevertheless they were reconciled; and there is no telling how long their discourse would have lasted, had not the bell from Soplicowo aroused them.

It was the signal for supper; it was time to return home, especially since in the distance the crackling of broken branches could be heard. Perhaps they were looking for them? To return together was not fitting; so Telimena stole to the right towards the garden, and [pg 133] Thaddeus ran to the left, to the highway. On this detour both were somewhat disturbed: it seemed to Telimena that once from behind a bush shone the thin, cowled face of Robak; Thaddeus saw distinctly that once or twice a long white phantom made its appearance on his left; what it was he knew not, but he had a suspicion that it was the Count in his long English frock coat.

They had supper in the old castle. The obstinate Protazy, not heeding the definite orders of the Judge, had again stormed the castle in the absence of the people of higher station, and, as he said, had foreclosed the mortgage on it. The guests entered in order and stood about the table. The Chamberlain took his place at the head; this honour befitted him from his age and his office; advancing to it he bowed to the ladies, the old men, and the young men. The Collector of Alms was not at the table; the Chamberlain's wife occupied the place of the Bernardine, on her husband's right. The Judge, when he had stationed the guests as was fitting, pronounced a Latin grace. Brandy was passed to the gentlemen; thereupon all sat down, and silently and with relish they ate the cold salad of beet leaves whitened with cream.

After the cold dish came crabs, chickens, and asparagus, along with glasses of Malaga and of Hungarian wine; all ate, drank, and were silent. Probably never since the time when the walls of this castle were erected, which had generously entertained so many noble gentlemen, and had heard and echoed so many vivats, had there been memory of so gloomy a supper. The great, empty hall of the castle echoed only the popping of corks and the clink of plates; you would have said that some evil spirit had tied up the lips of the guests. [pg 134]

Many were the causes of this silence. The sportsmen had returned from the forest talkative enough, but when their ardour had cooled, and they thought over the hunt, they realised that they had come out of it with no great glory: was it necessary that a monkish cowl, bobbing up from God knows where, like Philip from the hemp, 91 should give a lesson to all the huntsmen of the district? O shame! What would they say of this in Oszmiana and Lida, which for ages had been rivals of their own district for the supremacy in woodcrafts? So they were thinking this over.

But the Assessor and the Notary, besides their mutual grudges, had on their minds the recent shame of their greyhounds. Before their eyes hovered a rascally hare, leaping nimbly about and bobbing its little tail from the wood's edge, in mockery of them; with this tail it beat upon their hearts as with a scourge: so they sat with faces bent over their plates. But the Assessor had still more recent reasons for chagrin, when he gazed at Telimena and at his rivals.

Telimena was sitting half turned away from Thaddeus, and in her confusion hardly dared to glance at him; she wanted to amuse the gloomy Count, and to make him talk more freely, so as to get him into better humour; for the Count was strangely glum when he returned from his walk, or rather, as Thaddeus thought, from his ambuscade. While listening to Telimena he raised his brow haughtily, frowned, and looked at her almost with contempt; then he sat down as near Zosia as he could, filled her glass, and passed plates to her, saying a thousand polite things, and bowing and smiling; sometimes he rolled his eyes and sighed deeply. It was evident, however, despite such skilful deception, that [pg 135] he was flirting merely to spite Telimena; for every time that he turned his head away, apparently by accident, his threatening eye glittered upon Telimena.

Telimena could not understand what all this meant; shrugging her shoulders, she thought, "He's showing off!" After all she was rather glad of the Count's new courtship, and turned her attention to her other neighbour.

Thaddeus, also gloomy, ate nothing and drank nothing; he seemed to be listening to the conversation, and glued his eyes on his plate. When Telimena poured him out wine, he was angry at her importunity; when she asked about his health, he yawned. He took it ill (so much had he changed in one evening) that Telimena was too ready to flirt; he was vext that her gown was cut so low—immodestly—and now for the first time, when he raised his eyes, he was almost frightened! For his sight had quickened; hardly had he glanced at Telimena's rosy face, when all at once he discovered a great and terrible secret! For Heaven's sake, she was rouged!

Whether the rouge was of a bad sort, or somehow had been accidentally scratched upon her face, at all events, here and there it was thin, and revealed beneath it a coarser complexion. Perhaps Thaddeus himself, in the Temple of Meditation, speaking too near her, had brushed from its white foundation the carmine, lighter than the dust of a butterfly's wing. Telimena had come back from the wood in too much of a hurry, and had not had time to repair her colouring; around her mouth, in particular, freckles could be seen. So the eyes of Thaddeus, like cunning spies, having discovered one piece of treason, began to explore one after another [pg 136] her remaining charms, and everywhere discovered some falsity. Two teeth were missing in her mouth; on her brow and temples there were wrinkles; thousands of wrinkles were concealed beneath her chin.

Alas! Thaddeus felt how unwise it is to observe too closely a beautiful object; how shameful to be a spy over one's sweetheart; how even loathsome it is to change one's taste and heart—but who can control his heart? In vain he tried to supply the lack of love by conscience, to warm again the coldness of his soul with the flame of her glance; now that glance, like the moon, bright but without warmth, shone over the surface of a soul that was chilled to its depths. Making such complaints and reproaches to himself, he bent his head over his plate, kept silent, and bit his lips.

Meanwhile an evil spirit assailed him with a new temptation, to listen to what Zosia was saying to the Count. The girl, captivated by the Count's affability, at first blushed, lowering her eyes; then they began to laugh, and finally to talk about a certain unexpected meeting in the garden, about a certain stepping over the burdocks and the vegetable beds. Thaddeus, eagerly pricking up his ears, devoured the bitter words and digested them in his soul. He had a frightful meal. As a serpent in a garden drinks with its double tongue from poisonous herbs, then rolls into a ball and lies down upon the path, threatening the foot that may carelessly step upon it, so Thaddeus, filled with the poison of jealousy, seemed indifferent, but yet was bursting with malice.

In the merriest assembly, if a few are out of sorts, at once their gloom spreads to the rest. The sportsmen had long ceased to speak, and now the other side of [pg 137] the table became silent, infected with the spleen of Thaddeus.

Even the Chamberlain was unusually gloomy and had no wish to chat, observing that his daughters, handsome and well-dowered young ladies as they were, in the flower of youth, by universal opinion the best matches in the district, were silent and neglected by the young men, who were also silent. This also caused concern to the hospitable Judge; and the Seneschal, noticing that all were thus silent, called the meal not a Polish but a wolves' supper.

Hreczecha had an ear very sensitive to silence; he himself was a great talker, and he was inordinately fond of chatterers. It was no wonder! He had passed all his life with the gentry at banquets, hunts, assemblies, and district consultations; he was accustomed to having something always drumming in his ears, even when he himself was silent, or was stealing with a flapper after a fly, or sat musing with closed eyes; by day he sought conversation, by night they had to repeat to him the rosary prayers, or tell him stories. Hence also he was a staunch enemy of the tobacco pipe, which he thought invented by the Germans in order to denationalise us. He used to say, "To make Poland dumb is to Germanise Poland." 92 The old man, who had prattled all through his life, now wished to repose amid prattle; silence awoke him from sleep: thus millers, lulled by the clatter of the wheels, as soon as the axles stop, awake crying in fright: "The Lord be with us!" 93

The Seneschal by a bow made a sign to the Chamberlain, and, with his hand raised to his lips, motioned to the Judge, asking for the floor. The gentlemen both [pg 138]   returned that mute bow, meaning, "Pray speak." The Seneschal opened his address:—

"I might venture to beg the young men to entertain us at this supper, according to the ancient custom, not to sit silent and munch: are we Capuchin fathers? Whoever keeps silent among the gentry acts exactly like a hunter who lets his cartridge rust in his gun; therefore I praise highly the garrulity of our ancestors. After the chase they went to the table not only to eat, but that they might together speak forth freely what each one had within his heart; the faults and the merits of the huntsmen and the beaters, the hounds, the shots—all were included in the order of the day; there would arise a hubbub as dear to the ears of the sportsmen as a second rousing of the beast. I know, I know what ails you all; that cloud of black cares has undoubtedly arisen from Robak's cowl! You are ashamed of your bad shots! Let not your shame burn you; I have known better hunters than you, and they used to miss; to hit, to miss, to correct one's mistake, that is hunter's luck. I myself, though I have been carrying a gun ever since I was a child, have often missed; that famous sportsman Tuloszczyk used to miss, and even the late Pan Rejtan did not always hit the mark. Of Rejtan I will speak later. As for letting the beast escape from the line of beaters, as for the two young gentlemen's not holding their ground before the beast as they ought, though they had a pike in their hands, *that* no one can either praise or blame: for to retreat with one's gun loaded was, according to our old ideas, to be a coward of cowards; likewise to shoot blindly, as many do, without letting the beast come close or sighting at it, is a shameful thing; but whoever aims well, whoever lets the beast [pg 139]   come near him as is proper, even if he misses, may retire without shame; or he may fight with the pike, but at his own pleasure and not from compulsion; since the pike is put in a sportsman's hands not for attack but for defence alone. Such was the ancient custom; and so believe me, and do not take your retreat to heart, my beloved Thaddeus and Your Honour the Count. But whenever you call to mind the happenings of to-day, remember also the caution of the old Seneschal, that one hunter should never get in another's way, and that two should never shoot at the same time at the same game."

The Seneschal was just pronouncing the word *game*, when the Assessor whispered under his breath, *dame*. "Bravo," cried the young men; there arose a murmur and laughter; all repeated Hreczecha's caution, especially the last word: some cried *game*, and others, laughing aloud, *dame*; the Notary whispered *skirt*, the Assessor, *flirt*, fixing upon Telimena eyes like stilettos.

The Seneschal had not thought at all of making any personal allusions, and had not noticed what they were secretly whispering; glad that he had been able to stir up laughter among the ladies and the young men, he turned to the hunters, wishing to cheer them up also; and he began anew, pouring himself out a glass of wine:—

"In vain do my eyes seek the Bernardine; I should like to tell him a curious incident, similar to what occurred at our hunt to-day. The Warden told us that he had known but one man who could shoot at long range with as good aim as Robak, but I knew another; by an equally sure shot he saved the lives of two men of high rank. I saw it myself, when Rejtan, the deputy [pg 140] to the Diet, went hunting with the Prince de Nassau in the forests of Naliboki. Those lords were not jealous of the fame of an untitled gentleman, but were the first to propose his health at table, and gave him countless splendid presents, and the hide of the boar that had been slain. Of that wild boar and of the shot I will tell you as an eyewitness, for the incident was similar to that of to-day, and it happened to the greatest sportsmen of my time, to the deputy Rejtan and the Prince de Nassau."

But then the Judge spoke up, pouring out a beaker:—

"I drink the health of Robak; Seneschal, clink your glass with mine. If we cannot enrich the Alms-Gatherer with a gift, we will at least try to pay him for his powder; we promise solemnly that the bear killed this day in the wood shall suffice the cloister kitchen for two years. But the skin I will not give to the Monk; I will either take it by force or the Monk must yield it to me through humility, or I will buy it, though it cost me the pelts of ten sables. Of that skin we will dispose according to our will; the first crown and glory the servant of God has already received, the hide His Excellency the Chamberlain shall give to him who has deserved the second reward."

The Chamberlain rubbed his forehead and lowered his eyebrows. The sportsmen began to murmur, and each made some remark; one how he had discovered the beast, another how he had wounded it; this one had called on the dogs, and that turned back the beast into the forest once more. The Assessor and the Notary disputed, one exalting the merits of his Sanguszko gun, the other those of his Sagalas musket from Balabanowka.

"Neighbour Judge," pronounced the Chamberlain [pg 141] at last, "the servant of God has rightfully won the first reward; but it is not easy to decide who is the next to him, for all seem to me to have equal merits, all to be equal in skill, adroitness, and courage. Fortune, however, has this day distinguished two by the danger in which they were; two were nearest to the bear's claws, Thaddeus and the Count; to them the skin belongs. Thaddeus will yield, I am sure, as the younger, and as the kinsman of our host; hence Your Honour the Count will receive the spolia opima. 94 Let this trophy adorn your hunting chamber, let it be a reminder of to-day's sport, a symbol of fortune in the chase, a spur to future glory."

He concluded gaily, thinking that he had soothed the Count, and did not know how grievously he had stabbed his heart. For at the mention of his hunting chamber the Count involuntarily raised his eyes; and those horns of stags, those branching antlers like a forest of laurels, sown by the hands of the fathers to form crowns for the sons, those pillars adorned with rows of portraits, that coat of arms shining in the vaulting, the old Half-Goat, spoke to him from all sides with voices of the past. He awoke from his musings, and remembered where he was and whose guest; he, the heir of the Horeszkos, was a guest within his own threshold, was feasting with the Soplicas, his immemorial foes! And moreover the jealousy that he felt for Thaddeus incensed the Count all the more powerfully against the Soplicas. So he said with a bitter laugh:—

"My little house is too small; in it there is no worthy place for so magnificent a gift: let the bear rather abide amid these horned trophies until the Judge deign to yield it to me together with the castle."

[pg 142]

The Chamberlain, guessing whither things were tending, tapped his golden snuffbox, and asked for the floor.

"You deserve praise, my neighbour Count," he said, "for caring for your interests even at dinner time, not living thoughtlessly from day to day as do fashionable young fellows of your years. I wish and hope to end the trial in my Chamberlain's court by a reconciliation; hitherto the only difficulty has been over the improvements. I have formed a project of exchange, to make up for the improvements with land, in the following fashion."

Here he began to develop in due order, as he always did, a plan for the exchange that was to take place. He was already in the middle of the subject, when an unexpected movement started at the end of the table; some were pointing at something that they had noticed, and others were looking in the same direction, until finally all heads, like ears of grain bent down by a wind behind them, were turned away from the Chamberlain, to the corner.

From the corner, where hung the portrait of the late Pantler, the last of the Horeszko family, from a little door concealed between the pillars, had quietly come forth a form like a phantom. It was Gerwazy; they recognised him by his stature, by his face, and by the little silvery Half-Goats on his yellow coat. He walked straight as a post, silent and grim, without taking off his hat, without even inclining his head; in his hand he held a glittering key, like a dagger; he opened a case and began to turn something in it.

In two corners of the hall, against pillars, stood two musical clocks in locked cases; the queer old fellows, [pg 143] long at odds with the sun, often indicated noon at sunset. Gerwazy had not undertaken to repair the machines, but he would not give up winding them; he turned the key in the clocks every evening, and the time for winding had just come. While the Chamberlain was occupying the attention of the parties interested in the case, he drew up the weight; the rusty wheels gnashed their broken teeth; the Chamberlain shuddered and interrupted his dissertation. "Brother," he said, "postpone a bit your faithful toil;" and he went on with his plan of an exchange; but the Warden, to spite him, pulled still more strongly the other weight, and suddenly the bullfinch perched on the top of the clock began to flap its wings and pour forth one of its melodies. The bird, which had been artistically made, but was, unfortunately, out of order, began to moan and whistle, ever worse and worse. The guests burst out laughing; the Chamberlain had to break off again. "My dear Warden," he cried, "or rather screech owl,95 if you value your beak, quit that hooting."

But Gerwazy was not at all frightened by the threat; with dignity he put his right hand on the clock and rested the left on his hip; with both hands thus supported he cried:—

"My precious Chamberlain, a grandee is free to make jokes. The sparrow is smaller than the owl, but on its own shavings it is bolder than the owl in a mansion not its own. A Warden is no owl; whoever comes by night into another man's loft is an owl, and I will scare him hence."

"Put him out!" shouted the Chamberlain.

"Count, you see what is being done," called the Warden. "Is Your Honour not yet sufficiently tainted [pg 144] by eating and drinking with these Soplicas? In addition, must I, the keeper of the castle, Gerwazy Rembajlo, Warden of the Horeszkos, be insulted in the house of my lords?—and will you endure it!"

Thereupon Protazy called out three times.—

"Silence, clear the room! I, Protazy Baltazar Brzechalski, known under two titles, once General of the Tribunal, commonly called Apparitor, hereby make my apparitor's report and formal declaration—claiming as witnesses all free-born persons here present and summoning the Assessor to investigate the case in behalf of His Honour Judge Soplica—as to an incursion, that is to say, an infringement of the frontier, a violent entry of the castle, over which hitherto the Judge has had legal authority, an evident proof of which is the fact that he is eating in the castle."

"Wind-bag," yelled the Warden, "I'll show you now!"

And, taking from his belt his iron keys, he whirled them round his head and hurled them with all his might; the bunch of iron flew like a stone from a sling. It would surely have split Protazy's brow into quarters, but luckily the Apparitor ducked and escaped death.

All started from their places. For a moment there was a dead silence; then the Judge cried, "To the stocks with that bully! Ho, boys!" —and the servants rushed nimbly along the narrow passage between the wall and the bench. But the Count blocked their way with a chair, and, placing his foot firmly on that feeble entrenchment, called out:—

"Beware, Judge! No one shall do injury to my servant in my own house; whoever has a complaint against the old man, let him present it to me."
[pg 145]
The Chamberlain cast a sidelong glance into the eyes of the Count:—

"Without your valuable aid I shall manage to punish the insolent old fellow; but Your Honour the Count is appropriating the castle ahead of time, before the decree is pronounced. You are not lord here, you are not entertaining us. Sit quiet as you have been sitting; if you honour not my grey head, at least respect the first office in the district."

"What do I care?" muttered the Count in return. "Enough of this prattle! Bore other men with your respects and offices! I have been guilty of folly enough already, when I joined with you gentlemen in drinking bouts that end by becoming coarse brawls. Give me satisfaction for the injury to my honour! We shall meet again when you are sober— follow me, Gerwazy!"

The Chamberlain had never expected any such answer as this, and was just filling his glass, when he was smitten by the insolence of the Count as by thunder: resting the bottle motionless against the glass, he leaned his head to one side and pricked up his ears, opening wide his eyes and half unclosing his lips; he held his peace, but squeezed the glass in his hand so powerfully that it broke with a snap and sent the liquor spurting into his eyes. One would have said that with the wine fire was poured into his soul; so did his face flame, so did his eye blaze. He struggled to speak; the first word he ground indistinctly in his mouth, until it flew forth between his teeth:—

"Fool! you cub of a Count! I'll teach you! Thomas, my sabre! I'll teach you *mores*, you fool; get to hell out of here! Respects and offices wound your delicate ears! I'll pay you up right off over your pretty earrings. [pg 146] Get out of the door, draw your sword! Thomas, my sabre!"

Then friends rushed to the Chamberlain, and the Judge seized his hand.

"Hold, sir, this is our affair; I was challenged first. Protazy, my hanger! I will make him dance like a bear on a pole!"

But Thaddeus checked the Judge:—

"My dear uncle, and Your Honour the Chamberlain, is it fitting for you gentlemen to meddle with this fop? Are there not young men here? And you, my brave youth, who challenge old men to combat, we shall see whether you are so terrible a knight; we will settle accounts to-morrow, and chose our place and weapons. To-day depart, while you are still whole."

The advice was good; the Warden and the Count had fallen into no common straits. At the upper end of the table only a mighty shouting was raging, but at the lower end bottles were flying around the head of the Count. The frightened women began to beseech and weep; Telimena, with a cry of "Alas!" lifted her eyes, rose, and fell in a faint; and, inclining her neck over the Count's shoulder, laid upon his breast her swan's breast. The Count, infuriated though he was, checked himself in his mad career, and began to revive her and chafe her.

Meanwhile Gerwazy, exposed to the blows of stools and bottles, was already tottering; already the servants, doubling up their fists, were rushing on him from all sides in a crowd, when, fortunately, Zosia, seeing the assault, leapt up, and, filled with pity, sheltered the old man by extending her arms like a cross. They checked themselves; Gerwazy slowly retired and vanished from [pg 147] sight; they looked to see where he had hidden himself beneath the table, when suddenly he came out on the other side as if from under the earth, and, raising aloft a bench in his strong arms, whirled round like a windmill and cleared half the hall. He seized the Count, and thus both, sheltered by the bench, retired towards the little door; when they were already almost at the threshold, Gerwazy stopped, once more eyed his foes, and deliberated for an instant, whether to retire under arms, or with new weapons to seek fortune in war. He chose the second; already he had swung back the bench for a blow, like a battering-ram; already, with head bent down, breast thrust forward, and foot uplifted, he was about to attack—when he caught sight of the Seneschal, and felt terror in his heart.

The Seneschal, sitting quietly, with half-closed eyes, had seemed buried in deep thought; only when the Count had bandied words with the Chamberlain and threatened the Judge, the Seneschal had turned his head, had twice taken a pinch of snuff and rubbed his eyes. Although the Seneschal was only a distant relative of the Judge, yet he was established in his hospitable house, and was beyond measure careful about the health of his friend. Therefore he gazed with curiosity at the combat, and slowly extended on the table his arm, hand, and fingers; on his palm he laid a knife, with the haft extended to the tip of the index finger, and the point turned towards his elbow; then with his arm extended a trifle backward he poised it as if playing with it—but he watched the Count.

The art of throwing knives, terrible in hand to hand combat, had at that time already fallen into disuse in Lithuania, and was familiar only to old men; the [pg 148] Warden had tried it often in tavern quarrels, and the Seneschal was expert at it. From the motion of his arm one could see that he would hit hard, and from his eyes one could easily guess that he was aiming at the Count (the last of the Horeszkos, although in the female line); the young men, less observant, did not understand the motions of the old Seneschal, but Gerwazy turned pale, shielded the Count with the bench, and withdrew towards the door. — "Catch him!" shouted the crowd.

As a wolf when surprised over its carrion throws itself blindly into the pack that disturbs its meal; he is already chasing them, he is about to tear them, when amid the yelping of the dogs a gun hammer gently clicks; the wolf recognises it by the click, glances in that direction; he notices that in the rear, behind the hounds, a hunter, half crouching and upon one knee, is moving the gun barrel towards him and is just touching the trigger; the wolf droops its ears and scuttles off with its tail between its legs; the pack with a triumphant uproar rush on and pluck it by its shaggy flanks; the beast often turns, glances at them, snaps its jaws; and hardly does he threaten them with the gnashing of his white teeth when the pack scamper away whining: so did Gerwazy withdraw with threatening mien, checking his assailants by his eyes and by the bench, until the Count and he reached the back of the dark niche.

"Catch him!" they cried again; the triumph was not long: for over the heads of the throng the Warden appeared unexpectedly in the gallery, by the old organ, and with a crash began to tear out the leaden pipes; he would have worked great havoc by his blows from above.

But the guests were already leaving the hall in a throng; the terrified servants did not dare to hold [pg 149] their ground, but, seizing some of the platters, ran out after their masters; they left behind even the plates and a part of the service.

Who last, caring not for the threats and blows, retired from the scene of battle? Protazy Brzechalski. He, standing unmoved behind the Judge's chair, in his apparitor's voice recited his notification until he had reached the very end; then he abandoned the empty battlefield, where remained corpses, wounded, and ruins.

Among the men there were no casualties; but all the benches had legs dislocated, and the table was also crippled: stripped of its cloth, it lay upon plates dripping with wine—like a knight upon bloody shields—among numerous bodies of chickens and turkeys, from which protruded the forks lately stuck within their breasts.

In a moment all within the deserted building of the Horeszkos had returned to its wonted calm. The darkness thickened; the remnants of the magnificent feast lay like that nocturnal banquet to which the ghosts of the departed must gather when evoked at the festival of the *Forefathers* . 96 Now the owls had cried thrice from the garret, like conjurers; they seemed to greet the rising of the moon of which the form fell through the window on the table, trembling like a spirit in Purgatory; from the vaults beneath rats leapt out through holes, like the souls of the damned; they gnawed and drank; at times in a corner a forgotten champagne bottle would pop as a toast to the spirits.

But on the second story, in the room that was still called the mirror room, though the mirrors were gone, stood the Count on the balcony facing the gate. He was cooling himself in the breeze; he had put his long [pg 150] coat on only one arm, folding the other sleeve and the skirts about his neck and draping his breast with the coat as with a cloak. Gerwazy was walking with long steps through the apartment; both were deep in thought, and were talking together.

"Pistols," said the Count, "or, if they prefer, sabres."

"The castle," said the Warden, "and the village, both are ours."

"Challenge the uncle, the nephew," exclaimed the Count, "the whole family!"

"Seize the castle," exclaimed the Warden, "the village and the lands!" — As he said this he turned to the Count. — "If you wish to have peace, take possession of the whole. Of what use is the lawsuit, my boy! The affair is plain as day: the castle has been in the hands of the Horeszkos for four hundred years; a part of the estate was torn from it in the time of the Targowica confederacy, and, as you know, given into the possession of the Soplica. You ought to take from them not only that part, but the whole, for the costs of the suit, and as punishment for their plundering. I have always said to you, let lawsuits alone; I have always said to you, raid them, make a foray97 on them. That was the ancient custom: whoever once possessed an estate was the heir thereof; win in the field and you will win in the court too. As for our ancient quarrels with the Soplicas, for them I have a little penknife that is better than a lawsuit; and, if Maciej gives me the aid of his switch, then we two together will chop those Soplicas into fodder."

"Bravo!" said the Count, "your plan, of Gothico-Sarmatian stamp, pleases me better than the wrangling of advocates. See here! Through all Lithuania we will [pg 151] make a stir by an expedition such as has not been heard of for many a long day. And we shall enjoy it ourselves. For two years have I been abiding here, and what fighting have I ever seen? With boors over a boundary line! Our expedition, however, promises bloodshed; in one such I took part during my travels. When I tarried in Sicily with a certain Prince, brigands bore away his son-in-law into the mountains, and insolently demanded a ransom from his kinsfolk; we, hastily gathering our servants and vassals, attacked them: I killed two robbers with mine own hand; I was the first to break into their camp; I freed the prisoner. Ah, my Gerwazy, how triumphant, how beautiful was our return, in knightly-feudal style! The populace met us with flowers—the daughter of the Prince, grateful to the deliverer, with tears fell into my embraces. When I arrived at Palermo, they knew of it from the gazette, and all the women pointed at me. They even printed a romance about the whole event, where I am mentioned by name. The romance is entitled, The Count; or, The Mysteries of the Castle of Birbante-Rocca . Are there dungeons in this castle?"

"There are immense beer-cellars," said the Warden, "but empty, for the Soplicas have drunk up the wine!"

"We must arm the jockeys on the estate," added the Count, "and summon the vassals from the village."

"Lackeys? God forbid!" interrupted Gerwazy. "Is a foray a drunk and disorderly affair? Who ever heard of making a foray with boors and lackeys? Sir, you know nothing at all about forays! Vassals, that is, mustachioed champions,98 are something quite different; vassals of that sort can be found. But we must not look for them in the peasant villages, but through the hamlets [pg 152] of the gentry, in Dobrzyn, in Rzezikow, in Cientycze, in Rombanki; 99 the gentry of ancient lineage, in whom flows knightly blood, are all well disposed to the family of the Horeszkos, and are all mortal enemies of the Soplicas! Thence I will collect some three hundred mustachioed gentlemen; that is my affair. Do you return to your mansion and sleep your fill, for to-morrow there will be hard work; you are fond of sleeping, it is already late, the second cock is already crowing. I will guard the castle here until day breaks, and at sunrise I shall be in the hamlet of Dobrzyn."

At these words the Count withdrew from the balcony, but before he departed he glanced through the opening of an embrasure, and exclaimed, seeing a multitude of lights in the household of the Soplicas, "Illuminate if you will! To-morrow at this time it will be bright in this castle, but dark in your mansion."

Gerwazy sat down upon the floor, leaned against the wall, and bent down his thought-laden brow towards his breast. The light of the moon fell on his bald pate, and Gerwazy drew upon it various patterns with his finger; it was evident that he was spinning warlike plans for future expeditions. His heavy lids were more and more weighed down; his head nodded on his powerless neck; he felt that sleep was overcoming him, and began according to his wont his evening prayers. But between the Pater Noster and the Ave Maria arose strange phantoms, wavering, and jostling each other: the Warden sees the Horeszkos, his ancient lords; some carry sabres, and others maces; 100 each gazes menacingly and twirls his mustache, flourishing his sabre or brandishing his mace—after them flashed one silent, gloomy shadow, with a bloody spot upon its [pg 153] breast. Gerwazy shuddered, he had recognised the Pantler; he began to cross himself, and, the more surely to drive away his terrible visions, he recited the litany for souls in Purgatory. Again his eyes closed fast and his ears rang—he sees a throng of mounted gentry; their sabres glitter: "The foray, the foray against Korelicze, and Rymsza at the head!" And he beholds himself, how he flies on a grey horse, with his dreadful sword uplifted above his head; his taratatka, 101 opened wide, rustles in the breeze; his red plumed hat has fallen backward from his left ear; he flies on, and upon the road overthrows both horsemen and foot-travellers, and finally he burns the Soplica in his barn. Then his head, heavy with its musings, drooped upon his breast, and thus fell asleep the last Warden of the Horeszkos.
[pg 154]

BOOK VI.—THE HAMLET 102

ARGUMENT

Warlike preparations for the foray—Protazy's expedition—Robak and the Judge consult on public affairs—Continuation of Protazy's fruitless expedition—A digression on hemp—Dobrzyn, the hamlet of gentry—Description of the person and the way of life of Maciek Dobrzynski.

Imperceptibly there crept forth from the moist darkness a dawn with no red glow, bringing on a day with no brightness in its eye. It was day long since, and yet one could hardly see. The mist hung over the earth like a straw thatch over the poor hut of a Lithuanian; towards the east one could see from a somewhat whiter circle in the sky that the sun had risen, and that thence it must once more descend to the earth; but it did not advance gaily and it slumbered on the road.

Following the example of the sky, everything was late on earth; the cattle started late to pasture, and caught the hares at a late breakfast. These usually returned to the groves at dawn: to-day, covered by the thick fog, some were nibbling duckweed; others, gathered in pairs, were digging holes in the field, and thought to enjoy themselves in the open air; but the cattle drove them back to the forest.

Even in the forest there was quiet. The birds on awakening did not sing, but shook the dew from their feathers, hugged the trees, tucked their heads under their wings, closed their eyes again, and awaited the [pg 155] sun. Somewhere on the borders of a swamp a stork clacked with its bill; on the haycocks sat drenched ravens, which, with open beaks, poured forth ceaseless chatter—hateful to the farmers as an omen of damp weather. The farmers had long since gone out to work.

The women, reaping, had already begun their usual song, gloomy, melancholy, and monotonous as a rainy day, all the sadder since its sound soaked into the mist without an echo; the sickles clinked in the grain, and the meadow resounded. A line of mowers cutting the rowen whistled ceaselessly a jingling tune; at the end of each swath they stopped, sharpened their scythes, and rhythmically hammered them. The people could not be seen in the mist; only the sickles, the scythes, and the songs hummed together like the notes of invisible music.

In the centre, the Steward, seated on a pile of grain, turned his head gloomily, and did not look at the work; he was gazing on the highway, at the crossroads, where something unusual was going on.

On the highway and in the byways since early dawn there had been unusual animation; from one side a peasant's waggon creaked, flying like a postchaise; from another a gentleman's gig ratded at full gallop, and met a second and a third; from the left-hand road a messenger rushed like a courier, from the right raced a dozen horses; all were hurrying, though they were headed in different directions. What could this mean? The Steward arose from the pile. He wished to look into the matter, to make inquiries; he stood long on the road, and shouted vainly, but could stop no one, nor even recognise any one in the fog. The riders flashed [pg 156] by like spirits; there could only be heard from time to time the dull sound of hoofs, and, what was stranger yet, the clank of sabres; this greatly rejoiced the Steward and yet it terrified him: for, though at that time there was peace in Lithuania, dull rumours of war had long been current, of the French, Dombrowski, and Napoleon. Were these horsemen and these arms an omen of wars? The Steward ran to tell all to the Judge, hoping likewise to learn something himself.

At Soplicowo the inmates of the house and the guests, after the brawl of the day before, had arisen gloomy and discontented with themselves. In vain the Seneschal's daughter invited the ladies to tell fortunes with cards; in vain they suggested a game of marriage to the gentlemen. They would not amuse themselves or play, but sat silently in the corners; the men smoked pipes, the women knitted; even the flies were asleep. The Seneschal, who had thrown aside his flapper, was bored by the silence and went to join the servants; he preferred to listen in the kitchen to the cries of the housekeeper, the threats and blows of the cook, the noise of the serving boys; at last the monotonous motion of the spits that turned the roast gradually caused him to fall into pleasant musings.

Since early morning the Judge had been writing, locked in his room; since early morning the Apparitor had been waiting beneath the window, on a bench of turf. After finishing his summons, the Judge called in Protazy and read in a loud voice his complaint against the Count, for wounding his honour and for insulting expressions, and against Gerwazy, for violence and blows; both of them he cited before the criminal court in the district town for threats—and to pay the costs of [pg 157] the lawsuit between them. The summons must be served that very day, by word of mouth, in presence of the parties, before the sun went down. As soon as he caught sight of the summons, the Apparitor extended his hand and listened with a solemn air; he stood there with dignity, but he would have been glad to jump for joy. At the very thought of the lawsuit he felt himself young again; he remembered those years long gone by, when he used to serve many a summons, sure to receive bruises in return, but at the same time generous pay. Thus a soldier who has passed his life waging war, and in his old age rests crippled in a hospital, as soon as he hears a trumpet or a distant drum, starts up from his bed, cries in his sleep, "Smite the Muscovites!" and on his wooden leg rushes from the hospital so quickly that young men can hardly catch him.

Protazy hastened to put on his apparitor's costume; he did not however don his tunic or his kontusz: those were reserved for the pomp and ceremony of the court sessions. For the journey he had different clothes: broad riding trousers, and a coat, of which the skirts could be buttoned up or let fall over the knees; a cap with ear flaps, tied up with a string—they could be raised for fine weather and let down in case of rain. Thus clad he took his cane and set out on foot, for apparitors before a lawsuit, as spies before battle, must hide under various forms and costumes.

Protazy did well in hastening to depart, for he would have had no long comfort from his summons. In Soplicowo they changed their plans of campaign. Robak, thoughtful and perplexed, suddenly broke in upon the Judge and said:—

"Judge, we shall have trouble with that aunt, with [pg 158] that giddy-pated coquette, Telimena. When Zosia was left alone, a child and poor, Jacek gave her to Telimena to be brought up, hearing that she was a good sort of woman and knew the world; but I notice that she is stirring things up for us here; she is intriguing and seems to be flirting with Thaddeus. I have my eye on her. Or perhaps she is aiming at the Count, perhaps at both at once. So let us think over how to get rid of her, for from her actions may arise gossip, a bad example, and quarrels among the youngsters, which may be a hindrance to your legal negotiations."

"Negotiations?" cried the Judge with unusual warmth, "I'm done with negotiations; I've finished with them, broken them off."

"What's this?" interrupted Robak, "where's your sense, where's your head? What nonsense are you telling me? What new row has come up?"

"It is not my fault," said the Judge; "the trial will make the matter plain. That pompous, stupid Count was the cause of the squabble, and that rascal Gerwazy; but this is the business of the court. It is too bad that you were not in the castle at the supper, Father; you would have borne witness how fearfully the Count insulted me."

"My dear sir," cried Robak, "why did you insist on going to those ruins? You know that I cannot stand the castle; henceforth I will never set foot there again. Another brawl! The judgment of God be on us! How did it happen? Tell me! This matter must be hushed up. I am sick already of seeing so many acts of folly; I have more important business than to reconcile litigious squabblers; but I will reconcile you once again."
[pg 159]

"Reconcile? What do you mean! Go to the devil with your reconciliation!" interrupted the Judge, stamping his foot. "Look at this monk! Because I receive him courteously, he wants to lead me by the nose. Pray understand that the Soplicas are not wont to be reconciled; when they summon a man to court they must win their case. Sometimes a suit has continued in their name until they won it in the sixth generation. I committed folly enough by your advice when I convoked for the third time the Chamberlain's court. From this day on there shall be no compromise, none, none, none!" (As he shouted these words he walked up and down and stamped both feet.) "Besides that, he must beg my pardon for his discourteous act of yesterday, or fight a duel!"

"But, Judge, what will happen if Jacek learns of this? He will certainly die of despair! Have not the Soplicas done evil enough in this castle? Brother, I do not wish to mention that terrible event, but you too know that the Targowica confederates 103 took a part of the estate from the owner of the castle and gave it to the Soplicas. Jacek, repenting his sin, had to vow, when absolved, to restore those lands. So he took Zosia, the poor heiress of the Horeszkos, under his care, and he paid a great price for her bringing up. He wished to win her for his own son Thaddeus, and thus unite in brotherly affection two hostile houses, and yield without shame to the heiress what had been plundered from her."

"But what have I to do with all this?" cried the Judge. "I have never been acquainted with Jacek—have not even seen him; I had scarcely heard of his riotous life, since I was then studying rhetoric in a [pg 160] Jesuit school, and later served as page with the Wojewoda. They gave me the estate and I took it; he told me to receive Zosia, and I received her and cared for her, and am planning for her future. I am weary enough of all this old wives' tale! And then why did this Count intrude upon me here? With what right to the castle? You know, my friend, he's only some sixteenth cousin to the Horeszkos, the tenth water on the kisiel. 104 And he must insult me? and I invite him to a reconciliation!"

"Brother," said the Monk, "there are weighty reasons for this. You remember that Jacek wanted to send his son to the army, but later let him remain in Lithuania: what reason was there for that? Why, at home he will be more useful to his country. You have surely heard the news of which every one is talking, and of which I have often brought tidings: now is the time to tell it all, now is the time! An important matter, my brother! Now the war is upon us! A war for Poland, brother! We shall be Poles once more! War is inevitable. When I hurried here on a secret mission, the vanguard of the army was already on the Niemen. Napoleon is already gathering an immense army, such as man has never seen and history does not remember; by the side of the French the whole Polish army is advancing, our Joseph,105 our Dombrowski, our white eagles! They are already on the march, at the first sign from Napoleon they will cross the Niemen; and, brother, our Fatherland will be restored!"

The Judge, as he listened, slowly folded his spectacles, and gazed fixedly at the Monk, but said nothing; he sighed deeply, and tears stood in his eyes—finally he clasped Robak about the neck with all his might, exclaiming:—
[pg 161]
"My Robak, is this really true? My Robak," he repeated, "is this really true? How many times they have deceived us! Do you remember, they said that Napoleon was already on the road? And we were waiting! They said, he is already in the Kingdom,106 he has already beaten the Prussians, and is coming in among us! And what did he do? He made peace at Tilsit. 107 Is it really true? Are you not deceiving yourself?"

"It is the truth," cried Robak, "as God is in Heaven!"

"Blessed be the lips that bring these tidings!" said the Judge, raising his hands on high. "You shall not regret your mission, Robak; your monastery shall not regret it; two hundred choice sheep I give to your monastery. Monk, yesterday you expressed a desire for my chestnut and praised my bay; to-day the two shall at once be harnessed to the waggon in which you gather alms. To-day ask me for what you wish, for whatever pleases you, and I will not refuse!

But as to all that business with the Count, let me alone; he has wronged me, I have already summoned him to court—is it fitting that I should propose an accommodation?"

The astonished Monk wrung his hands. Fixing his eyes upon the Judge and shrugging his shoulders, he said:—

"So, when Napoleon is bringing liberty to Lithuania, when all the world trembles, then you are thinking of your lawsuit? And after all that I have told you will you sit calmly, folding your hands, when one must act?"

"Act? How?" asked the Judge.

"Have you not yet read it in my eyes?" replied Robak. "Does your heart still tell you nothing? Ah, brother, if you have one drop of the Soplicas' blood in [pg 162] your veins, just consider: the French are striking from in front— what if we stir up a rising of the people from the rear? What do you think? Let our Warhorse neigh, let the Bear roar in Zmudz! 108 Ah, if only a thousand men, if but five hundred should press from behind upon the Muscovites, and spread abroad the rising like fire; if we, seizing cannon and standards from the Muscovites, should go as conquerors to greet the deliverers of our kinsmen? We advance! Napoleon, seeing our lances, asks, 'What army is that?' We shout, 'The insurgents, Most August Emperor; the volunteers of Lithuania!' He asks, 'Who is their commander?' — 'Judge Soplica!' Ah, who then would dare to breathe a word of Targowica? Brother, while Ponary stands, while the Niemen flows, so long will the name of the Soplicas be famous in Lithuania; to their grandsons and great-grandsons the capital of the Jagiellos 109 will point, saying, 'There is a Soplica, one of those Soplicas who first started the revolt.' "

"People's talk is of small account," answered the Judge. "I have never greatly cared for the praises of the world. God is my witness that I am innocent of my brother's sins; in politics I have never meddled much, but have performed the duties of my office and ploughed my patch of ground. But I am a gentleman by birth, and should be glad to wipe out the blot on my escutcheon; I am a Pole, and should be glad to do some service for my country—even to lay down my life. With the sabre I was never over skilled, and yet some men have received slashes even from me. The world knows that at the time of the last Polish district assemblies I challenged and wounded the two brothers Buzwik, who—— But enough of this. What is your idea, sir? [pg 163]

Should we take the field at once? To gather musketeers is easy; I have plenty of powder, and at the parish house the priest has some small cannon; I remember that Jankiel has told me that he has some points for lances, which I may take in case of need. He smuggled these lance-points in cases of goods, from Königsberg; we will take them, and make shafts at once. There will be no lack of sabres; the gentry will mount their steeds, my nephew and I at the head, and——? Somehow we'll manage it!"

"O Polish blood!" exclaimed the Bernardine with emotion, leaping towards the Judge with open arms; "true child of the Soplicas! God ordains you to wipe out the sins of your vagabond brother. I have always respected you, but from this instant I love you, as though we were own brothers. Let us prepare everything, but it is not yet time to take the field; I myself will indicate the place and will inform you of the time. I know that the Tsar has sent messengers to Napoleon to ask for peace; the war is not yet proclaimed. But Prince Joseph has heard from Pan Bignon,110 a Frenchman, a member of the Imperial Council, that all these negotiations will come to nothing, that there will be war. The Prince sent me as a scout with instructions that the Lithuanians should be ready to announce to Napoleon when he came that they wish to unite anew with their sister, the Kingdom, and desire that Poland be restored. Meanwhile, brother, you must be reconciled with the Count; he is a crank, a trifle fantastic in his notions, but he is a good, honest young Pole; we need such; cranks are very necessary in revolutions, as I know from experience; even stupid fellows will be of service, so long as they are honest and under the [pg 164] authority of clever men. The Count is a magnate, and has great influence among the gentry; the whole district will rise if he joins the revolt; knowing his estate, every gentleman will say, 'It must be a sure thing, since the magnates are in it; I will join directly.' "

"Let him make the first move," said the Judge, "let him come here, let him beg my pardon. At any rate I am older than he, and hold an office! As for the lawsuit, we will refer it to arbitration."

The Bernardine slammed the door.

"Well, a happy journey to you!" said the Judge.

The Monk mounted a vehicle standing by the threshold, lashed the horses with the whip, tickled their sides with the reins, and the carriage flew off and vanished in billows of fog; only now and then the grey cowl of the Monk rose above the mist like a vulture above the clouds.

The Apparitor had long ago arrived at the Count's house. As an experienced fox, when the scent of bacon allures it, runs towards it but bears in mind the secret tricks of hunters; it runs, stops, sits up frequently, raises its brush, and with it as with a fan waves the breeze to its nostrils, and asks the breeze whether the hunters have not poisoned the food: so Protazy left the road and circled over the meadow around the house; he twirled his stick in his hand and pretended that he had somewhere seen some stray cattle; thus skilfully manœuvring he arrived close to the garden; he bent down and ran so that you would have said that he was trailing a land rail; then he suddenly jumped over the fence and plunged into the hemp.

In that thick, green, fragrant growth around the house there is a sure refuge for beasts and men. Often [pg 165] a hare, caught among the cabbages, leaps to find surer hiding in the hemp than in the shrubbery, for among the close-set stalks no greyhound can catch it, nor foxhound smell it out because of the strong odour. In the hemp a serving man, fleeing from the whip or the fist, sits quietly until his master has spent his wrath. And often even runaway peasant recruits, while the government is tracking them in the woods, are sitting in the hemp. And hence at the time of battles, forays, and confiscations, each side uses immense exertions to occupy a position in the hemp, which commonly extends forward to the walls of the mansion, and backward until it joins the hop fields, and thus covers their attack and retreat from the enemy.

Protazy, though a bold fellow, felt some terror, for the very smell of the leaves called to his mind various of his former adventures as apparitor—one after another—of which the hemp had been a witness: how once a gentleman of Telsze, Dzindolet, whom he had summoned to court, had put a pistol against his breast, and bidden him crawl under the table and from there bark out a recantation of that summons with a dog's voice, 111 so that the Apparitor had to run full speed for the hemp; how later Wolodkowicz, 112 a haughty and insolent grandee, who used to break up district diets and violate courts of justice, receiving his official summons, had torn it into bits, and stationing footmen with clubs at the doors, had with his own hand held a bare sword over the Apparitor's head, crying: "Either I will cut you down or you will eat your paper." The Apparitor, like a cautious man, had pretended to begin to eat it, until, stealing up to the window, he had plunged into the hemp garden.
[pg 166]
To be sure, at this time it was no longer the custom in Lithuania to defend oneself from a summons with the sabre or the whip, and an apparitor only got cursed now and then for his pains; but Protazy could not know of that change of customs, for it was long since he had carried any summons. Though he was always ready, though he himself had begged the Judge to let him, up till now the Judge, from a due regard for his advanced age, had refused his requests; today he had accepted his offer because of pressing need.

The Apparitor gazed and listened—all was quiet—slowly he thrust forward his hand through the hemp, and, separating the dense mass of stalks, swam through the greenery as a fisherman dives beneath the water. He raised his head—all was quiet—he stole up to the windows—all was quiet—through the windows he surveyed the interior of the mansion—all was empty. He stepped up on the porch, not without terror, and undid the latch—all was empty as in an enchanted house; he took out his summons, and read aloud the notification. But suddenly he heard a clatter, and felt a trembling of the heart, and wanted to run away; when from the door there came towards him a person—luckily well known to him! Robak! Both were surprised.

Evidently the Count had departed somewhere with all his train, and in a great hurry, for he had left the doors open. It was evident that he had been arming himself; on the floor lay double-barrelled muskets and carbines, besides ramrods and gunhammers and locksmith's tools with which they had been repairing the arms. There were also gunpowder and paper; they had been making cartridges. Had the Count gone hunting with all his train? But why should he take [pg 167] hand arms? Here lay a rusty, hiltless sabre, there a sword with no belt; they must have been selecting weapons from this rubbish, and have ransacked even the old armouries. Robak surveyed with care the guns and swords, and then went out to the farmhouse to explore, looking for servants of whom he might inquire about the Count. In the deserted farmhouse he at length found two peasant women, from whom he learned that the master and his whole household had departed in a body, armed, along the road to Dobrzyn.

The hamlet of Dobrzyn has a wide reputation in Lithuania for the bravery of its gentlemen and the beauty of its gentlewomen. It was once powerful and populous, for when King Jan III. Sobieski had summoned the general militia by the "twigs," 113 the ensign of the wojewodeship had led to him from Dobrzyn alone six hundred armed gentry. The family had now grown small and poor; formerly at the courts of the magnates or in their troops, at forays, and at the district assemblies the Dobrzynskis used to find an easy living. Now they were forced to work for themselves, like mere serfs, except that they did not wear peasants' russet doublets, but long white coats with black stripes, and on Sunday kontuszes. Also the dress of even the poorest of their women was different from the jackets of the peasants; they usually wore drilling or percale, herded their cattle in shoes not of bark but of leather, and reaped and even spun with gloves on.

The Dobrzynskis were distinguished among their Lithuanian brethren by their language and likewise by their stature and their appearance. They were of pure Polish blood, and all had black hair, high foreheads, black eyes, and aquiline noses. From the land of [pg 168] Dobrzyn 114 they derived their ancient family, and, though they had been settled in Lithuania for four hundred years, they preserved their Masovian speech and customs. Whenever any one of them gave his son a name at baptism, he always used to choose as a patron a saint of the Kingdom, either Bartholomew or Matthias [Matyasz]. Thus the son of Maciej was always called Bardomiej, 115 and again the son of Bartlomiej was called Maciej; the women were all christened Kachna or Maryna. In order to distinguish themselves amid such confusion, they took various nicknames, from some merit or defect, both men and women. Sometimes they would give a man several surnames, as a mark of the contempt or of the regard of his compatriots; sometimes the same gentleman was known by one name in Dobrzyn, and by a different title in the neighbouring hamlets. Imitating the Dobrzynskis, the rest of the gentry of the vicinity likewise assumed nicknames, or by-names. 116 Now almost every family employs them, but only a few know that they originated in Dobrzyn, and were necessary there, while in the rest of the country they became a custom through mere stupid imitation.

So Matyasz Dobrzynski, who was at the head of the whole family, had been called Cock-on-the-Steeple. Later, after the year seventeen hundred and ninety-four, he changed his nickname and was christened Hand-on-Hip; the Dobrzynskis themselves also called him Bunny our King, 117 but the Lithuanians styled him the Maciek of Macieks.

As he over the Dobrzynskis, so his house ruled over the village, standing between the tavern and the church. To all appearances it was rarely visited and mere trash lived in it, for at the entrance stood posts without gates, [pg 169] and the garden was neither fenced nor planted; in the vegetable beds birches had grown up. Yet this old farmhouse seemed the capitol of the village, for it was handsomer and more spacious than the other cottages, and on the right side, where the living-room was placed, it was of brick. Near by were a storehouse, granary, barn, cow shed, and stable, all close together, as is usually the case among the gentry. The whole was uncommonly old and decayed; the house roofs shone as if made of green tin, because of the moss and grass, which grew as luxuriantly as on a prairie. The thatches of the barns were like hanging gardens of various plants, the nettle and the crimson crocus, the yellow mullen and the bright-coloured tassels of mercury. In them too were nests of various birds; in the lofts were dove-cotes, nests of swallows in the windows; white rabbits hopped about at the threshold and burrowed in the untrodden turf. In a word the place was like a birdcage or a warren.

But of old it had been fortified! Everywhere there were plenty of traces that it had undergone great and frequent attacks. Near the gateway there still lay in the grass a relic of the Swedish invasion, an iron cannon ball, as large as a child's head; once the open gate had rested on that ball as on a stone. In the yard, among the weeds and the wormwood, rose the old stumps of some dozen crosses, on unconsecrated ground, a sign that here lay buried men who had perished by a sudden and unexpected death. When one eyed from close by the storehouse, granary, and cottage, he saw that the walls were peppered from ground to summit as with a swarm of black insects; in the centre of each spot sat a bullet, like a bumble-bee in its earthy burrow.
[pg 170]
On the doors of the establishment all the latches, nails, and hooks were either cut off or bore the marks of sabres; evidently here they had tested the temper of those swords of the time of the Sigismunds, with which one might boldly cut off the heads of nails or cleave hooks in two without making a notch in the blade. Over the doors could be seen coats of arms of the Dobrzynskis, but shelves of cheeses veiled the bearings, and swallows had walled them in thickly with their nests.

The interior of the house itself and of the stable and carriage-house you would find as full of accoutrements as an old armoury. Under the roof hung four immense helmets, the ornaments of martial brows; to-day the birds of Venus, the doves, cooing, fed their young in them. In the stable a great cuirass extended over the manger and a corselet of ring mail served as a chute through which the boy threw down clover to the colts. In the kitchen the godless cook had spoiled the temper of several swords by sticking them into the oven instead of spits; with a Turkish horsetail, captured at Vienna, she dusted her handmill. In a word, housewifely Ceres had banished Mars and ruled along with Pomona, Flora, and Vertumnus over Dobrzynski's house, stable, and barn. But to-day the goddesses must yield anew; Mars returns.

At daybreak there had appeared in Dobrzyn a mounted messenger; he galloped from cottage to cottage and awoke them as if to work for the manor: the gentry arose and filled with a crowd the streets of the hamlet; cries were heard in the tavern, candles seen in the priest's house. All were running about, each asked the other what this meant; the old men took counsel together, the young men saddled their [pg 171] horses while the women held them; the boys scuffled about, in a hurry to run and fight, but did not know with whom or about what! Willy-nilly, they had to stay behind. In the priest's dwelling there was in progress a long, tumultuous, frightfully confused debate; at last, not being able to agree, they finally decided to lay the whole matter before Father Maciej.

Seventy-two years of age was Maciej, a hale old man, of low stature, a former Confederate of Bar. 118 Both his friends and his enemies remembered his curved damascened sabre, with which he was wont to chop spears and bayonets like fodder, and to which in jest he had given the modest name of switch . From a Confederate he became a partisan of the King, and supported Tyzenhaus, 119 the Under-Treasurer of Lithuania; but when the King joined the men of Targowica, Maciej once more deserted the royal side. And hence, since he had passed through so many parties, he had long been called Cock-on-the-Steeple, because like a cock he turned his standard with the wind. You would in vain search for the cause of such frequent changes; perhaps Maciej was too fond of war, and, when conquered on one side, sought battle anew on the other; perhaps the shrewd politician judged well the spirit of the times, and turned whither he thought the good of his country called him. 120 Who knows! This much is sure, that never was he seduced either by desire for personal fame, or by base greed, and that never had he supported the Muscovite party; for at the very sight of a Muscovite he frothed and grimaced. In order not to meet a Muscovite, after the partition of the country, he sat at home like a bear that sucks its paw in the woods.

His last experience in war was when he went with Oginski 121 to Wilno, where they both served under [pg 172] Jasinski, and there with his switch he performed prodigies of valour. Everybody knew how he had jumped down alone from the ramparts of Praga to defend Pan Pociej, 122 who had been deserted on the field of battle and had received twenty-three wounds. In Lithuania they long thought that both had been killed; but both returned, each as full of holes as a sieve. Pan Pociej, an honourable man, immediately after the war had wished to reward generously his defender Dobrzynski; he had offered him for life a farm of five houses, and assigned him yearly a thousand ducats in gold. But Dobrzynski wrote back: "Let Pociej remain in debt to Maciej, and not Maciej to Pociej." So he refused the farm and would not take the money; returning home alone, he lived by the work of his own hands, making hives for bees and medicine for cattle, sending to market partridges which he caught in snares, and hunting wild beasts.

In Dobrzyn there were numbers of sagacious old men—men versed in Latin, who from their youth up had practised at the bar; there were numbers of richer men: but of all the family the poor and simple Maciek was the most highly honoured, not only as a swordsman made famous by his *switch* , but as a man of wise and sure judgment, who knew the history of the country and the traditions of the family, and was equally well versed in law and farming. He knew likewise the secrets of hunting and of medicine; they even ascribed to him (though this the priest denied) a knowledge of higher, superhuman things. This much is sure, that he knew with precision the changes of the weather, and could guess them oftener than the farmer's almanac. It is no marvel then that, whether it was a question of beginning the sowing, or of sending out the river barges, or of reaping the grain; whether it was a matter of going to [pg 173] law, or of concluding a compromise, nothing was done in Dobrzyn without the advice of Maciek. Such influence the old man did not in the least seek for; on the contrary, he wished to be rid of it, scolded his clients, and usually pushed them out of the door of his house without opening his lips; he rarely gave advice, and never to common men; only in extremely important disputes or agreements, when asked, would he utter an opinion—and then in few words. It was thought that he would undertake to-day's affair and put himself in person at the head of the expedition; for in his youth he had loved a combat beyond measure, and he was an enemy of the Muscovite race.

The aged man was walking about in his solitary yard, humming a song, "When the early dawn ariseth," 123 and was happy because the weather was clearing; the mist was not rising up as it usually does when clouds are gathering, but kept falling: the wind spread forth its palms and stroked the mist, smoothed it, and spread it on the meadow; meanwhile the sun from on high with a thousand beams pierced the web, silvered it, gilded it, made it rosy. As when a pair of workmen at Sluck are making a Polish girdle; a girl at the base of the loom smooths and presses the web with her hands, while the weaver throws her from above threads of silver, gold and purple, forming colours and flowers: thus to-day the wind spread all the earth with mist and the sun embroidered it.

Maciej was warming himself in the sun after finishing his prayers, and was already setting about his household work. He brought out grass and leaves; he sat down in front of his house and whistled: at this whistle a multitude of rabbits bobbed up from beneath the ground. Like narcissuses suddenly blooming above [pg 174] the grass, their long ears shine white; beneath them their bright eyes glitter like bloody rubies thickly sown in the velvet of the greensward. Now the rabbits sit up, and each listens and gazes around; finally the whole white, furry herd run to the old man, allured by leaves of cabbage; they jump to his feet, on his knees, on his shoulders: himself white as a rabbit, he loves to gather them around him and stroke their warm fur with his hand; but with his other hand he throws millet on the grass for the sparrows, and the noisy rabble drop from the roofs.

While the aged man was amusing himself with the sight of this gathering, suddenly the rabbits vanished into the earth, and the flocks of sparrows fled to the roof before new guests, who were coming into the yard with quick steps. These were the envoys whom the assembly of gentry at the priest's house had sent to consult Maciek. Greeting the old man from afar with low bows, they said: "Praised be Jesus Christ." — "For ever and ever, amen," 124 answered the old man; and, when he had learned of the importance of the embassy, he asked them into his cottage. They entered and sat down upon a bench. The first of the envoys took his stand in the centre and began to render an account of his mission.

Meanwhile more and more of the gentry were arriving; almost all the Dobrzynskis, and no few of the neighbours from the hamlets near by, armed and unarmed, in carts and in carriages, on foot and on horseback. They halted their vehicles, tied their nags to the birches, and, curious as to the outcome of the deliberations, they formed a circle about the house: they soon filled the room and thronged the vestibule; others listened with their heads crowded into the windows.
[pg 175]

BOOK VII.—THE CONSULTATION

ARGUMENT

Salutary counsels of Bartek, called the Prussian—Martial argument of Maciek the Sprinkler—Political argument of Pan Buchmann—Jankiel advises harmony, which is cut off abruptly by the penknife—Speech of Gerwazy, which makes apparent the great potency of parliamentary eloquence—Protest of old Maciek—The sudden arrival of reinforcements interrupts the consultation—Down with the Soplica!

It came the turn of the deputy Bartek to state his case. He was a man who often travelled with rafts to Königsberg; he was called the Prussian by the members of his family, in jest, for he hated the Prussians horribly, although he loved to talk of them. He was a man well advanced in years, who on his distant travels had learned much of the world; a diligent reader of gazettes, well versed in politics, he could cast no little light on the subject under discussion. Thus he concluded his speech:—

"This is not, Pan Maciej, my brother, and revered father of us all—this is not aid to be despised. I should rely on the

French in time of war as on four aces; they are a warlike people, and since the times of Thaddeus Kosciuszko the world has not had such a military genius as the great Emperor Bonaparte. I remember when the French crossed the Warta; I was on a trip abroad at the time, in the year of our Lord one thousand eight hundred and six; I was just then doing some trading with Dantzic, and, since I have many kinsmen in the district [pg 176] of Posen, I had gone to visit them. So it happened that Pan Joseph Grabowski 125 and I—he is now colonel of a regiment, but at that time he was living in the country near Obiezierz—were out hunting small game together.

"In Great Poland126 there was then peace, as there is now in Lithuania; suddenly the tidings spread abroad of a fearful battle; a messenger from Pan Todwen rushed up to us. Grabowski read the letter and cried: 'Jena! Jena!127 The Prussians are smitten hip and thigh; victory!' Dismounting from my horse, I immediately fell on my knees to thank the Lord God. We rode back to the city as if on business, as if we knew nothing of the matter; there we saw that all the landraths, hofraths, commissioners and all similar rubbish were bowing low to us; they all trembled and turned pale, like those cockroaches we call Prussians, when one pours boiling water on them. Laughing and rubbing our hands we asked humbly for news, and inquired what they had heard from Jena. Thereupon terror seized them, they were astonished that we already knew of that disaster. The Germans cried, 'Ach Herri Gott! O Weh!' and, hanging their heads, they ran into their houses, and then pell-mell out of their houses again. O that was a scramble! All the roads in Great Poland were full of fugitives; the Germans crawled along them like ants, dragging their carts, or rather waggons and drays, as the people call them there; men and women, with pipes and coffee-pots, were dragging boxes and feather beds; they scuttled off as best they could. But we quietly took counsel together: 'To horse! Let us harass the retreat of the Germans; now we will give it to the landraths in the neck, cut chops from the hofraths, and catch the herr officers by the cues.' And now General Dombrowski [pg 177] entered the district of Posen and brought the orders of the Emperor to stir up an insurrection! In one week our people so whipped and banished the Prussians that you couldn't have found a German to make medicine of! 128 What if we could turn the trick just as briskly and smartly now, and here in Lithuania give the Muscovites just such another sweating? Hey? What think you, Maciej? If Moscow picks a bone with Bonaparte, then he will make a war that will be no joke: he is the foremost hero in the world, and has armies unnumbered! Hey, what think you, Maciej, our Father Bunny?"

He concluded. All awaited the verdict of Maciej. Maciej did not move his head or raise his eyes, but only struck himself several times on the side, as though he were feeling for his sabre. (Since the partition of the country he had worn no sabre; however, from old habit, at the mention of a Muscovite he always clapped his hand to his left side; he was evidently groping for his switch; and hence everybody called him Hand-on-Hip.) Now he raised his head, and they listened in deep silence. Maciej disappointed the general expectation; he only frowned and again dropped his head on his breast. Finally he spoke out, pronouncing every word slowly and with emphasis, and nodding his head in time with them:—

"Silence! Whence comes all this news? How far off are the French? Who is their leader? Have they already begun war with Moscow? Where and on what pretext? Which way are they going to move? and with what numbers are they comings? Have they a large force of infantry and cavalry? Whoever knows, let him tell!"
[pg 178]
The crowd was silent, each man gazing at his neighbour.

"I should be glad," said the Prussian, "to wait for the Bernardine Robak, for all the tidings come from him. Meanwhile we should send trusty spies across the border and quietly arm all the country round; but meanwhile we should conduct the whole matter with caution, in order not to betray our intentions to the Muscovites."

"Hah! Wait, prate, debate?" interrupted another Maciej, christened Sprinkler, 129 from a great club that he called his *sprinkling-brush*; he had it with him to-day. He stood behind it, rested both hands on the knob, and leaned his chin on his hands, crying: "Delay, wait, debate! Hem, hum, haw, and then run away! I have never been in Prussia; Königsberg sense is good for Prussia, but I have my plain gentleman's sense. This much I know: whoever wants to fight, let him seize his sprinkling-brush; whoever prefers to die, let him call the priest—that's all! I want to live and fight! Of what use is the Bernardine? Are we schoolboys? What do I care for that Robak? Now we will all be Robaks, that is, worms, and proceed to gnaw at the Muscovites! Hem, haw! spies! to explore! Do you know what that means? Why, that you are impotent old beggars! Hey, brothers! It is a setter's work to follow a trail, a Bernardine's to gather alms, but my work is—to sprinkle, sprinkle, sprinkle, and that's all!"

Here he patted his club; after him the whole crowd of gentry yelled, "Sprinkle, sprinkle!"

The side of Sprinkler was supported by Bartek, called Razor from his thin sabre; and likewise by Maciej, known as Bucket, from a blunderbuss that he [pg 179] carried, with a muzzle so broad that from it as from a pail a thousand bullets poured in a stream. Both cried, "Long live Sprinkler and his brush." The Prussian tried to speak, but he was drowned by uproar and laughter. "Away, away with the Prussian cowards," they shouted; "let cowards go and hide in Bernardine cowls!"

Then once more old Maciej slowly raised his head, and the tumult began somewhat to subside.

"Do not scoff at Robak," he said; "I know him; he is a clever priest. That little worm130 has gnawed a larger nut than you; I have seen him but once, but as soon as I set eyes on him I noticed what sort of bird he was; the Monk turned away his eyes, fearing that I might summon him to confession. But that is not my affair—of that there would be much to say! He will not come here; it would be vain to summon the Bernardine. If all this news came from him, then who knows what was his object, for he is the devil of a priest! If you know nothing more than this news, then why did you come here, and what do you want?"

"War!" they cried. "What war?" he asked. "War with the Muscovites!" they shouted, "to fight! Down with the Muscovites!"

The Prussian kept shouting and raising his voice higher and higher, until he finally obtained a hearing, which he owed partly to his polite bows, and partly to his shrill and piercing tones.

"I too want to fight," he shouted, pounding his breast with his fist; "though I don't carry a sprinkling-brush, yet with a pole from a river barge I once gave a good christening to four Prussians who tried to drown me in the Pregel when I was drunk."

[pg 180]

"Good for you, Bartek," said Sprinkler, "good for you; sprinkle, sprinkle!"

"But in the name of the most dear Jesus, we must first know with whom the war is and about what; we must proclaim that to the world," shouted the Prussian, "for what is going to make the people follow us? Where they are to go, and when, and how, we do not know ourselves. Brother gentlemen, we need discretion! My friends, we need order and method! If you wish war, let us make a confederacy,131 and discuss where to form it and under whose leadership. That was the way in Great Poland—we saw the retreat of the Germans, and what did we do? We consulted secretly together; we armed both the gentry and a company of peasants; and, when we were ready, we waited Dombrowski's orders; at last, to horse! We rose as one man!"

"I beg the floor," called out the manager of Kleck, a spruce young man, dressed in German costume. His name was Buchmann, but he was a Pole, born in Poland; it was not quite certain that he was of gentle birth, but of that they asked no questions, and everybody respected Buchmann, because he was in service with a great magnate, was a good patriot, and full of learning. From foreign books he had learned the art of farming, and conducted well the administration of his estate; on politics he had also formed wise opinions; he knew how to write beautifully and how to express himself with elegance: therefore all became silent when he began to discourse.

"I beg the floor," he repeated; he twice cleared his throat, bowed, and with tuneful lips thus proceeded:—

"My predecessors in their eloquent speeches have touched on all the principal and decisive points, and [pg 181] have raised the discussion to a higher plane; it only remains for me to unite into one focus the pertinent thoughts and considerations that have been put forward: I have the hope of thus reconciling contrary opinions. I have noted that the entire discussion consists of two parts; the division is already made, and that division I follow. First: why should we undertake an insurrection? in what spirit? That is the first vital question. The second concerns the revolutionary authority. The division is a proper one, only I wish to reverse it, and begin with the authority: when once we understand the authority, from it I will deduce the nature, spirit, and aim of the insurrection. As for the authority then—when I survey with my eyes the history of all humanity, what do I perceive therein? Why, that the human race, savage, and scattered in forests, gathers together, collects, unites for common defence, and considers it; that is its first consultation. Then each lays aside a part of his own liberty for the common good; that is the first foundation, from which, as from a spring, flow all laws. We see then that government is created by agreement, and does not proceed, as men erroneously hold, from the will of God. Thus, since government rests upon the social contract, the division of power is only its necessary consequence."

"So there you are at contracts! Do you mean those of Kiev or of Minsk?" 132 said old Maciej. "You must mean the Babin government!133 Pan Buchmann, whether God or the devil chose to cast the Tsar upon us I will not dispute with Your Honour; Pan Buchmann, tell us, please, how to cast off the Tsar."

"There's the rub," shouted Sprinkler; "if I could only jump to the throne, and with my brush—splash—once [pg 182] moisten the Tsar, then he wouldn't come back, either through the Kiev tract or the Minsk tract, or by any one of Buchmann's contracts; the Russian priests would not revive him either by the power of God or by that of Beelzebub—the only brave way is to sprinkle. Pan Buchmann, your speech was very eloquent, but eloquence is nothing but noise; sprinkling is the principal thing."

"Good, good, good!" squealed Bartek the Razor, rubbing his hands, and running from Sprinkler to Maciek like a shuttle thrown from one side of the loom to the other. "Only do you, Maciek of the switch, and you, Maciek of the club, make up your disagreement, and, so help me Heaven, we will knock the Muscovites to splinters; Razor advances under the orders of Switch."

"Orders are good on parade," interrupted Sprinkler. "We had a standing order in the Kowno brigade, a short and pointed one: 'Strike terror and be not terrified; fight and do not surrender; advance always, and make quick strokes, slish, slash!' "

"Those are my principles," squealed Razor. "What's the use of spilling ink and drawing up acts of confederation? Do you want one? That's the whole question. Maciej is our marshal and his little switch is his baton of office."

"Long live Cock-on-the-Steeple!" shouted Baptist. The gentry answered, "Vivant the sprinklers!"

But in the corners a murmur had arisen, though it was stifled in the centre; evidently the council was dividing into two sides. Buchmann shouted: "I will never approve an agreement; that's my system." Somebody else yelled "Veto," 134 and others seconded [pg

183] him from the corners. Finally the gruff voice of Skoluba was heard, a gentleman from another hamlet.

"What is this, my friends of the Dobrzynski family? What does all this mean? How about us, shall we be deprived of our rights? When we were invited from our hamlet—and the Warden, My-boy Rembajlo invited us—we were told that great things were to be done, that the question did not affect the Dobrzynskis alone, but the whole district, the entire gentry; Robak mumbled the same thing, though he never finished his talk and always stammered and expressed himself obscurely. Well, finally we have gathered, and have called in our neighbours by messengers. You Dobrzynskis are not the only men here; from various other hamlets there are about two hundred of us here; so let us *all* consult together. If we need a marshal, let us all vote, with an equal voice for each; long live equality!"

Then two Terajewiczes and four Stypulkowskis and three Mickiewiczes shouted, "Vivat equality," taking the side of Skoluba. Meanwhile Buchmann was crying, "Agreement will be our ruin!" Sprinkler yelled: "We can get along alone without you; long live our marshal, the Maciek of Macieks! Let him have the baton!" The Dobrzynskis cried, "We beg you to take it!" but the rest of the gentry shouted with one voice, "We forbid it!" The throng was breaking up into two groups, and, nodding their heads in contrary directions, one faction cried, "We forbid," and the other, "We beg you."

Old Maciek sat in their midst the one dumb man, and his head alone was unmoved. Opposite him stood Baptist, resting his hands on his club, and, moving his [pg 184] head, which was supported on the end of the club, like a pumpkin stuck on the end of a long pole, he nodded it, now forward and now backward, and cried incessantly, "Sprinkle, sprinkle!" Up and down the room the mobile Razor ran constantly from Sprinkler to Maciej's bench, but Bucket slowly walked across the room from the Dobrzynskis to the other gentry, as if he were trying to reconcile them. One shouted continually, "Shave," and the other, "Pour"; Maciek held his peace, but he was evidently beginning to be angry.

For a quarter of an hour the uproar seethed, when above the bawling crowd, out of the throng of heads, there leapt aloft a shining pillar. This was a sword two yards long and a whole palm broad, sharp on both edges. Evidently it was a German sword, forged of Nuremberg steel; all gazed at the weapon in silence. Who had raised it up? They could not see, but at once they guessed.

"That is the penknife, long live the penknife!" they shouted; "vivat the penknife, the jewel135 of Rembajlo hamlet! Vivat Rembajlo, Notchy, Half-Goat, My-boy!"

At once Gerwazy, for it was he, pressed through the crowd into the middle of the room, carrying his flashing penknife; then, lowering the point before Maciek as a sign of greeting, he said:—

"The penknife bows to the switch. Brothers, gentlemen of Dobrzyn, I will give you no advice. Not at all; I will only tell you why I have assembled you; but what to do and how to do it, decide for yourselves. You know the rumour has long been current among the hamlets that great things are preparing in the world. Father Robak has been talking of this; do not you all [pg 185] know this?" ("We know it," they shouted.) "Well, so for a wise head," continued the orator, looking sharply at them, "two words are enough. Is not that true?" ("It is," they said.) "Since the French Emperor is coming from one direction," said the Warden, "and the Russian Tsar from the other, there will be war; the Tsar and the Emperor, kings and kings, will start to pummel one another as monarchs usually do—and shall we sit quiet? When the great begin to choke the great, let us choke the smaller, each his own man. When we set to smiting above and below, great men great ones, and small men small ones, then all the rascals will be overthrown, and thus happiness and the Polish Commonwealth will bloom again. Is not this so?"

"As true as if you were reading it out of a book," they said.

"It is true!" repeated Baptist, "drop after drop, every bit."

"I am always ready to shave!" exclaimed Razor.

"Only make an agreement," courteously begged Bucket, "under whose leadership Baptist and Maciej shall proceed."

But Buchmann interrupted him: "Let fools agree; discussions do not harm the common weal. I beg you to be silent." ("We are listening.") "The case gains thereby; the Warden is considering it from a new point of view."

"Not at all," shouted the Warden, "I follow the old fashion. Of great things great men should think; for them there is an Emperor, and there will be a King, a Senate, and Deputies. Such things, my boy, are done in Cracow or in Warsaw, not here among us, in the [pg 186] hamlet of Dobrzyn. Acts of confederation are not written on a chimney with chalk, nor on a river barge, but on parchment; it is not for us to write such acts. Poland has the secretaries of the Kingdom and of Lithuania; such was the ancient custom: my business is to whittle with my penknife."

"To sprinkle with my brush," added Sprinkler.

"And to bore with my awl," cried Bartek the Awl, drawing his sword.

"I summon you all to witness," concluded the Warden; "did not Robak tell you, that before you receive Napoleon into your house you should sweep out the dirt? You all heard it, but do you understand? Who is the dirt of the district? Who traitorously killed the best of Poles; who robbed and plundered him? Who? Must I tell you?"

"Why, it is Soplica," interrupted Bucket; "and now he even wants to snatch the remnants from the hands of the heir; he is a scoundrel."

"O, he is a tyrant!" squealed Razor.

"Then sprinkle him!" added Baptist.

"If he is a traitor," said Buchmann, "to the gallows with him!"

"Hurrah!" they all cried, "down with Soplica!"

But the Prussian ventured to undertake the defence of the Judge, and cried with arms held up towards the gentry:—

"Brother gentlemen! O! O! By God's wounds, what means this? Warden, are you mad? Was it this we were discussing? Because a man had a crazy, outlaw brother, shall we punish him on his brother's account? That is a Christian way of doing things! The Count is behind all this. As for the Judge's being [pg 187] hard on the gentry, that is not true! In Heaven's name! Why, it is you who summon *him* to court, but he always seeks a peaceful settlement with you; he yields his rights and even pays the costs. He has a lawsuit with the Count, but what of that? Both are rich; let magnate fight magnate: what do we people care? The Judge a tyrant! He was the first to forbid that the peasants should bow low before him, saying that that was a sin. Often a company of peasants—I have seen this myself—sit at table with him; he has paid the taxes for the village, and it is quite different at Kleck, though there, Pan Buchmann, you run things in German fashion. The Judge a traitor! I have known him since we were in the primary school; as a lad he was honest, and to-day he is the same; he loves Poland above everything, he keeps up Polish customs, he will not yield to Muscovite fashions. Whenever I return from Prussia, and want to wash off the German taint, I drop in at Soplicowo, as the centre of Polish ways; there a man drinks and breathes his Country! In God's name, brothers Dobrzynski; I am one of you, but I will not let the Judge be wronged; nothing will come of that. It was not thus in Great Poland, brothers: what a spirit! what harmony! It is pleasant to remember it! There no one dared to interrupt our counsels with such a trifle."

"It is no trifle to hang scoundrels!" shouted the Warden.

The murmur was increasing. Suddenly Jankiel asked a hearing, jumped on a bench, took his stand on it, and thus raised above their heads a beard like a tavern bush, which hung down to his belt. With his right hand he slowly took from his head his foxskin hat, with his left [pg 188] he adjusted his disordered skull-cap; then he tucked his right hand in his girdle and spoke thus, bowing low to all with his foxskin hat:—

"Well, gentlemen of Dobrzyn, I am nothing but a Jew; the Judge is no kith or kin of mine; I respect the Soplicas as very good gentlemen and my landlords; I respect also the Bartek and Maciej Dobrzynskis, as good neighbours and my benefactors; but I say thus: if you want to do violence to the Judge, that is very bad; some of you may get hurt and be killed. But how about the assessors? and the police-captain? and the prison? For in the village near Soplica's house there are heaps of soldiers, all yagers! The Assessor is at the house; he need only whistle, and they will march right up and stand there ready for action. And what will happen then? But if you are expecting the French, why the French are still far off, a long road. I'm a Jew and know nothing of war, but I have been in Bielica, where I met Jews straight from the boundary. The report is that the French were stationed on the river Lososna, and that if there is to be war, it will not come till spring. Well, I tell you, wait; the farm of Soplicowo is not a fair booth, that is taken apart, put in a waggon, and carried off; the farm will stand as it is until spring. And the Judge is no Jew in a rented tavern; he won't run away, you can find him in the spring. But now pray disperse, and don't speak aloud of what has occurred, for to talk of it will do no good. And I beg you all, kind gentlemen, follow me: my Sarah has given birth to a little Jankiel, and to-day I treat the crowd; and the music is splendid! I will order bagpipes, a bass viol, and two fiddles; and Pan Maciek, my friend, likes old July mead and a new mazurka. I have new mazurkas, and I have taught my kids to sing just fine."

[pg 189]
The eloquence of the universally beloved Jankiel touched the hearts of his hearers; there arose cries and exclamations of joy; the murmur of approbation was even spreading beyond the house, when Gerwazy aimed his penknife at Jankiel. The Jew jumped down and disappeared in the crowd; the Warden shouted:—

"Begone, Jew, don't stick your fingers into the door; this is not your business! Prussian, because you, sir, conduct your trading with the Judge's pair of miserable boats, are you shouting for him? Have you forgotten, my boy, that your respected father used to make the trip to Prussia with twenty Horeszko boats? Thence he and his family grew rich; yes, and every one of you that are living here in Dobrzyn. For you old men remember, and you young men have heard, that the Pantler was the father and benefactor of you all. Whom did he send as manager to his Pinsk estates? A Dobrzynski. Who were his accountants? Dobrzynskis. He chose none for majordomos and none for butlers except Dobrzynskis; his house was full of Dobrzynskis. He pressed your cases before the courts, he gained pensions for you from the king; he put your children by droves in the Piarist136 schools, and paid for their clothes, board, and lodging; when they grew up he even got places for them, also at his own expense. Why did he do this? Because he was your neighbour. To-day Soplica's landmarks touch your borders; what good has *he* ever done you?"

"Not a bit!" interrupted Bucket, "for he is an upstart that rose from being a petty landholder. But how haughtily he blows out his cheeks, pooh, pooh, pooh; how high he holds his head! You remember, I invited him to my daughter's wedding; I offered him drink, [pg 190] but he wouldn't take it; he said: 'I don't drink as much as you gentry; you gentry swill like bitterns.' What a magnate! a milksop made of pastry flour! 137 He wouldn't drink, so we poured it down his throat; he cried, 'This is an act of violence!' Just wait; I'll pour it into him out of my bucket!"

"The knave!" exclaimed Baptist; "I'll just sprinkle him on my own account. My son used to be a clever lad; now he's turned so stupid that they call him Buzzard,138 and he has become such a ninny all because of the Judge. I said to him once, 'What do you run off to Soplicowo for? If I catch you there, God help you!' Immediately he slunk off to

Zosia again, and stole through the hemp; I caught him, and then took him by the ears and sprinkled him. But he blubbered and blubbered like a peasant's baby: 'Father, you may kill me, but I must go there!' and he kept on sobbing. 'What's the matter with you?' I asked, and he told me that he was in love with Zosia, and wanted to have a look at her! I felt sorry for the poor lad, and said to the Judge: 'Judge, give me Zosia for Buzzard.' 'She is still too young,' he answered. 'Wait about three years, and then she may do as she likes.' The scoundrel! He lies; he's already arranging another match for her. I have heard of it; just let me screw myself in there at the wedding, and I'll bless their marriage bed with my sprinkler."

"And shall such a scoundrel hold sway," cried the Warden, "and ruin ancient magnates, better men than he? And shall both the memory and the name of the Horeszkos perish! Where is there gratitude in the world? There is none in Dobrzyn. Brothers, do you wish to wage war with the Russian Emperor and yet [pg 191] do you fear a battle with Soplicowo farm? Are you afraid of prison! Do I summon you to brigandage? God forbid! Gentlemen and brothers, I stand on my rights. Why, the Count has won several times and has obtained no few decrees; the only trouble is to execute them! This was the ancient custom: the court wrote the decree, and the gentry carried it out, and especially the Dobrzynskis, and thence grew your fame in Lithuania! Yes, at the foray of Mysz the Dobrzynskis alone fought with the Muscovites, who were led by the Russian general Voynilovich, and that scoundrel, his friend, Pan Wolk of Logomowicze. You remember how we took Wolk captive, and how we were going to hang him to a beam in the barn, because he was a tyrant to the peasantry and a servant of the Muscovites; but the stupid peasants took pity on him! (I must roast him some time on this penknife.) I will not mention countless other great forays, from which we always emerged as befitted gentlemen, both with profit and with general applause and glory! Why should I remind you of this! To-day the Count, your neighbour, carries on his lawsuit and gains decrees in vain, for not one of you is willing to aid the poor orphan! The heir of that Pantler who nourished hundreds, to-day has no friend except me, his Warden, and except this faithful penknife of mine!"

"And my brush," said Sprinkler. "Where you go, dear Gerwazy, there will I go too, while I have a hand, and while this splish-splash is in my hands. Two are a pair! In Heaven's name, my Gerwazy! You have your sword, I have my sprinkling-brush! In Heaven's name, I will sprinkle, and do you strike; and thus slish and slash, splish and splash; let others prate!"
[pg 192]
"But, my brothers," said Razor, "you will not exclude Bartek; all that you may soap I will shave."

"I too prefer to move on with you," added Bucket, "since I cannot make them agree on the choice of a marshal. What care I for votes and balls for voting? I have other balls." (Here he took from his pocket a handful of bullets and rattled them.) "Here are balls!" he cried, "all these balls are for the Judge!"

"We will join you," shouted Skoluba, "indeed we will!"

"Where you go," cried all the gentry, "where you go, there will we go also! Long live the Horeszkos! Vivant the Half-Goats! Vivat the Warden Rembajlo! Down with the Soplica!"

And thus the eloquent Gerwazy carried them all away, for all had their grudges against the Judge, as is usual among neighbours; now complaints of damage done by cattle, now for the cutting of wood, now squabbles over boundary lines: some were aroused by anger, others merely by envy for the wealth of the Judge—all were united by hatred. They crowded about the Warden, and raised aloft sabres and sticks.

At last Maciek, hitherto sullen and motionless, rose from his bench and with slow steps came out into the middle of the room and put his hands on his hips: looking straight before him and nodding his head, he began to speak, pronouncing slowly every word, pausing between them and emphasising them:—

"O stupid, stupid idiots! Whoever dances, you will pay the piper. So long as the discussion was over the resurrection of Poland and had to do with the public weal, idiots, all this time you quarrelled! It was impossible, idiots, either to debate, idiots, or to get order [pg 193] among you, idiots, or to put a leader over you, idiots! But let any one raise his private grudges, idiots, then straightway you agree! Get out of here! for, as my name is Maciek, I wish you to millions, hundreds of hundreds of thousands of waggons of hogsheads, of drays of devils!!!"

All were hushed as if struck by lightning! But at the same moment a terrible shouting arose outside the house, "Vivat the Count!" He was riding into Maciej's yard, armed himself, and followed by ten armed jockeys. The Count was mounted on a mettled steed and dressed in black garments; over them a nut-brown cloak of Italian cut, broad and without sleeves, and fastened at the neck with a buckle, fell from his shoulders like a great shroud. He wore a round hat with a feather, and carried a sword in his hand; he wheeled about and saluted the throng with the sword.

"Vivat the Count!" they cried; "we will live and die with him!" The gentry began to gaze out of the cottage through the windows, and to press continually towards the door behind the Warden. The Warden went out, and behind him the crowd tumbled through the door; Maciek drove out the remnant, shut the door, bolted it, and, looking out through the window, said once more, "Idiots!"

But meanwhile the gentry had rallied to the Count. They went to the tavern; Gerwazy called to mind the days of old, and bade them give him three Polish girdles, by means of which he drew from the vaults of the tavern three casks, one of mead, the second of brandy, and the third of beer. He took out the spigots, and immediately three streamlets spurted forth, gurgling, one white as silver, the second red as carnelian, the third yellow: [pg 194] with a triple rainbow they played on high;

they fell in a hundred cups and hummed in a hundred glasses. The gentry ran riot: some drank, others wished a hundred years to the Count, all shouted, "Down with the Soplica!"

Jankiel rode off on horseback, silently, without saddle; the Prussian likewise, unheard, though he still discoursed eloquently, tried to slip away; the gentry chased him, crying that he was a traitor. Mickiewicz stood apart, at some distance, without either shouting or giving counsel, but from his air they perceived that he was plotting something evil: so they drew their blades, and at the shout of "Down with him" he retreated, and defended himself; he was already wounded and leaning on the fence, when Zan and the three Czechots sprang to his aid. After this the men were separated, but in that scuffle two had been wounded in the hand, and one had got cut over the ear. The rest were mounting their horses.

The Count and Gerwazy marshalled them and distributed arms and orders. At last, all started at a gallop down the long street of the hamlet, crying, "Down with the Soplica!"
[pg 195]

BOOK VIII.—THE FORAY

ARGUMENT

The Seneschal's astronomy—The Chamberlain's remarks on comets—Mysterious scene in the Judge's room—Thaddeus, wishing to extricate himself dexterously, gets into serious trouble—A new Dido—The foray—The last protest by an Apparitor—The Count conquers Soplicowo—Storm and massacre—Gerwazy as butler—The banquet after the foray.

Before a thunderstorm there is a quiet, sullen moment, when the cloud that has gathered over men's heads stops and with threatening countenance checks the breath of the winds; it is silent, but surveys the earth with the eyes of the lightnings, marking the spots where soon it will cast bolt after bolt: such a moment of calm rested over the house at Soplicowo. You would have thought that a presentiment of unusual events had closed all lips, and had borne off the spirits of all into the land of dreams.

After supper the Judge and his guests went out into the yard to enjoy the evening, and seated themselves on benches of turf built along the house wall. The whole company, in gloomy, quiet attitudes, gazed at the sky, which seemed to grow lower and narrower, and to approach the earth nearer and nearer, until both, hiding beneath a dark veil, like lovers, began a mysterious discourse, interpreting their feelings in the stifled sighs, whispers, murmurs, and half-uttered words, of which the marvellous music of the evening is composed.
[pg 196]
The owl began it, hooting from beneath the house roof; the bats rustled with flimsy wings, and flew towards the house, where shone the panes of the windows and human faces; but nearer, the little sisters of the bats, the moths, hovered in a swarm, attracted by the white garments of the women; they were especially troublesome to Zosia, beating against her face and her bright eyes, which they mistook for two candles. In the air an immense cloud of insects gathered and whirled about, playing like the music of the spheres; Zosia's ear distinguished amid the thousand noises the accord of the flies and the false half-tone of the mosquitoes.

In the fields the evening concert had hardly begun; the musicians were just finishing the tuning of their instruments: already the land rail, the first violin of the meadow, had shrieked thrice; already from afar the bitterns seconded it with a bass boom below in the marshes; already the woodcocks were rising up with whirling flight, uttering repeated cries, as though they were beating on drums.

As a finale to the humming of the insects and the din of the birds there resounded in a double chorus two ponds, like enchanted lakes in the Caucasus mountains, silent through all the day and playing at evening. One pond, which had clear depths and a sandy shore, gave forth from its blue chest a gentle, solemn call; the other pond, with a muddy bottom and a turbid throat, answered it with a mournfully passionate cry. In both ponds sang countless hordes of frogs; the two choruses were attuned into two great accords: one thundered fortissimo, the other gently warbled; one seemed to complain, the other only sighed; thus the [pg 197] two ponds conversed together across the fields, like two Æolian harps that play alternately.

The darkness was thickening; only in the woods and among the willows along the streamlet the eyes of wolves shone like candles, and farther off, on the narrowed borders of the horizon, here and there were the fires of shepherds' camps. Finally the moon lighted her silver torch, came forth from the wood, and illumined both sky and land. Now they both, half uncovered from the darkness, slept side by side, like a happy married pair; the heaven took into its pure arms the breast of the earth, which shone silvery in the moonlight.

Now, opposite the moon, first one star and then another began to shine; now a thousand of them, and now a million twinkled. Castor and his brother Pollux glittered at their head, once called among the Slavs Lele and Polele; 139 now they have been christened anew in the people's zodiac; one is called Lithuania and the other the Kingdom. 140

Farther off glitter the two pans of the heavenly Scales. Upon them God on the day of creation—as old men say—weighed in turn the earth and all the planets before he set the burden of them in the abysses of the air; then he hung up in heaven the gilded scales: on these men have modelled their balances and scale pans.

To the north shines the circle of the starry Sieve, 141 through which God, as they say, gifted grains of corn, when he cast them down from heaven for Adam our father, who had been banished for his sins from paradise.

Somewhat higher, David's Car, 142 ready for mounting, turns its long pole towards the north star. The old Lithuanians know, concerning this chariot, that the populace err in calling it David's, since it is the Angel's [pg 198] Car. On it long ago rode Lucifer, when he summoned God to combat, rushing at full gallop along the Milky Way towards the threshold of heaven, until Michael threw him from his car, and cast the car from the road. Now it is stretched out ruined amid the stars; the Archangel Michael will not allow it to be repaired.

And it is also well known among the old Lithuanians—but this knowledge they probably derived from the rabbins—that the huge, long Dragon of the zodiac, which winds its starry coils over the sky, and which astronomers erroneously christen a serpent, is not a serpent, but a fish, and is named Leviathan. Long ago it dwelt in the seas, but after the deluge it died for lack of water; hence on the vault of heaven, both as a curiosity and as a reminder, the angels hung up its dead remains. In the same way the priest of Mir has hung up in his church the ribs and shanks of giants that have been dug from the earth. 143

Such stories of the stars, which he had conned from books or learned from tradition, did the Seneschal relate. Though in the evening the old Seneschal's sight was weak, and he could see nothing in the sky through his spectacles, yet he knew by heart the name and form of every constellation; with his finger he indicated their places and their paths.

To-day they listened little to him, and gave no heed at all to the Sieve, or to the Dragon, or even to the Scales; to-day the eyes and thoughts of all were absorbed by a new guest, recently observed in the sky. This was a comet of the first magnitude and power, 144 which had appeared in the west and was flying towards the north; with a bloody eye it looked askance upon the Chariot, as though it wished to seize the empty place of Lucifer; [pg 199] behind, it threw out a long tail, and with it encircled a third part of the sky, gathered in hundreds of stars as with a net, and drew them after it; but it aimed its own head higher, towards the north, straight for the polar star.

With inexpressible apprehension all the Lithuanian folk gazed each night at this heavenly marvel, foreboding ill from it, and likewise from other signs: for too often they heard the cries of ill-omened birds, which, gathering in throngs on empty fields, sharpened their beaks as if awaiting corpses. Too often they noticed that the dogs rooted up the earth, and, as if scenting death, howled piercingly, which was an omen of famine or of war. But the forest guards beheld how through the graveyard walked the Maid of Pestilence, whose brow rises above the highest trees, and who waves in her left hand a bloody kerchief. 145

From all this the Overseer drew various conclusions, as he stood by the fence after coming to report on the work; so likewise did the Bookkeeper, who was whispering with the Steward.

But the Chamberlain was seated on the bench of turf before the house. He interrupted the conversation of the guests, a sign that he was preparing to speak; in the moonlight shone his great snuffbox (all of pure gold, set with diamonds; in the middle of it was a portrait of King Stanislaw, under glass); he tapped on it with his fingers, took a pinch, and said:—

"Thaddeus, your talk about the stars is only an echo of what you have heard in school; as to marvels I prefer to take the advice of simple people. I too studied astronomy for two years at Wilno, where Pani Puzynin, a wise and a rich woman, had given the income of a [pg 200] village of two hundred peasants for the purchase of various glasses and telescopes. Father Poczobut, 146 a famous man, was in charge of the observatory, and at that time rector of the whole university; however he finally abandoned his professor's chair and his telescope and returned to his monastery, to his quiet cell, and there he died as a good Christian should. I am also acquainted with Sniadecki, 147 who is a very wise man, though a layman. Now the astronomers regard planets and comets just as plain citizens do a coach; they know whether it is drawing up before the king's palace, or whether it is starting abroad from the city gates; but who was riding in it, and why, of what he talked with the king, and whether the king dismissed the ambassador with peace or war—of all that they do not even inquire. I remember in my time when Branicki started in his coach to Jassy, 148 and after that dishonourable coach streamed a train of Targowica confederates, as the tail follows that comet. The plain people, though they did not meddle in public deliberations, guessed at once that that train was an omen of treason. The report is that the folk has given the name of broom to this comet, and says that it will sweep away a million men." And in reply the Seneschal said with a bow:—

"That is true, Your Excellency the Chamberlain. I remember myself what was once told me when I was a little child; I remember, though I was not ten years old at the time, how I saw at our house the late Sapieha, lieutenant of a regiment of cuirassiers, who later was Court Marshal of the Kingdom, and finally died as Grand Chancellor of Lithuania, at the age of one hundred and ten years; when Jan III. Sobieski was king, he had served in the Vienna campaign under the [pg 201] command of the hetman Jablonowski. So this Chancellor related that just at the moment when King Jan III. was mounting his horse, when the papal nuncio had blest him for the journey, and the Austrian ambassador was kissing his foot as he handed him the stirrup (the ambassador was named Count Wilczek), the King cried: 'See what is going on in Heaven!' They beheld that over their heads was advancing a comet by the same path that the armies of Mahomet had taken, from the east to the west. Later Father Bartochowski, who composed a panegyric for the triumph at Cracow, under the title Orientis Fulmen , 149 discoursed much about that comet; I have also read of it in a work called Janina , 150 in which the entire expedition of the late King Jan is described, and where there is engraved the great standard of Mahomet, and just such a comet as we see to-day."

"Amen," said the Judge in reply, "I

accept your augury that a Jan III. may appear along with the star! To-day there is a great hero in the west; perhaps the comet will bring him to us: which may God grant!"

Sorrowfully drooping his head, the Seneschal replied:—

"A comet sometimes forebodes wars, and sometimes mere brawls! It is not good that it has appeared here over Soplicowo; perhaps it threatens us with some household misfortune. Yesterday we had wrangling and disputes enough, both at the time of the hunt and during the banquet. In the morning the Notary quarrelled with the Assessor, and Thaddeus challenged the Count in the evening. The disagreement seems to have arisen from the bear's hide, and if my friend the Judge had not hindered me, I should have reconciled the two [pg 202] adversaries right at the table. For I should have liked to tell a curious incident, similar to what occurred at our hunt yesterday, which happened to the foremost sportsmen of my time, the deputy Rejtan and the Prince de Nassau. The occurrence was as follows:—

"Prince Czartoryski,151 the general of Podole, was travelling from Volhynia to his Polish estates, or, if I remember correctly, to the Diet at Warsaw. On his way he visited the gentry, partly for amusement, and partly to win popularity; so he called upon Pan Thaddeus Rejtan, 152 to-day of holy memory, who was later our deputy from Nowogrodek, and in whose house I grew up from childhood. So Rejtan, on the occasion of the Prince's coming, had invited guests, and the gentry had gathered in large numbers. There were theatrical entertainments (the Prince was devoted to the theatre); Kaszyc, who lives in Jatra, gave fireworks; Pan Tyzenhaus 153 sent dancers; and Oginski 154 and Pan Soltan, who lives in Zdzienciol, furnished musicians. In a word, at home they offered entertainments gorgeous beyond expectation, and in the forest they arranged a mighty hunt. It is well known to you gentlemen that almost all the Czartoryskis within the memory of man, though they spring from the blood of the Jagiellos, are nevertheless not over keen on hunting, though certainly not from laziness, but from their foreign tastes; and the Prince General looked oftener into books than into kennels, and oftener into ladies' alcoves than into the forests.

"In the Prince's suite was a German, Prince de Nassau,155 of whom they related that, when a guest in the Libyan country, he had once gone hunting with the Moorish kings, and there with a spear had overcome a [pg 203] tiger in hand to hand combat, of which feat that Prince de Nassau boasted greatly. In our country, at that time, they were hunting wild boars; Rejtan had killed with his musket an immense sow, at great risk to himself, for he shot from close by. Each of us admired and praised the sureness of the aim; only the German, de Nassau, listened with indifference to such compliments, and, walking off, muttered in his beard that a sure aim proved only a bold eye, but that cold steel proved a bold hand; and once more he began to talk big about his Libya and his spear, his Moorish kings and his tiger. This began to be annoying to Pan Rejtan, who, being a quick-tempered man, smote his sword and said: 'My Lord Prince, whoever looks boldly, fights boldly; wild boars are equal to tigers, and sabres to spears.' Then the German and he began somewhat too lively a discussion. Luckily the Prince General interrupted their dispute, and reconciled them, speaking in French; what he said to them I know not, but that reconciliation was only ashes over live coals: for Rejtan took the matter to heart, bided his time, and promised to play the German a good trick. This trick he almost atoned for with his own life, but he played it the next day, as I will tell you immediately."

Here the Seneschal paused, and, raising his right hand, asked the Chamberlain for his snuffbox; he took several pinches, but did not vouchsafe to finish his tale, as though he wished to sharpen the curiosity of his hearers. At last he was beginning—when that tale, so curious and so diligently hearkened to, was again interrupted! For some one had unexpectedly sent a man to the Judge, with the message that he was waiting on business that brooked no delay. The Judge, wishing [pg 204] them good night, bade farewell to the company: immediately they scattered in various directions; some went into the house to sleep, others into the barn, to rest on the hay; the Judge went to give audience to the traveller.

The others were already asleep. Thaddeus wandered about the hallway, pacing like a watchman near his uncle's door, for he had to seek his counsel about important affairs, on that very day, before he went to sleep. He did not dare to knock, for the Judge had locked the door and was talking secretly with somebody; Thaddeus awaited the end of the interview and pricked up his ears.

From within he heard a sobbing; without touching the latch he cautiously looked through the keyhole. He saw a marvellous thing! The Judge and Robak were kneeling on the floor in each other's embrace, and were weeping hot tears; Robak was kissing the Judge's hands, while the Judge, weeping, embraced Robak around the neck; finally, after a pause of a quarter of an hour in their talk, Robak softly spoke these words:— 156

"Brother, God knows that till now I have never betrayed the secrets that, in repentance for my sins, I vowed at my confession to keep inviolate; that, entirely devoted to God and to my country, not serving pride, nor seeking earthly glory, I have lived till now and wished to die a Bernardine monk, concealing my name not only from the crowd, but from you and from my own son! However, the provincial has given me permission to make the disclosure in articulo mortis. Who knows whether I shall return alive! Who knows what will happen in Dobrzyn! Brother, affairs are frightfully, frightfully confused! The French are still [pg 205] far away, we must wait till the winter is over, but the gentry may not restrain themselves. Perhaps I have been too active in stirring up the insurrection! They may have understood me ill! The Warden has spoiled all! That crazy Count, I hear, has rushed away to Dobrzyn; I could not head him off, for an important reason: old Maciek has recognised me, and if he betrays me I must needs bow my neck beneath the penknife. Nothing will restrain the Warden! My life matters little, but by that disclosure I should destroy the foundations of the plot.

"And yet! I must be there to-day, and see what is going on, though I perish! Without me the gentry will run wild! Farewell, my dearest brother! Farewell, I must hasten. If I perish, you alone will sigh for my soul; in case of war, the whole secret is known to you—finish what I have begun, and remember that you are a Soplica."

Here the Monk wiped away his tears, buttoned his gown, drew on his cowl, and quietly opened the shutters of the rear window; evidently he jumped through the window into the garden. The Judge, left alone, sat down in a chair and began to weep.

Thaddeus waited a moment, before he jingled at the latch; when the door was opened he went in quietly and bowed low.

"My dear uncle," he said, "I have spent here but a few days, and the days have passed like a flash. I have not yet had time to enjoy fully your house and your own company, but I must depart, I must hasten away at once; to-day, uncle, or to-morrow at the latest. You remember that we have challenged the Count; to fight him is my affair, and I have sent a challenge. Since [pg 206] duelling is prohibited in Lithuania, I am going to the borders of the Grand Duchy of Warsaw; the Count, of course, is a braggart, but he does not lack courage, and will appear without fail at the appointed place. We will settle accounts; and, if God grants me his blessing, I will punish him, and then will swim over the Lososna, where the ranks of my brothers await me. I have heard that my father in his will bade me enter the army, and I have not heard that that will has been cancelled."

"My dear Thaddeus," said his uncle, "have you been scalded with boiling water, or are you dodging like a hunted fox that waves its brush in one direction and itself runs in another? We have challenged him, to be sure, and you will have to fight, but why are you so bent on going to-day? Before a duel it is the custom to send friends and settle the terms; the Count may still beg our pardon and make amends: just wait, there is still time enough. Some other whimsy must be driving you away from here; speak it out frankly: why such excuses? I am your uncle, and, though old, I know what young hearts are; I have been a father to you." (As he spoke he stroked his nephew beneath the chin.) "My little finger has already been whispering in my ear that you, sir, have been carrying on some intrigues here with the ladies. Nowadays young men take to the ladies devilish quick. But, my dear Thaddeus, confess it to me, and frankly."

"That is the truth," mumbled Thaddeus, "there are other causes, my beloved uncle! Perhaps it was my own fault! A mistake! No, a misfortune! It is now hard to correct it! No, dear uncle, I can stay here no longer. An error of youth! Uncle, do not question me further; [pg 207] I must depart from Soplicowo as quickly as may be."

"Oho!" said his uncle, "this is certainly some love tiff. I noticed yesterday that you bit your lips while you looked from under your eyebrows at a certain little girl; I saw that she too had a sour expression. I know all that nonsense; when a pair of children fall in love, then they have no end of misfortunes. Now they feel happy, now again they are afflicted and cast down; now again, for God knows what reason, they are ready to bite each other; now they stand in corners as if playing blind man's buff, and won't say a word to each other; sometimes they even run out into the fields. If such an attack is upon you, just be patient, there is a cure for all that; I will undertake to reconcile you shortly. I know all that nonsense, I have been young myself. Tell me all about it; in return I too may reveal something, and thus we will confess ourselves to each other."

"Uncle," said Thaddeus, kissing his hand and blushing, "I will tell you the truth. I have taken a great liking to that little girl, Zosia, your ward, though I have seen her only a couple of times; but they tell me that you design for my wife the Chamberlain's daughter, a beautiful girl, and a rich man's daughter. Now I could not marry Panna Rosa when I am in love with Zosia; it is hard to change one's heart, but dishonourable to marry when one loves another. Perhaps time will heal me; I shall depart—for a long absence."

"Thaddeus," interrupted his uncle, "that is a strange way of being in love, to run away from one's belovèd. It is well that you are frank; you see, you would have committed an act of folly by going away. But what [pg 208] should you say if I helped you to obtain Zosia? Hey? Well, aren't you jumping for joy?"

"Your goodness amazes me," said Thaddeus after a pause, "but yet—the favour of my kind uncle will avail me nothing! Ah, my hopes are vain, for Pani Telimena will not yield me Zosia!"

"We will ask her," said the Judge.

"No one can prevail upon her," interrupted Thaddeus hastily. "No, I cannot wait, uncle; I must be on my way quickly, to-morrow. Only give me your blessing, uncle; I have made all my preparations, and am now leaving for the Grand Duchy."

The Judge, twirling his mustaches, gazed angrily at the lad:—

"Are you so frank? Have you opened your heart to me so fully? First that duel! Then again love and this departure; O, there is something behind all this! They have been telling me, I have watched your steps! You are a deceitful, giddy fellow; you have been telling lies. Where were you going that evening, and what were you tracking like a setter outside the house? See here, Thaddeus, maybe you have seduced Zosia and are now running away? If so, booby, you will not succeed! Whether you like it or not, I tell you that you shall marry Zosia. Otherwise, the horsewhip—to-morrow you shall stand before the altar! And you talk to me of feelings—of an unchanging heart! You are a liar! Foh! I'll look into your case, Pan Thaddeus, I'll make your ears smart for you! I've had enough trouble to-day—till my head aches with it—and now you come to keep me from going to sleep in peace! Now go to bed!"

So speaking he threw open the door and called the Apparitor to undress him. [pg 209]

Thaddeus went out quietly, hanging his head, and thought over his bitter interview with his uncle. It was the first time that he had ever been scolded so severely! He appreciated the justice of the reproaches and blushed at himself. What should he do? What if Zosia should learn the whole story? Should he ask for her hand? But what would Telimena say? No—he felt that he could remain no longer in Soplicowo.

Thus buried in thought, he had hardly made two steps when something crossed his path; he looked—and saw a phantom all in white, tall, frail, and slender. It approached him with an outstretched arm, from which was reflected the trembling light of the moon, and, stepping up to him, softly moaned:—

"Ungrateful man! You sought my glance, and now you avoid it; you sought for speech with me, and to-day you close your ears, as though in my words and in my glance there were poison! I deserve my fate; I knew who you were! A man! Guiltless of coquetry, I did not wish to torture you, but made you happy; and is this the gratitude you show me! A triumph over my soft heart has hardened your heart; since you won it so easily, too quickly have you despised it! I deserve my fate; but, taught by bitter experience, believe me, that I despise myself more than you can despise me!"

"Telimena," said Thaddeus, "I vow to Heaven that my heart is not hard, nor do I avoid you through contempt. But just consider, they are watching us, following us; can we act so openly? What will people say? Why, this is improper, I vow—it is a sin!"

"A sin!" she answered him with a bitter smile. "O you young innocent! you lamb! If I, who am a woman, from very force of love care not though I be [pg 210] discovered, and though I be put to shame—but you! you a man? What matters it to one of you men, even though he may confess that he has intrigues with a dozen sweethearts at a time? Speak the truth, you wish to desert me."

She dissolved in tears.

"Telimena," answered Thaddeus, "what would the world say of a man, who now, at my time of life, in good health, should settle down in a village and pass his time making love—when so many young men, so many married men are leaving their wives and children and fleeing abroad, to the standards of their country? Although I might wish to remain, does it depend on me? My father in his will bade me enter the Polish army, and now my uncle has repeated that command; to-morrow I depart; I have already made my resolution, and with Heaven's aid, Telimena, I shall not change it."

"I do not wish to bar your path to glory," said Telimena, "or to hinder your happiness! You are a man, you will find a sweetheart worthier of your love; you will find one richer and fairer! Only for my consolation, let me know before we part that your liking for me was a true affection, that it was not merely a jest or wanton lust, but love; let me know that my Thaddeus loves me! Let me hear once more from your lips the words 'I love,' let me grave them in my heart, and write them in my thoughts; I shall forgive more easily, though you cease to love me, remembering how you have loved me!"

And she began to sob.

Thaddeus, seeing that she wept and implored him so feelingly, and that she required of him only such a trifle, was moved; sincere sorrow and pity overcame [pg 211] him, and if he had searched the secrets of his heart, perhaps at that moment he himself could not have told whether he loved her or not. So he spoke eagerly:—

"Telimena, so may God's bright lightning strike me, if it be not true that I have been fond of you—yes, that I have loved you deeply; short were the moments that we spent together, but so sweetly and so tenderly did they pass that for long, forever, will they be present to my thoughts, and Heaven knows that I shall never forget you!"

With a bound Telimena fell upon his neck:—

"This is what I have hoped for; you love me, so I still live! For to-day I was going to end my life by my own hand! Since you love me, my dear one, can you abandon me? To you I have given my heart, and to you I will give my worldly goods; I will follow you everywhere; with you each corner of the world will be charming; of the wildest wilderness love, believe me, will make a paradise!"

Thaddeus tore himself from her embrace by force. "What?" said he, "are you mad? Follow me? Where? How? Shall I, being a common soldier, drag you after me, as a sutleress?"

"Then we will be espoused," said Telimena.

"No, never!" shouted Thaddeus. "At present I have no intention whatever of marrying, nor of making love—nonsense! Let's drop the matter! I beg you, my dear, bethink yourself! Be calm! I am grateful to you, but it is impossible for us to marry; let us love each other, but just—in different places. I cannot remain longer; no, no, I must go. Farewell, my Telimena, I leave to-morrow."

He spoke, pulled his hat over his eyes, and turned [pg 212] aside, meaning to depart; but Telimena checked him with an eye and countenance like those of Medusa's head: against his will he had to remain; he looked with terror on her form; she had become pale, without motion, breath, or life. At last, stretching out an arm like a sword to transfix him, with her finger aimed straight at the eyes of Thaddeus, she cried:—

"This is what I wished! Ha, tongue of dragon, heart of viper! I care not that, infatuated with you, I scorned the Assessor, the Count, and the Notary, that you seduced me and have now abandoned me in my orphanhood; for that I care not! You are a man, I know your falsity; I know that, like others, you too would be capable of breaking your plighted troth; but I did not know that so basely you could lie! I have been listening by your uncle's door! So what about that child Zosia? Has she attracted your regard? And do you traitorously lay claim to her! Hardly had you deceived one unfortunate, when already beneath her very eyes you were seeking new victims! Flee, but my curses will reach you—or remain, and I will publish your perfidies to the world; your arts will no longer corrupt others as they have corrupted me! Away! I despise you! You are a liar, a base man!"

At this insult, mortal for a gentleman's ears, the like of which no Soplica had ever heard, Thaddeus trembled, and his face grew pale as that of a corpse. Stamping his foot and biting his lips, he muttered, "Idiotic woman!"

He walked away, but the epithet "base" echoed in his heart; the young man shuddered, and felt that he had deserved it; he felt that he had inflicted a great wrong on Telimena; his conscience told him that she [pg 213] had reproached him justly: yet he felt that after those reproaches he loathed her more violently than ever. Of Zosia, alas! he did not venture to think; he was ashamed. However, that very Zosia, so lovely and so charming, his uncle had been seeking to win for him! Perhaps she would have been his wife, had not a demon, after entangling him in sin after sin, lie after lie, at last bade him adieu with a mocking laugh. He was rebuked and scorned by all! In a few short days he had ruined his future! He felt the just punishment of his crime.

In this storm of feelings, like an anchor of rest there suddenly flashed upon him the thought of the duel. "I must slay the Count, the scoundrel!" he cried, "I must perish or be avenged!" But for what? That he did not know himself. And that great burst of anger, as it had come over him in the twinkling of an eye, so it vanished away; he was seized anew by a deep sadness. He meditated whether his observation might not be true, that the Count and Zosia had some mutual understanding. "And what of that? Perhaps the Count sincerely loves Zosia; perhaps she loves him, and will choose him for her husband! By what right could I desire to break off that marriage; and, unhappy myself, to destroy the happiness of every one?"

He fell into despair and saw no other means except speedy flight. Whither? To the grave!

So, pressing his fist against his bent brow, he ran to the meadows, where, below, the ponds glittered, and took his stand above the one with marshy banks; in its greenish depths he buried his greedy gaze and drew into his breast with joy the swampy odours, and opened his lips to them; for suicide, like all wild passions, springs from the imagination: in the giddy whirling [pg 214] of his brain he felt an unspeakable longing to drown himself in the swamp.

But Telimena, guessing the young man's despair from his wild gestures, and seeing that he had run towards the ponds, although she burned with such just wrath against him, was nevertheless alarmed; in reality she had a kind heart. She had felt sorrow that Thaddeus dared to love another; she had wished to punish him, but she had not thought of destroying him. So she rushed after him, raising both her arms and crying: "Stop! What folly! Love me or not! Get married or depart! Only stop!——" But in his swift course he had far outstripped her; he already—was standing at the shore!

By a strange decree of fate, along that same shore was riding the Count, at the head of his band of jockeys; and, carried away by the charm of so fair a night, and by the marvellous harmony of that subaqueous orchestra, of those choruses that rang like Æolian harps (for no frogs sing so beautifully as those of Poland), he checked his horse and forgot about his expedition. He turned his ear to the pond and listened curiously; he ran his eyes over the fields, over the expanse of the heavens: he was evidently composing in his thoughts a nocturnal landscape.

In very truth, the neighbourhood was picturesque! The two ponds inclined their faces towards each other like a pair of lovers. The right pond had waters smooth and pure as a maiden's cheeks; the left was somewhat darker, like the swarthy face of a youth, already shaded with manly down. The right was encircled with glittering golden sand as if with bright hair; but the brow of the left bristled with osiers, and was tufted with [pg 215] willows: both ponds were clothed in a garment of green.

From them there flowed and met two streams, like hands clasped together: farther on the stream formed a waterfall; it fell, but did not perish, for into the darkness of the ravine it bore upon its waves the golden shimmer of the moon. The water fell in sheets, and on every sheet glittered skeins of moonbeams; the light in the ravine was dispersed into fine splinters, which the fleeing flood seized and carried off below, but from on high the moonbeams fell in fresh skeins. You might have thought that by the pond a nixie 157 was sitting, and with one hand was pouring forth a fountain from a bottomless urn, while with the other she cast sportively into the water handfuls of enchanted gold that she took from her apron.

Farther on, the brook, running out from the ravine, wound over the plain, and became quiet, but one could see that it still flowed, for along its moving, shimmering surface the quivering moonlight twinkled. As the fair serpent of Zmudz called giwojtos, though, lying amid the heather, it seems to slumber, still crawls along, for by turns it shows silver and golden, until it suddenly vanishes from the eye in the moss or ferns; so the brook wound and hid among the alders, which showed black on the far horizon, raising their light forms, indistinct to the eye, like spirits half seen and half in mist.

Between the ponds in the ravine a mill was hidden. As an old guardian who is spying on two lovers and has heard their talk together, grows angry, storms, shakes his head and hands and stutters out threats against them; so that mill suddenly shook its brow overgrown with moss and twirled around its many-fingered fist: [pg 216] hardly had it begun to clatter and stir its sharp-toothed jaws, when at the same moment it deafened the love talk of the ponds, and awoke the Count.

The Count, seeing that Thaddeus had

approached so near the spot where he had halted under arms, shouted: "To arms! Seize him!" The jockeys rushed forward, and, before Thaddeus could comprehend what was happening to him, they had already caught him; they ran towards the mansion and poured into the yard. The mansion awoke, the dogs barked, the watchmen shouted, the Judge rushed out half clad; he saw the armed throng and thought that they were robbers until he recognised the Count. "What does this mean?" he asked. The Count flashed his sword over him, but, when he saw that he was unarmed, his fury grew cool.

"Soplica," he said, "ancestral enemy of my family, to-day I punish thee for ancient and for fresh offences; to-day thou wilt render me an account for the seizure of my fortune before I avenge me for the insult to my honour!"

But the Judge crossed himself and cried:—

"In the name of the Father and of the Son! foh! My Lord the Count, are you a robber? By God, does this befit your birth, your education, and the station you occupy in the world? I will not permit myself to be wronged!"

Meanwhile the servants of the Judge had run up, some with clubs, others with guns; the Seneschal, standing some distance away, looked curiously into the eyes of the Count—and held a knife in his sleeve.

They were already on the point of beginning battle, but the Judge prevented them; it was vain to offer any defence, for a new enemy was coming up. Among the alders they saw a flash, and heard the report of a carbine! [pg 217]

The bridge over the river rattled with the trampling of cavalry, and a thousand voices thundered, "Down with the Soplica!" The Judge shuddered, for he recognised Gerwazy's watchword.

"This is nothing," cried the Count, "there will soon be more of us here; submit, Judge, these are my allies."

Thereupon the Assessor ran up shouting:—

"I arrest you in the name of His Imperial Majesty! Yield your sword, Count, for I shall summon the aid of the army; and you are aware, that if any one dares to make a night attack under arms, it is provided by ukaz one thousand two hundred, that as a malef——"

Thereupon the Count struck him across the face with the flat of his sword. The Assessor fell stunned, and disappeared among the nettles; all thought that he was wounded or dead.

"I see," said the Judge, "that this looks like brigandage."

Every one shrieked; all were deafened by the wailing of Zosia, who, throwing her arms around the Judge, cried like a child pricked with needles by Jews.

Meanwhile Telimena had rushed among the horses and extended her clasped hands towards the Count.

"Upon your honour!" she cried with a piercing voice, with head thrown back and with streaming hair. "By all that is holy, we implore you on our knees! Count, will you dare to refuse? Ladies beg you; savage man, you must first murder *us* !"

She fell in a faint.—The Count sprang to her aid, amazed and somewhat disconcerted by this scene.

"Panna Sophia," he said, "Pani Telimena, never shall this sword be stained with the blood of an unarmed foe! Soplicas, you are my prisoners. Thus did I in Italy, when beneath the crag that the Sicilians call [pg 218] Birbante-Rocca I overcame a camp of brigands; the armed I slew, those that laid down their weapons I captured and had bound: they walked behind the steeds and adorned my glorious triumph; then they were hanged at the foot of Etna."

It was an especial piece of good luck for the Soplicas that the Count, having better horses than the gentry, and wishing to be the first in the engagement, had left them behind, and had galloped at least a mile 158 in advance of the rest of the cavalry, along with his jockeys, who were obedient and well disciplined, and formed a sort of regular army. For the rest of the gentry, as is usually the case with insurgents, were turbulent, and beyond measure quick at hanging. As it was, the Count had time to recover from his heat and wrath, and to deliberate how to end the battle without bloodshed; so he gave orders to lock the Soplica family in the mansion as prisoners of war, and stationed guards at the doors.

Then with a shout of "Down with the Soplicas!" the gentry rushed on in a body, surrounded the estate and took it by storm, so much the more easily since the leader had been captured and the garrison had run away; but the conquerors wanted to fight and looked for an enemy. Not being admitted to the mansion, they ran to the farmhouse, to the kitchen—when they entered the kitchen, the sight of the pots, the hardly extinct fire, the fresh smell of cooked food, the crunching of the dogs, which were gnawing the remains of the supper, appealed to the hearts of all, and changed the current of their thoughts; it cooled their wrath, but inflamed their desire for food. Wearied by the march and by an entire day of debate, they thrice shouted with one voice, "Eat, eat!" to which there came a reply of "Drink, drink!" from among the throng [pg 219] of gentry. There arose two choruses, some crying "Drink!" and others "Eat!" —the watchwords flew and echoed, and wherever they reached they made mouths water and stomachs feel empty. And so, at a signal given from the kitchen, the army unexpectedly dispersed for foraging.

Gerwazy, repulsed from the Judge's rooms, had to retire, out of regard for the Count's watchmen. So, not being able to take vengeance on his enemy, he bethought himself of the second great aim of this expedition. As a man experienced and adept in legal matters, he wished to establish the Count in his new possessions legally and formally; so he ran for the Apparitor, and at last, after long search, discovered him behind the stove. Straight-way he seized him by the collar, dragged him to the yard, and, pointing his penknife at his breast, spoke thus:—

"Mr. Apparitor, my Lord the Count ventures to ask Your Honour that you would be so kind as immediately to proclaim before the gentlemen and brethren the establishment of the Count in the castle, in the estate of the Soplicas, the village, the sown fields, the fallow land, in a word, cum grovibus, forestis et borderibus; peasantibus, bailiffis, et omnibus rebus et quibusdam aliis . You know the formula; so bark it out: don't leave out anything."

"Mr. Warden, wait awhile," said Protazy boldly, thrusting his hands into his belt. "I am ready to carry out all the orders of the contending parties, but I warn you that the act will not be valid, being extorted by violence and proclaimed by night."

"What violence?" said the Warden. "There is no assault here. Why, I am asking you politely; if it is too dark for you, then I will kindle a fire with my penknife so that it will be as bright in your peepers as in seven churches."
[pg 220]
"My dear Gerwazy," said the Apparitor, "why be so huffy? I am an apparitor; it is not my business to discuss the case. Everybody knows that a party to a suit summons an apparitor and dictates to him whatever he chooses, and the apparitor proclaims it. The apparitor is the ambassador of the law, and ambassadors are not subject to punishment, so that I do not know why you keep me under guard. I will immediately write an act if some one will only bring me a lantern, but meanwhile I proclaim: Brothers, come to order!"

And in order to make his voice carry better, he stepped up on a great heap of beams (near the garden fence beams were drying; he climbed on them, and at once, as if the wind had blown him away, he vanished from sight; they heard how he plumped into the cabbage patch, they saw how his white hat flitted like a dove over the dark hemp. Bucket shot at the hat, but missed his aim; then there was a crackling of poles—Protazy was already in the hop patch. "I protest," he shouted; he was sure of escape, for behind him he had swamps and the bed of the stream.

After this protest, which resounded like the last cannon shot on conquered ramparts, all resistance subsided in the mansion of the Soplicas. The hungry gentry pillaged and seized upon whatever they could find. Sprinkler, taking his stand in the cow-shed, sprinkled an ox and two calves on the brows, and Razor plunged his sabre in their throats. Awl with equal diligence employed his sword, sticking hogs and sucking pigs beneath the shoulder blades. And now slaughter threatened the poultry—a watchful flock of those geese that once saved Rome from the treachery of the Gauls, in vain cackled for aid; in place of Manlius, Bucket attacked the coop, strangled some of the birds, and tied [pg 221] others alive to the girdle of his kontusz. In vain the geese called out hoarsely, winding their necks about; in vain the ganders hissed and nipped their assailant. He ran; besprinkled with the glittering down, borne forward as if on wheels by the motion of the close-packed wings, he seemed to be Chochlik, the winged evil spirit. 159

But the most terrible slaughter, though the least uproar, was among the hens. Young Buzzard assaulted the hen-coop, and, catching them with a cord, he pulled down from the roosts the cocks and the rough-feathered and crested hens; one after another he strangled them and laid them in a heap; lovely birds, fed upon pearl barley. Heedless Buzzard, what fervour carried thee away! Never after this wilt thou win thy pardon from the angry Zosia!

Gerwazy called to mind the days of old, and bade them give him the belts from their kontuszes, and with them he drew from the Soplicas' cellar casks of old brandy, mead, and beer. Some they broached at once; others the gentry, thick as ants, seized with a will and rolled to the castle. There the whole throng gathered for the night encampment; there were established the Count's headquarters.

They laid a hundred fires, boiled, broiled, and roasted; the tables bent beneath the meat, and drink flowed in a river. The gentry were minded to eat, drink, and sing the whole night through, but slowly they began to doze and yawn; eye after eye was extinguished, and the whole company nodded their heads; each fell where he sat, one with a platter, one over a tankard, one by a quarter of beef. Thus the victors were conquered at last by Sleep, the brother of Death.
[pg 222]

BOOK IX.—THE BATTLE

ARGUMENT

Of the dangers arising from the disorderly conduct of a camp—Unexpected succour—The gloomy situation of the gentry—The visit of the Bernardine, collecting alms, is an omen of rescue—Major Plut by excessive gallantry draws down a storm upon himself—A pistol shot, the signal for combat—The deeds of Sprinkler; the deeds and dangers of Maciek—Bucket by an ambuscade preserves Soplicowo—Reinforcements of cavalry; attack on the infantry—The deeds of Thaddeus—Duel of the leaders interrupted by treason—The Seneschal by a decisive manœuvre inclines the scales of combat—Bloody deeds of Gerwazy—The Chamberlain as a magnanimous victor.

And they snored in so sound a sleep that they were not wakened by the gleam of lanterns and the entry of some dozens of men, who fell upon the gentry as wall spiders, called *mowers* , upon drowsy flies; scarcely does one of them have time to buzz before the grim master encircles it around with long legs and strangles it. The sleep of the gentry was still sounder than the sleep of flies: not a one buzzed; all lay as if lifeless, though they were seized by strong arms, and thrown about like straw when it is bound into sheaves.

Bucket alone, whose head was strongest at a banquet of all those in the district; Bucket, who could drink two butts of mead before his tongue faltered and his legs tottered—Bucket, though long had he feasted and deeply did he slumber, still gave a sign of life; he blinked with one eye, and saw!—real nightmares! two dreadful faces directly above him, and each had a pair of mustaches. [pg 223] They breathed upon him, and touched his lips with their mustaches, and flourished about four hands like wings. He was terrified, and wanted to cross himself, but he tried in vain to stir his arm; his right arm seemed pinned to his side. He strove to move his left—alas! he found that the spirits had wrapt him tight as a babe in swaddling bands. He was terrified still more frightfully; immediately he closed his eyes and lay without breathing; he grew cold and was near to death.

But Sprinkler made an effort to defend himself, too late! For he was already bound fast in his own belt. However, he twisted himself about and leapt up with such a spring that he fell back on the breasts of the sleeping men and rolled over their heads; he tossed like a pike, when it writhes on the sand, and roared like a bear, for he had strong lungs. He roared: "Treachery!" At once the whole company awoke and answered in chorus: "Treachery! Violence! Treachery!"

The cry went echoing to the mirror room, where slept the Count, Gerwazy, and the jockeys. Gerwazy awoke, and in vain struggled to free himself, for he was tied fast at full length to his own sword; he looked about, and saw by the window armed men, in short, black helmets and green uniforms. One of them, girt with a scarf, held a sword, and with its point directed his company of men, whispering: "Bind! Bind!" Around him lay the jockeys, tied up like sheep; the Count was sitting unbound but without arms, and by him stood two private soldiers with bare bayonets—Gerwazy recognised them: alas! the Muscovites!!!

Often had the Warden been in like distress, often had he felt ropes on his arms and legs; and yet he had freed himself, for he knew a way of breaking bands: [pg 224] he was very strong and trusted in himself. He planned to save himself by silence; he closed his eyes as if he were asleep, slowly stretched out his arms and legs, held his breath, and contracted his belly and his chest to the utmost; then suddenly he grew short, puffed himself out, and doubled up: as a serpent, when it hides its head and tail in its coils, so Gerwazy became short and thick instead of long. The cords stretched and even creaked, but did not break! From very shame and terror the Warden turned over and hid his angry face upon the floor; closing his eyes he lay senseless as a log.

Then the drums began to roll, at first slowly, then with a rumble that became ever faster and louder; at this signal the Muscovite officer gave orders to lock up the Count and the jockeys in the hall, under guard, but to take the gentry out into the yard, where the other company was stationed. In vain Sprinkler fumed and struggled.

The staff was stationed in the yard, and with it many armed gentry, the Podhajskis, Birbaszes, Hreczechas, Biergels, all friends or kinsmen of the Judge. They had hastened to his relief when they heard of the attack upon him, the more eagerly since they had long been at odds with the Dobrzynskis.

Who had summoned the battalion of Muscovites from the villages? Who had gathered so quickly the neighbours from the hamlets? Was it the Assessor or Jankiel? As to this there were various rumours, but no one knew with certainty either then or later.

Already the sun was rising, and showed blood-red; its blunt edge, as if stripped of beams, was half visible and half hidden in the black clouds, like a heated horseshoe in the charcoal of a forge. The wind was rising, and it drove on the clouds from the east, crowded and [pg 225] jagged as blocks of ice; each cloud as it passed over sprinkled cold rain; behind it rushed the wind and dried the rain again; after the wind again a damp cloud flew by; and thus the day by turns was cold and drizzly.

Meanwhile the Major had given orders to drag up the beams that were drying near the yard, and in each beam to cut with an axe semicircular notches; into these notches he thrust the legs of the prisoners and closed them with another beam. The two logs, nailed together at the ends, fastened upon the legs like the jaws of a bulldog; with cords they tied the arms of the gentry still more tightly behind their backs. The Major for their further torment had already had their caps pulled from their heads, and from their backs their cloaks, their kontuszes, and even their jackets—even their tunics. Thus the gentry, fastened in the stocks, sat in a row, chattering their teeth in the cold and the rain, for the drizzle kept increasing. In vain Sprinkler fumed and struggled.

Vainly the Judge interceded for the gentry, and vainly Telimena joined her entreaties to the tears of Zosia, that they should have more regard for the captives. Captain Nikita Rykov, to be sure—a Muscovite but a good fellow—allowed himself to be mollified; but this was of no avail, since he himself had to obey Major Plut. 160

This Major, by birth a Pole from the little town of Dzierowicze, according to report, had been named Plutowicz in Polish, but had changed his name; he was a great rascal, as is usually the case with Poles that turn Muscovites in the Tsar's service. Plut, with his pipe in his mouth and his hands on his hips, stood in front of the ranks of soldiers; when people bowed to him, he turned up his nose, and in answer, as a sign of [pg 226] his wrathful humour, he puffed out a cloud of smoke and walked towards the house.

But meanwhile the Judge had been appeasing Rykov, and likewise taking aside the Assessor. They were consulting how to end the affair out of court, and, what was still more important, without interference from the government. So Captain Rykov said to Major Plut:—

"Major, what do we want of all these captives? If we send them up for trial, there will be great trouble for the gentry of the district, and no one will give you any reward for it, sir. I tell you, Major, it will be better to settle the matter quietly; the Judge will have to reward you for your pains, and we will say that we came here on a visit: thus the goats will be whole and the wolf will be full. There is a Russian proverb: 'All can be done—with caution!' and another proverb, 'Roast your own meat on the Tsar's spit,' and a third proverb, 'Harmony is better than discord.' Tie the knot tight and put the ends in the water. We will not make a report, so that nobody will find out. 'God gave hands to take with' —that is a Russian proverb."

When he heard this the Major rose and exploded with wrath:—

"Are you mad, Rykov? This is the Imperial service, and service is not friendship, you idiotic old Rykov! Are you mad? Shall I discharge rebels! In these warlike times! Ha, my Polish friends, I'll teach you rebellion! Ha, you rascally Dobrzynski gentlemen; O, I know you—let the rascals soak!" (And he guffawed, as he looked out of the window.) "Why, that same Dobrzynski who is sitting with his coat on—hey, take off his coat!—last year at the masked ball started that squabble with me. Who began it? He—not I. I was dancing, and he yelled, 'Turn the scoundrel out!' [pg 227] Since I was just then under investigation for stealing from the regimental treasury, I was much embarrassed; but what business was it of his? I was dancing the mazurka, and he shouted from behind, 'Scoundrel!' The gentry after him cried 'Hurrah!' They insulted me. Well? The beggarly gentleman has fallen into my claws. I said to him: 'See here, Dobrzynski, the goat will come to the butcher's waggon!' Well, Dobrzynski, switches are cut for you, you see!"

Then he bent over and whispered into the Judge's ear:—

"Judge, if you want to have this matter hushed up, a thousand rubles cash for each head. A thousand rubles, Judge, that's my last word."

The Judge tried to bargain, but the Major would not listen; once more he stalked about the room and puffed out clouds of smoke, like a squib or a rocket. The women followed him, imploring and weeping.

"Major," said the Judge, "even if you go to law, what will you gain? There has been no bloody battle here, and no wounds; for their eating of hens and geese they will pay fines according to the statute. I shall not make complaint against the Count; this was only an ordinary squabble between neighbours."

"Judge," said the Major, "have you read the Yellow Book ?" 161

"What yellow book?" asked the Judge.

"A book," said the Major, "that is better than all your statutes, and in it every other word is *halter* , *Siberia* , *the knout* ; the book of martial law, now proclaimed throughout all Lithuania: your tribunals are now on the shelf. According to martial law, for such pranks you will at the very least be sent to hard labour in Siberia."
[pg 228]
"I appeal to the Governor," said the Judge.

"Appeal to the Emperor if you want to," said Plut. "You know that when the Emperor confirms decrees, he often by his grace doubles the penalty. Appeal, and perhaps in case of need, my dear Judge, I shall get a good hold on you too. Jankiel, a spy whom the government has long been tracking, is a frequenter of your house and the tenant of your tavern. I may now put every one of you under arrest at once."

"Arrest me?" said the Judge. "How do you dare without orders?"

And the dispute was becoming more and more lively, when a new guest rode into the farmyard.

A strange throng was coming in. In front, like a courier, ran an immense black ram, whose brow bristled with four horns, two of which were decked with bells and curled about his ears, and two jutted out sidewise from his forehead and were hung with small, round, tinkling brass balls. After the ram came oxen and a flock of sheep and goats; behind the cattle were four heavily loaded waggons.

All divined that Father Robak, the Alms-Gatherer, had arrived. So the Judge, knowing his duty as host, took his stand on the threshold, to welcome the guest. The Monk rode on the first wain, his face half hidden by his cowl; but they immediately recognised him, for, when he passed the prisoners, he turned his countenance towards them and made a sign to them with his finger. And the driver of the second wain was equally well known, old Maciek, the Switch, disguised as a peasant. The gentry began to shout as soon as he appeared; he said only "Idiots!" and imposed silence by a gesture. On the third waggon was the Prussian, in a torn overcoat; and Zan and Mickiewicz rode on the fourth.
[pg 229]
Meanwhile the Podhajskis and the Isajewiczes, the Birbaszes, Wilbiks, Biergels, and Kotwiczes, seeing the Dobrzynskis under so severe constraint, began slowly to cool down from their former wrath; for the Polish gentry, though beyond measure quarrelsome and eager for fighting, are nevertheless not vindictive. So they ran to old Maciej for counsel. He stationed the whole crowd about the waggons and told them to wait.

The Bernardine entered the room. They hardly recognised him, though he had not changed his clothes—his bearing was so different. He was ordinarily gloomy and thoughtful, but now he held his head high, and with a radiant mien, like a jolly monk, he laughed long before he began to talk:—

"Ha! ha! ha! ha! My respects, my respects! Ha! ha! ha! Excellent, first-class! Officers, some people hunt by day, but you by night! The hunting was good; I have seen the game. Pluck, pluck the gentry, peel them well; bridle them, for the gentry sometimes kick! I congratulate you, Major, that you have caught the young Count; he is a fat morsel, a rich fellow, a young man of old family; don't let him out of the cage without getting three hundred ducats for him; and when you have them, give some three-pence for my monastery and for me, for I always pray for your soul. As I am a Bernardine, I am very anxious about your soul! Death pulls even staff-officers by the ears. Baka162 wrote well—that Death seizes on sinners at dinners, and on silken frocks she often knocks, and monks' cowls she slashes like satin sashes, and the curb of girls she raps like shoulder-straps. Mother Death, says Baka, like an onion, brings tears from the dears she embraces, and fondles alike both the baby that drowses and the rake that carouses! Ah! ah! Major, to-day [pg 230]   we live and tomorrow we rot; that only is ours which to-day we eat and drink! Judge, doesn't it seem to you time for breakfast? I take my seat at the table, and beg all to be seated with me. Major, how about some stewed beef and gravy? Lieutenant, what's your idea? Should you like a bowl of good punch?"

"That's a fact, Father," said two officers; "it's time to be eating, and to drink the Judge's health!"

The household, gazing at Robak, marvelled whence he had got such a bearing and such jollity. The Judge at once repeated the orders to the cook; they brought in a bowl, sugar, bottles, and stewed beef. Plut and Rykov set to work briskly; and so greedily did they feed and so copiously did they drink, that in a half hour they had eaten twenty-three plates of the stewed beef and emptied an enormous half bowl of punch.

So the Major, full and merry, lolled in his chair, took out his pipe, lighted it with a bank note, and, wiping the breakfast from his lips with the end of a napkin, turned his laughing eyes on the women, and said:—

"Fair ladies, I like you as dessert! By my major's epaulets, when a man has eaten breakfast, the best relish after the stewed beef is chatting with such fair ladies as you fair ladies! I tell you what: let's have a game of cards, of vingt et un or whist; or shall we start a mazurka? Hey, in the name of three hundred devils, why, I am the best dancer of the mazurka in the whole yager regiment!"

Thereupon he leaned forward closer to the ladies, and puffed out smoke and compliments by turns.

"Let's dance!" cried Robak. "When I have finished my bottle, though a monk, I occasionally tuck up my gown, and dance a bit of a mazurka! But you see, Major, we are drinking here and the yagers are freezing there [pg 231] in the yard. Sport is sport! Judge, give them a keg of brandy; the Major will permit it; let the bold yagers have a drink!"

"I might beg the favour," said the Major, "but you are not forced to grant it."

"Judge," whispered Robak, "give 'em a keg of spirits."

And thus, while the merry staff tippled in the mansion, outside the house there began a drinking bout among the troops.

Captain Rykov drained cup after cup in silence; but the Major drank and at the same time paid court to the ladies, and the ardour for dancing continually increased within him. He threw aside his pipe and seized Telimena's hand; he was eager to dance, but she ran away; so he went up to Zosia, and bowing and tottering invited her to open the mazurka.

"Hey you, Rykov, stop pulling at your pipe! Put away your pipe; you play the balalaika well. You see that guitar there; go, get the guitar and give us a mazurka! I, the Major, will lead out in the first couple."

The Captain took the guitar and began to tune it; Plut again urged Telimena to dance:—

"On the word of a Major, madam, I am not a Russian if I lie! May I be the son of a bitch if I lie! Ask, and all the officers will bear witness, all the army will tell you that in the second army, ninth corps, second division of infantry, fiftieth yager regiment, Major Plut is the foremost dancer of the mazurka. Come on, young lady! Don't be so skittish, for I shall punish you in officer's fashion."

So saying he jumped up, seized Telimena's hand, and imprinted a broad kiss on her white shoulder; but [pg 232] Thaddeus, darting in from the side, slapped his face. The kiss and the blow resounded together, one after the other, as word after word.

The Major was dumbfounded, rubbed his eyes, and, pale with wrath, shouted, "Rebellion, a rebel!" —and, drawing his sword, rushed to run him through. Then the Monk took a pistol from his sleeve, and cried: "Shoot, Thaddeus, aim for the bull's eye." Thaddeus at once seized it, aimed, and shot; he missed, but he deafened and scorched the Major. Rykov started up with his guitar, crying, "Rebellion! rebellion!" and made for Thaddeus; but from the other side of the table the Seneschal swung his arm with a left-hand motion, and a knife whistled through the air between the heads of the company and struck before they saw it flash. It struck the bottom of the guitar and pierced it through and through; Rykov dodged and thus escaped death, but he was frightened; with a cry of "Yagers! Rebellion! In God's name!" he drew his sword, and, defending himself, he retreated to the threshold.

Then on the other side of the room many of the gentry poured in through the windows with swords, Switch at their head. In the hall Plut and Rykov behind him were calling the soldiers; already the three nearest the house were running to their aid; already three glittering bayonets were gliding through the door, and behind them there were bent forward three black helmets. Maciek stood by the door with his switch raised on high, and, squeezing close to the wall, lay in wait for them as a cat for rats; then he struck a fearful blow. Perhaps he would have felled three heads, but the old man either had poor eyesight, or else he was too much wrought up; since, before they put forward their necks, he smote on their helmets, and stripped them off; [pg 233] the switch, falling, clinked on the bayonets.—The Muscovites started back, and Maciek drove them out to the yard.

There the confusion was still worse. There the partisans of the Soplicas vied with each other in setting free the Dobrzynskis by tearing apart the beams. Seeing this, the yagers seized their arms and made for them; a sergeant rushed ahead and transfixed Podhajski with a bayonet; he wounded two others of the gentry and was shooting at a third; they fled: this was close to the log in which Baptist was fastened. He already had his arms free and ready for fight; he rose, lifted his hand with its long fingers and clenched his fist; and from above he gave the Russian such a blow on the back that he knocked his face and temples into the lock of his carbine. The lock clicked, but the powder, moist with blood, did not catch; the sergeant fell on his arms at the feet of Baptist. Baptist bent down, seized the carbine by the barrel, and, brandishing it like his sprinkling-brush, lifted it aloft; he whirled it about and straightway smote two privates on the shoulders and gave a corporal a blow on the head; the rest, terrified, recoiled in dismay from the log: thus Sprinkler sheltered the gentry with a moving roof.

Then they pulled apart the logs and cut the cords; the gentry, once free, descended upon the waggons of the Alms-Gatherer, and from them procured swords, sabres, cutlasses, scythes, and guns. Bucket found two blunderbusses and a bag of bullets; he poured some of these into his own blunderbuss; the other gun he loaded in the same way and gave over to Buzzard.

More yagers arrived, fell into disorder, and knocked against one another; the gentry in the tumult could not cut and slash; the yagers could not shoot, for they [pg 234] were fighting hand to hand. Like tooth on tooth, steel on steel clashed and snapped; bayonet broke on sabre and scythe on sword hilt; fist met fist and arm met arm.

But Rykov, with a part of the yagers, ran up to where the barn adjoined the fence; there he made a stand and called to his soldiers that they should stop so disorderly a fight, since, without having a chance to use their weapons, they were falling beneath the fists of the enemy. Angry that he himself could not fire, for in the press he could not distinguish Muscovites from Poles, he shouted, "Fall in" (which means form in line); but his command could not be heard in the midst of the shouting.

Old Maciek, who was not good at hand to hand combat, retreated, clearing a place before him to the right and to the left; now with the tip of his sabre he sheared a bayonet from a gun barrel as a wick from a candle; now with a slashing blow from the left he cut or stabbed. Thus the cautious Maciek retired to the open field.

But an old corporal, who was the instructor of the regiment, a great master of the bayonet, pressed upon him with the utmost obstinacy; he gathered himself together, bent down, and grasped his carbine with both hands, holding the right on the lock and the left at the middle of the barrel; he dodged and skipped, and at times crouched down; he let go with his left hand, and thrust forward the weapon with his right, like the sting from the jaws of a serpent; and again he withdrew it and rested it on his knees; and thus dodging and jumping he pressed upon Maciek.

Old Maciek appreciated the skill of his adversary, and with his left hand adjusted his spectacles on his nose; with his right he held the hilt of his switch close [pg 235] to his breast, and withdrew, following the motions of the corporal with his eyes; he himself tottered on his legs as though he were drunk. The corporal pressed on the more quickly; sure of his triumph, and in order the more easily to reach his retiring foe, he arose and stretched forward his right arm at full length, pushing forward his carbine; he made such an effort in thrusting with his heavy weapon, that he even leaned forward. Maciek shoved the hilt of his sword just under the spot where the bayonet is set upon the gun barrel, and knocked up the weapon; then, suddenly lowering his switch, he wounded the Muscovite in the arm, and again, with a slash from the left, cut through his jaw. Thus fell the corporal, the finest fencer among the Muscovites, a cavalier of three crosses and four medals.

Meanwhile, near the logs, the left wing of the gentry was already near victory. There fought Sprinkler, visible from afar, there Razor hovered around the Muscovites; the latter slashed at their waists, the former pounded their heads. As a machine that German workmen have invented and that is called a thrasher, but is at the same time a chopper—it has chains and knives, and cuts up the straw and thrashes the grain at the same time—so did Sprinkler and Razor work together, slaughtering their enemies, one from above and the other from below.

But Sprinkler now abandoned sure victory and ran to the right wing, where a new danger was threatening Maciek. Eager to avenge the death of the corporal, an ensign was attacking him with a long spontoon—the spontoon is a combination of pike and axe, now discarded, and employed only in the fleet, but then it was used also in the infantry. The ensign, a young man, ran nimbly back and forth; whenever his adversary [pg 236] beat the weapon to one side, he retired; Maciek, not being able to drive off the young man, was obliged merely to defend himself without inflicting wounds. Already the ensign had given him a slight wound with the spear; already, raising the halberd aloft, he was collecting himself for a blow. Baptist was unable to reach him in time, but stopping half way, he whirled his weapon, and cast it under the feet of his enemy; he broke a bone, and the ensign immediately dropped the spontoon from his hands. He staggered; Baptist rushed on him, and after him a throng of gentry, and after the gentry the Muscovites from the left wing ran up in disorder, and the battle raged around Sprinkler.

Baptist, who had lost his arms in defence of Maciek, almost paid for that service with his life; for two strong Muscovites fell on him from behind, and twisted four hands at once into his hair; bracing their feet, they pulled as on springy cables, hitched to the mast of a barge. In vain Sprinkler struck out blindly behind him; he tottered—but suddenly he saw that Gerwazy was fighting close by; he shouted, "Jesus Maria! the penknife!"

The Warden, hearing Baptist's cry, knew that he was in mortal terror; he turned back, and plunged the sharp steel blade between the head of Baptist and the hands of the Muscovites. They withdrew, uttering piercing cries, but one hand, more firmly entwined in the hair, remained hanging and spurted forth blood. Thus an eagle, when it buries one talon in a hare, catches with the other at a tree, in order to hold back the beast; but the hare, pulling, splits the eagle in two; the right talon remains on the tree in the forest; the left, covered with blood, the beast bears away to the fields.

Sprinkler, free once more, cast his eyes about, [pg 237] stretched out his hands, sought for a weapon, shouted for a weapon; meanwhile he brandished his fists, standing his ground manfully, but keeping close to the side of Gerwazy, until he caught sight of his son Buzzard in the press. Buzzard with his right hand was aiming a blunderbuss, and with his left was pulling after him a great club, a fathom long, armed with flints and knobs and knots. 163 (No one could have lifted it except Baptist.) Baptist, when he saw his darling weapon, his sprinkling-brush, seized it, kissed it, jumped into the air for joy, whirled it over his head and straightway moistened it.

What deeds he then performed, what disasters he spread abroad, it were vain to sing, for none would believe the Muse: even so they did not believe the poor woman in Wilno, who, standing on the summit of the holy Ostra Gate, saw how Deyov, the Muscovite general, coming on with a regiment of Cossacks, was already opening the gate, and how a single burgher, named Czarnobacki, killed Deyov and routed a whole regiment of Cossacks. 164

Suffice it to say, that things came to pass as Rykov had foreseen; the yagers in the crowd yielded to the power of their foes. Twenty-three rolled slain on the ground, thirty and more lay groaning with frequent wounds, many fled and hid in the garden, the hops, or along the river; some took refuge in the house under the protection of the women.

The victorious gentry ran with a cry of joy, some to the casks, others to tear booty from the enemy; Robak alone did not share their exultation. Hitherto he had not fought himself (for the canons forbid a priest to take part in combat), but as an experienced man he had been giving counsel, had run about the battlefield in all [pg 238] directions, and with his glance and his arm had urged on and guided those who were fighting. And now he shouted for them to assemble around him, attack Rykov, and complete the victory. Meanwhile by a messenger he informed Rykov that if he would lay down his arms he would preserve his life; but, in case the surrender of arms were delayed, Robak gave orders to surround the remnant and cut them down.

Captain Rykov was far from asking quarter. Gathering about him half a battalion, he shouted, "Ready!" Immediately the line seized their carbines and the arms rattled; they had long since been loaded. He shouted, "Aim!" and the barrels glittered in a long row. He shouted, "Fire in turn!" and one report followed another; one man shot, another loaded, a third clutched his musket. One could hear the whistling of bullets, the rattle of locks, the clink of ramrods; the whole line seemed to be a moving reptile, which moved a thousand glittering legs at the same time.

To be sure, the yagers were drunk with strong liquor; they aimed poorly and missed their mark; few inflicted wounds and hardly a single one killed his man: however, two of the Maciejs were already wounded, and one of the Bartlomiejs had fallen. The gentry replied but sparingly from their few guns, and were eager to attack the enemy with swords; but the older men restrained them: each moment the bullets whistled, struck, and forced the gentry to retreat—soon they would have cleared the yard; already they began to ring on the windows of the house.

Thaddeus, who by his uncle's orders had remained in the house to protect the women, hearing how the battle was becoming ever fiercer and fiercer, ran out, and after him rushed the Chamberlain, to whom Thomas [pg 239] had at last brought his sabre; he hurriedly joined the gentry and took his place at their head. He ran forward, raising his weapon, and the gentry moved after him. The yagers, letting them come near, poured upon them a hail of bullets; Isajewicz, Wilbik, and Razor fell wounded; then the gentry were checked by Robak on one side and Maciej on the other. The gentry cooled in their ardour, glanced about, and retired; the Muscovites saw this, and Captain Rykov planned to give the final blow, to drive the gentry from the yard and seize the mansion.

"Form for the attack!" he cried. "Charge bayonets! Forward!"

Immediately the line, levelling their gun barrels like poles, bent down their heads, moved on and quickened their step; in vain the gentry endeavoured to check them from in front and shot from the side; the line passed over half the yard without resistance. The Captain, pointing with his sword to the door of the mansion, shouted:—

"Surrender, Judge, or I will order your house to be burned!"

"Burn it," cried the Judge, "and I will roast you in that fire!"

O mansion of Soplicowo! if thy white walls are still whole and glitter beneath the lindens; if a throng of the neighbouring gentry still sit at the Judge's hospitable board, they surely often drink the health of Bucket, for without him Soplicowo would to-day be no more!

Bucket had so far given few proofs of valour. Though he was the first of the gentry to be freed from the stocks, and though he had straightway found in the waggon his darling bucket, his favourite blunderbuss, and with it a pouch of bullets, he did not care to fight. He said that [pg 240] he did not trust himself when dry, and so he went to a cask of spirits standing near, and, using his hand as a spoon, dipped up a stream into his lips. Only when he had well warmed and strengthened himself did he adjust his cap, take up his bucket from his knees, ram home a charge, sprinkle the pan, and gaze at the battlefield. He saw that a glittering wave of bayonets was smiting and dispersing the gentry, and he swam to meet that wave; he bent down and dived through the dense grass, across the centre of the yard, until he paused in ambush where the nettles were growing; with gestures he summoned Buzzard.

Buzzard, who was on guard at the mansion, was standing with his blunderbuss by the threshold, for in that mansion dwelt his dear Zosia, whom he loved eternally (though she had scorned his courtship), and in whose defence he was glad to perish.

The line of yagers was already entering the nettles, on the march, when Bucket touched the trigger, and from the broad mouth of his blunderbuss let fly a dozen chopped bullets into the midst of the Muscovites; Buzzard let fly another dozen, and the yagers fell into confusion. Dismayed by the ambuscade, the line folded back into a disorderly mass, retreated, and abandoned the wounded; Baptist finished their slaughter.

The barn was already far off; fearing a long retreat, Rykov made for the garden fence, and there checked his fleeing company in its course. He drew them up, but changed their formation; instead of a line he made a triangle, with its point to the front and its base protected by the garden fence. He did well, for the cavalry descended on him from the castle.

The Count, who had been in the castle under the guard of the Muscovites, when his terrified guards had [pg 241] dispersed, had mounted his followers, and hearing shots, was leading his cavalry into the firing line, himself at their head, with his steel raised aloft. At once Rykov cried, "Platoon fire!" A fiery thread flew along over the locks, and from the black levelled barrels three hundred bullets whistled. Three riders fell wounded, and one lay dead. The Count's steed fell, and the Count with it; with a cry the Warden ran to the rescue, for he saw that the yagers had aimed at the last of the Horeszkos—though in the female line. Robak was nearer, and covered the Count with his body; he received the bullets in his stead, drew him from under his horse, and led him away; but the gentry he bade disperse, take better aim, spare vain shots, and hide behind the fences, the well, and the walls of the stable. The Count and his cavalry had to wait a more fitting season.

Thaddeus comprehended Robak's plans and carried them out splendidly, seeking cover behind the wooden well; and, since he was sober and was a fine shot with his fowling piece (for he could hit a gold coin thrown in the air), he did terrible execution on the Muscovites, picking out their chiefs; with his first shot he at once killed the sergeant-major. Then with his two barrels, one after the other, he mowed down two sergeants, aiming now at the gold lace, now at the middle of the triangle, where stood the staff. Thereupon Rykov grew angry and chafed, he stamped his feet and bit the hilt of his sword.

"Major Plut," he cried, "what will come of this? Soon not one of us will be left here to give orders!"

So Plut shouted at Thaddeus in great wrath:—

"Shame on you, you Pole, for hiding behind a plank [pg 242] shelter; don't be a coward, come out into the open and fight honourably, as a soldier should."

To this Thaddeus replied:—

"Major, if you are so bold a knight, why do you hide behind a company of yagers? I am not afraid of you—come out from behind the fence; you have had your face slapped, but still I am ready to fight with you! Why all this bloodshed? The quarrel was between us two; so let the pistol or the sword settle it. I give you your choice of weapons, from a cannon to a pin. Otherwise, I will shoot you and your men like wolves in a cave."

So saying, he shot, and aimed so well that he hit the lieutenant by Rykov's side.

"Major," whispered Rykov, "go out and fight a duel with him, and take vengeance on him for what he did some time ago. If anybody else kills that young gentleman, then, Major, you see that you will not wash off your disgrace. You must coax out that gentleman into the field; if you can't kill him with a carbine, you may with a sword. Old Suvorov used to say, 'Rifles are trifles, but hand arms are grand arms.' Go out into the field, Major, for he is shooting at us; look, he is aiming now."

"Rykov, my dear friend," replied the Major, "you are a fine boy with a sword; go out yourself, brother Rykov—or, I tell you what, we will send one of our lieutenants. I, the Major, I cannot desert the soldiers; to me belongs the command of the battalion."

Rykov, hearing this, lifted his sword and went out boldly; he ordered the firing to cease and waved a white handkerchief. He asked Thaddeus what weapon he preferred; after discussion, they agreed on swords. Thaddeus had no weapon; while they were looking for [pg 243] swords, the Count rushed out armed and interrupted the negotiations.

"Pan Soplica," he shouted. "begging your pardon, you challenged the Major! I have a grudge of longer standing against the Captain; he has broken into my castle" — "Please say our castle," interrupted Protazy— "at the head of a band of robbers," the Count concluded. "He—I recognised Rykov—tied up my jockeys; I will punish him as I punished the brigands beneath the crag that the Sicilians call Birbante-Rocca."

All became silent, and the firing ceased; the armies gazed eagerly at the meeting of their leaders. The Count and Rykov advanced, standing sidewise, threatening each other with the right hand and the right eye; then with their left hands they uncovered their heads and bowed courteously—it is the custom of men of honour, before proceeding to murder, first to exchange greetings. Their swords were already crossed and had begun to clash. The knights, each lifting one foot, bent their right knees, and jumped forward and back by turns.

But Plut, seeing Thaddeus in front of his line, had a quiet consultation with Corporal Gont, who passed for the best shot in the company.

"Gont," said the Major, "you see that rascal there; if you will put a bullet into him right under the fifth rib I'll give you four silver rubles."

Gont cocked his carbine and bent over the lock; his faithful comrades sheltered him with their cloaks. He aimed, not at the rib, but at the head of Thaddeus; he shot and hit the centre of his hat, close to his mark. Thaddeus whirled about, then Sprinkler rushed on Rykov, and after him the gentry, crying "Treason!" [pg 244] Though Thaddeus shielded him, Rykov barely managed to retreat and find refuge in the centre of his ranks.

Again the Dobrzynskis and the other Lithuanians vied with one another in pressing forward, and, despite the former disagreements of the two factions, they fought like brothers, each urging on his comrade. The Dobrzynskis, seeing how a Podhajski was prancing before the line of yagers and slashing them with his scythe, shouted joyfully: "Long live the Podhajskis! Forward, brother Lithuanians! hurrah! hurrah for Lithuania!" And the Skolubas, seeing how the valiant Razor, despite his wound, was dashing on with his sabre raised aloft, cried: "Hurrah for the Macieks! long live the Masovians!" Inspiring one another with courage, they ran upon the Muscovites; in vain Robak and Maciek tried to restrain them.

While they were thus smiting the company of yagers from the front, the Seneschal abandoned the battlefield and went into the garden. By his side strode the cautious Protazy, to whom the Seneschal was quietly issuing orders.

In the garden, close to the fence against which Rykov had supported his triangle, stood a large old cheese house, built of lattice work made of beams nailed across one another, like a cage. In it there shone many scores of white cheeses; around them bunches of sage, bennet, cardoon, and wild thyme hung drying, the entire herb apothecary shop of the Seneschal's daughter. The cheese house was some twenty feet square, but it rested only on a single great pillar, like a stork's nest. The old oaken pillar slanted, for it was already half decayed, and threatened to fall. The Judge had often been advised to destroy the age-worn structure, but he always said that he preferred to repair it rather than to destroy it, or even [pg 245] to rebuild it. He kept postponing the task to a more convenient season, and in the meantime bade put two props under the pillar. The structure, thus strengthened, but still not firm, looked over the fence at Rykov's triangle.

Toward this cheese house the Seneschal and the Apparitor walked silently, each armed with an immense pole, as with a pike; after them the housekeeper stole through the hemp, with the scullion, a small but very strong lad. Arriving at the spot, they rested their poles against the rotted top of the pillar, and, clinging to the ends, pushed with all their might, as when boatmen with long poles push from the bank into the deep water a barge that has grounded on a reef.

The pillar snapped, and the cheese house tottered and fell with its load of beams and cheeses on the triangle of Muscovites; it crushed, wounded, and killed; where the ranks had just now been standing lay beams, corpses, and cheeses white as snow, stained with blood and brains. The triangle was shattered into bits, and now in the centre of it the sprinkling-brush thundered, the razor flashed, and the switch slashed; from the mansion rushed a throng of gentry, and the Count from the yard gate sent his cavalry against the scattered fugitives.

Now, only eight yagers with a sergeant at their head still defended themselves; the Warden ran against them, but they boldly stood their ground and aimed nine musket barrels straight at the brow of the Warden; he flew to meet the shot, brandishing the blade of his penknife. The Monk saw it, and ran across Gerwazy's path; he fell and tripped Gerwazy. They fell at the very moment when the platoon fired; hardly had the bullets whistled over him, when Gerwazy rose, and jumped up into the smoke. He straightway sheared off the heads of two yagers; the rest fled in confusion, the [pg 246] Warden chased and slashed them. They ran across the yard, Gerwazy on their track; they rushed into the door of a shed standing open, and Gerwazy entered the shed at their heels. He vanished in the darkness, but did not quit fighting, for through the door could be heard groans, yells, and frequent blows. Soon all became silent; Gerwazy came out alone, with a bloody sword.

Now the gentry had won the field; they pursued, slashed, and stabbed the dispersed yagers. Rykov alone remained, and cried that he would not lay down his arms; he was still fighting, when the Chamberlain went up to him, and, raising his sabre, said in an impressive tone:—

"Captain, you will not soil your honour by accepting quarter; unhappy, but valiant knight, you have given ample proof of your daring: now abandon hopeless resistance; lay down your arms, before we disarm you with our sabres. You will preserve life and honour; you are my prisoner."

Rykov, overcome by the dignity of the Chamberlain, complied, and gave over to him his naked sword, bloody to the hilt, saying:—

"Brother Poles, woe is me that I did not have even a single cannon! Suvorov said well: 'Remember, comrade Rykov, never to attack the Poles without cannon!' Well! The yagers were drunk, the Major let them drink! Ah, Major Plut! He has played sad tricks to-day. He will answer for them to the Tsar, for he was in command. I will be your friend, Chamberlain. There is a Russian proverb, Chamberlain, 'Who loves well, shoves well!' You are good at a bottle and good at a battle—but stop playing your rough jokes on my yagers."
[pg 247]
Hearing this, the Chamberlain raised his sabre and, through the Apparitor, proclaimed a general pardon; he gave orders to tend the wounded, to clear the field of troops, and to disarm and imprison the yagers. They searched long for Plut; he had buried himself deep in a nettle bush and lay there as if dead; at last he came out when he saw that the battle was over.

Thus ended the last foray in Lithuania. 165
[pg 248]

BOOK X—THE EMIGRATION. JACEK

ARGUMENT

Consultation in regard to securing the fortunes of the victors—Negotiations with Rykov—The farewell—An important discovery—Hope.

The morning clouds, dispersed for a moment, like black birds, kept gathering and flying towards the summit of the heavens; hardly had the sun declined from noon when their flock had covered half the sky with an immense mantle; the wind drove it on faster and faster, the cloud grew more and more dense and hung lower and lower: finally, half torn away from the sky on one side, bending towards the earth, and spread out far and wide like a great sail, it gathered into itself all the winds and flew over the sky from the south to the west.

There was an instant of calm, and the air became dull and silent, as if dumb with terror. And the fields of grain, which just before, bowing to the earth and again shaking their golden ears on high, had tossed like waves, now stood motionless and gazed at the sky with bristling stalks. And the green willows and poplars by the roadside, which, like mourners by an open grave, had been bowing their heads to the earth, and brandishing their long arms, with their silver tresses spread out on the winds, now stood as if dead, with an expression of dumb grief like the statue of Niobe on Sipylos. Only the trembling aspen shook its grey leaves.

The cattle, usually loath to return homeward, now [pg 249] rushed together, and, without waiting for their keepers, deserted their pasturage and ran towards the barn. The bull dug up the ground with his hoof and ploughed it with his horns, frightening all the herd with his ill-omened bellowing; the cow kept raising her large eyes to the sky, opening her mouth in wonder, and lowing deeply. But the boar lagged behind, fretting and gnashing his teeth, and stole sheaves of grain and seized them for his stores.

The birds hid in the woods, in the thatched roofs, in the depths of the grass; the ravens, surrounding the ponds in flocks, walked to and fro with measured steps; they turned their black eyes on the black clouds, and, protruding their tongues from their broad, dry throats and spreading out their wings, they awaited their bath. Yet even they, foreseeing too fierce a storm, already were making for the wood, like a rising cloud. The last of the birds, the swallow, made bold by its fleetness of wing, pierced the cloud like an arrow, and finally dropped from it like a bullet.

Just at that moment the gentry had finished their terrible combat with the Muscovites, and one and all were seeking shelter in the houses and stables, deserting the battlefield, where soon the elements joined in combat.

To the west, the earth, still gilded by the sun, shone with a gloomy, yellowish-red tint; already the cloud, spreading out its shadows like a net, was catching the remnants of the light and flying after the sun as if it wished to seize upon it before it set. Blasts of wind whistled sharply below; they rushed by, one after another, bringing drops of rain, large, clear, and rounded as hailstones.

Suddenly the winds grappled, split asunder, struggled, [pg 250] whirled about, and in whistling columns circled over the ponds, stirring the waters in the ponds to their depths; they fell upon the meadows and whistled through the willows and the grass. The willow branches snapped, the swaths of grass were borne on the wind like hair torn out by handfuls, mixed with ringlets from the sheaves. The winds howled; they fell upon the field, wallowed, dug into the earth, snatched up clods, and made an opening for a third wind, which tore itself from the field like a pillar of black earth, and rose and whirled like a moving pyramid, boring into the ground with its brow and from its feet sprinkling sand in the eyes of the stars; it broadened at every step and opened out at the summit, and with its immense trumpet it proclaimed the storm. At last with all this chaos of water and dust, of straw, leaves, branches, and torn-up sod, the winds smote on the forest and roared through the depths of the thicket like bears.

And now the rain poured as from a sieve, in great, swift drops; then the thunder roared and the drops united; now like straight strings they bound the sky to the earth with long tresses, now, as from buckets, they poured down in great masses. Now the sky and the earth were quite hidden; the night, and the storm more black than night, shrouded them. At times the horizon cracked from side to side, and the angel of the storm, like an immense sun, showed his glittering face; and again, wrapped in a shroud, he fled into the sky and the doors of the clouds crashed together with a thunder-clap. Again the gale increased and the driving rain, and the dense, thick, almost impenetrable darkness. Again the drops murmured more gently, the thunder for a moment subsided; again it awoke and roared and water once more gushed forth. At last all became calm; [pg 251] one heard only the soughing of the trees around the house and the patter of the rain.

On a day such as had just passed the wildest storm was to be desired, since the tempest, which covered the battlefield with darkness, drenched the roads and destroyed the bridges over the river, and made of the farm an inaccessible fortress. So of what had been done in the Soplicas' camp the news could not spread abroad on that day—and it was precisely upon secrecy that the fate of the gentry depended.

In the Judge's room an important consultation was in progress. The Bernardine lay on the bed, exhausted, pale, and blood-stained, but wholly sound in his mind; he issued orders and the Judge carried them out to the letter. He invited the Chamberlain to join them, summoned the Warden, had Rykov brought in, and then shut the door. For a whole hour the secret conversation continued, until Captain Rykov, throwing on the table a heavy purse of ducats, interrupted it with these words:—

"My Polish friends, it is common talk among you that every Muscovite is a rascal: now tell any one who asks, that you have found a Muscovite who was named Nikita Nikitich Rykov, a captain in the army, and who wore eight medals and three crosses—I beg you remember that. This medal was for Ochakov,166 this for Izmailov, 167 this for the battle at Novi, 168 this for Preisizh-Ilov; 169 that for Korsakov's famous retreat from Zurich. 170 And tell them that he received also a sword for valour, and likewise three expressions of approval from the field-marshal, two compliments from the Emperor, and four honourable mentions, all in writing."

"But, but, captain," interrupted Robak, "what is [pg 252] going to happen to *us* if you will not come to terms? You know that you have given your word to hush up this matter."

"Certainly, and I will give my word again," said Rykov; "there you have it! Why should I want to ruin you? I am an honest man; I like you Poles, for you are jolly fellows, good at a bottle, and likewise bold fellows, good at a battle. We have a Russian saying: 'Who rides in the cart often falls under the cart; who is in front to-day may be behind to-morrow; to-day you beat and to-morrow they beat you.' Why be angry over it? Such is the way of life among us soldiers. Why should a man be so mean as to be angry over a defeat! The fight at Ochakov was bloody, at Zurich they crushed our infantry, at Austerlitz I lost my whole company; but before that, when I was a sergeant, your Kosciuszko cut up my platoon with scythes at Raclawice. 171 What did it matter? Later on, at Maciejowice 172 I killed with my own bayonet two brave gentlemen; one of them was Mokronowski, who was advancing with a scythe in front of his troops and who had cut off the hand of a cannoneer, with the match in it. Ah, you Poles! The Fatherland! I feel it all, I, Rykov. The Tsar gives the order—but I am sorry for you. What have we against the Poles? Let Moscow be for the Muscovites and Poland for the Poles! But what is to be done? The Tsar will not permit it!"

The Judge replied to him:—

"Captain, that you are an honest man all in this district know, where you have been quartered for many years. Good friend, be not angry at this gift; we did not wish to offend you. These ducats we have ventured to collect because we know that you are not a rich man."

"O my yagers!" cried Rykov, "the whole company [pg 253] cut to pieces! My company! And all the fault of that Plut! He was the chief in command; he will have to answer for it to the Tsar. But, gentlemen, take those pennies for yourselves; I have my captain's pay, such as it is—enough for my punch and for a pipe of tobacco. But I like you, gentlemen, because with you I eat, drink, and am merry—with you I can have a friendly talk, and thus my life passes. So I will protect you, and when the inquiry comes up, on my word of honour, I will testify in your favour. We will say that we came here on a visit, had a drink, danced, got a trifle tipsy, and that Plut accidentally gave the word to fire; then came a battle, and the battalion somehow melted away. If you gentlemen will only grease the inquiry with gold it will come out all right. But now I will repeat to you what I have already said to that gentleman with the long sword, that Plut is the first in command, I the second; Plut is still alive, and he may play you a trick that will be your ruin, for he is a cunning specimen—you need to stuff his mouth with bank notes. Well, my friend, you with the long sword, have you called on Plut already? Have you had a talk with him?"

Gerwazy looked around and stroked his bald pate; he made a careless motion of his hand as if to signify that he had already arranged the whole matter. But Rykov persisted:—

"Well, will Plut keep quiet? Has he given his word to do so?"

The Warden, vexed that Rykov should torment him with questions, solemnly bent down his thumb to the ground, and then, with a wave of the hand, as if to cut short further discourse, he said:—

"I swear by my penknife that Plut will not betray us! He will talk no more with any one!"
[pg 254]
Then he let his hands fall and cracked his fingers, as if he were shaking the whole mystery out of his hands.

This dark gesture the hearers understood; they began to gaze in amazement at one another, each trying to guess his neighbour's thoughts, and the gloomy silence lasted for several minutes. At last Rykov said:—

"The wolf was a robber, and robbers have caught him!"

"Requiescat in pace ," added the Chamberlain.

"In this was the finger of God!" said the Judge. "But I am not guilty of this blood; I did not know of this."

The Monk rose on the pillows and sat up with gloomy mien. At last he said, looking sharply at the Warden:—

"It is a great sin to slay an unarmed captive! Christ forbids us to take vengeance even on our enemies! Ah! Warden, you will answer heavily for this to God. There is but one ground of pardon—if the deed was done not from stupid vengeance but pro publico bono ."

The Warden made a motion with his head and with his outstretched hand, and, blinking, repeated, "Pro publico bono ."

There was no more talk of Major Plut. Next day they sought vainly for him in the yard, and vainly offered a reward for his body: the Major had perished without leaving a trace behind, as though he had fallen into the water; as to what had become of him there were various rumours, but no one knew with certainty, either then or later. In vain they tormented the Warden with questions; he said nothing but these words, "Pro publico bono ." The Seneschal was in the secret, but, bound by his word of honour, the old man kept silent as if under a spell.

After the conclusion of the agreement, Rykov left the [pg 255] room and Robak had the warrior gentry called in, to whom the Chamberlain gravely discoursed as follows:—

"Brothers, to-day God has favoured our arms, but I must confess to you in plain terms that evil results will follow these untimely battles. We have erred, and each one of us here is to some degree at fault: the Monk Robak, for spreading tidings too zealously; the Warden and the gentry, for completely misunderstanding them. The war with Russia will not begin for some time; meanwhile, those who took the most active part in the battle cannot without danger remain in Lithuania. So, gentlemen, you must flee to the Grand Duchy of Warsaw; to be specific: Maciej, called Baptist, Thaddeus, Bucket, and Razor must depart over the Niemen, where the hosts of our nation await them. We will throw the whole blame on you who are gone, and on Plut, and thus we shall save the rest of your kindred. I bid you farewell, but not for long; there are sure hopes that in spring the dawn of freedom will arise for us, and Lithuania, who now bids you farewell as wanderers, will soon behold you again as her victorious deliverers. The Judge is preparing everything needful for the journey, and, so far as I am able, I will aid you with money."

The gentry felt that the Chamberlain counselled wisely. It is well known that whoever has once quarrelled with the Russian Tsar, can never conclude a lasting peace with him on this earth, and must either fight or rot in Siberia. So, saying nothing, they looked gloomily at one another and sighed; in token of agreement they nodded their heads.

The Pole, though famous among the nations because he loves his native land more than life, is nevertheless always prepared to abandon it, and to travel to the ends [pg 256] of the earth, to live long years in poverty and contempt, struggling with men and with fate—so long as amid the storm there shines upon him this hope, that he is serving the Fatherland.

They declared that they were ready to depart at once. However, this plan did not meet with Pan Buchmann's approval: Buchmann, prudent man that he was, had not meddled in the battle, but as soon as he heard that they were having a consultation, he hastened to put in his word; he thought the project good, but wanted to alter it, to develop it with more precision, to explain it more clearly, and, first of all, legally to appoint a commission, which should consider the aims of the emigration, the means and methods, and likewise various other matters. Unfortunately the shortness of the time prevented them from adopting Buchmann's advice. The gentry took a hasty farewell and at once started on their journey.

But the Judge retained Thaddeus in the room and said to the Monk:—

"It is time for me to tell you what I learned with certainty only yesterday, that our Thaddeus is sincerely in love with Zosia; let him ask her hand before his departure! I have spoken with Telimena, and she no longer opposes the match; Zosia also agrees to the wishes of her guardians. If we cannot to-day make the pair happy by marriage, then at least, brother, we may betroth them before his departure; for the heart of a young traveller, as you know well, is exposed to various temptations. And yet, when a young man glances at his ring and calls to mind that he is already a husband, at once the fever of temptations in a foreign land subsides. Believe me, a wedding ring has great force.

"I myself, thirty years ago, had a great passion for Panna Marta, whose heart I won; we were betrothed, [pg 257] but God did not bless that union; he left me alone on earth, taking to his glory the fair daughter of my friend the Seneschal Hreczecha. There was left to me only the memory of her virtues and her charms, and this golden wedding ring. Whenever I have looked upon it, the hapless girl has always appeared before my eyes; and thus, by the grace of God, I have preserved till now my plighted faith, and, without ever having been a husband, I am now an old widower, though the Seneschal has another daughter, very fair and very like my beloved Marta:"

So saying, he gazed tenderly at the ring, and wiped the tears from his eyes with the back of his hand.

"Brother, what think you?" he concluded. "Shall we betroth them? He loves her, and I have the consent of the aunt and of the girl."

But Thaddeus, stepping quickly up to him, said eagerly:—

"How can I thank you enough, my good uncle, for the constant care that you take for my happiness! Ah, my good uncle, I should be the happiest of men if Zosia were betrothed to me to-day, if I knew that she were to be my wife! However, I tell you frankly, this betrothal cannot take place to-day; there are various reasons. Question me no further; if Zosia will consent to wait, she may perhaps soon find in me a better man—and a man more worthy of her; perhaps by my constancy I shall gain her affection, perhaps I shall adorn my name with some trifling glory, perhaps I shall soon return to the home of my fathers. Then, uncle, I shall remind you of your promise, then on my knees I shall greet my dear Zosia, and, if she is free, I shall beg her hand; but now I am abandoning Lithuania, perhaps for long, and perhaps in the meantime another man may win Zosia's favour. I [pg 258] do not wish to bind her will, and to beg for an affection that I have not deserved would be a base act."

While the young man, much moved, was uttering these words, two tears, like two great round pearls, shone in his great blue eyes and rolled down quickly over his rosy cheeks.

But the curious Zosia from the depths of the alcove had been following this mysterious conversation through a crack; she had heard Thaddeus tell frankly and boldly of his love, and with fluttering heart she had seen those two great tears in his eyes. Though she could not find the key to his mystery, why he had fallen in love with her, why he was abandoning her, and where he was departing, nevertheless this departure made her sad. For the first time in her life she heard from the lips of a youth the great and marvellous news that she was beloved. So she ran to the little altar of the house and took from it a picture, and a small reliquary; the picture was of Saint Genevieve, and in the reliquary was a bit of the robe of Saint Joseph the Bridegroom, the patron of youths and maidens who are betrothed. With these sacred objects she entered the room:—

"Are you going away so soon? I want to give you a little present for the journey and a bit of warning too: always carry with you these relics and this picture, and remember Zosia. May the Lord God guide you in health and happiness and may he soon guide you back prosperously to us!"

She ceased, and lowered her head; hardly had she closed her blue eyes, when floods of tears escaped from under her lashes, and Zosia stood there silent, with closed eyelids, shedding tears like diamonds.

Thaddeus, taking his gifts, kissed her hand, and said: "Panna Sophia, now I must bid you good-bye! Farewell, [pg 259] do not forget me, and deign sometimes to repeat a prayer for me! Sophia!——" He could say no more.

But the Count, who had entered unexpectedly with Telimena and had observed the tender farewell of the young pair, was much moved, and said with a glance at Telimena:—

"How much beauty is there even in this simple scene, when the soul of the shepherdess and the soul of the warrior, like a boat and a ship during a storm at sea, must at last be parted! In very truth nothing so kindles the feelings in the heart as when heart separates from heart. Time is like a blast of wind; it extinguishes only the little candle; a great flame it fans to an even mightier conflagration. And my heart also is capable of loving even more mightily at a distance. Pan Soplica, I regarded you as my rival; that mistake was one of the causes of our lamentable quarrel, which forced me to draw the sword against your household. I perceive my mistake, for you sighed to the little shepherdess, while I had given my heart to this fair nymph. Let our differences be drowned in the blood of our country's enemies; we will no longer fight each other with the murderous steel! Let our amorous strife be settled otherwise; let us contend which shall surpass the other in the feeling of love! Let us both leave behind the dear objects of our hearts, let us both hasten against swords and spears; let us contend with each other in constancy, sorrow, and suffering, and pursue our country's enemies with our manly arms!"

He spoke and glanced at Telimena, but she made no reply, being overcome with amazement.

"My dear Count," interrupted the Judge, "why do you insist on departing? Believe me, you had best remain in security on your estate. The poor gentry may [pg 260] be skinned and scourged by the government, but you, Count, are sure of being left whole. You know what sort of government you have to deal with; you are fairly wealthy, and may ransom yourself from prison at the cost of only half your income for one year."

"That is not in concord with my character," said the Count. "Since I cannot be a lover, I will be a hero. Amid the cares of love I will call on glory as my comfortress; since I am a beggar of heart, I will be mighty of hand."

"Who hinders you from loving and being happy?" inquired Telimena.

"The power of my destiny," said the Count, "mysterious forebodings that with a secret impulse urge me to foreign lands and to unwonted deeds. I confess that to-day I wished in honour of Telimena to light the flame on the altars of Hymen, but this youth has given me too fair an example by tearing off his marriage wreath of his own free will and rushing to test his heart amid the hindrances of changeful fortune and amid the bloody chances of war. To-day for me, too, a new epoch is opened! Birbante-Rocca has resounded with the renown of my arms; may this renown spread far and wide in Poland also!"

He concluded, and proudly smote his sword hilt.

"It is hard to blame such a desire," said Robak. "Depart, but take money with you; you may equip a company of soldiers, like Wlodzimierz Potocki, who amazed the French by contributing a million to the treasury, or like Prince Dominik Radziwill, who abandoned his lands and goods and furnished two fresh regiments of cavalry. Go, go, but take money; across the Niemen we have hands enough, but money is scarce in the Grand Duchy; go, we bid you farewell!"

[pg 261]

"Alas!" said Telimena with a mournful glance, "I see that nothing will restrain you! My knight, when you enter the lists of battle, turn a feeling gaze on the colours of your belovèd." (Here she tore a ribbon from her dress, made a cockade, and pinned it on the Count's bosom.) "May these colours guide you against fiery cannon, against shining spears and sulphurous rains; and when you make yourself famous by warlike deeds, and when you shade with immortal laurels your blood-stained helmet and your casque, bold in victory, even then look once more on this cockade! Remember whose hand pinned upon you these colours!"

Here she offered him her hand. The Count knelt and kissed it; Telimena raised her handkerchief to one eye, but with the other eye she looked down on the Count, who was bidding her farewell with deep emotion. She sighed, but shrugged her shoulders.

But the Judge said: "Hurry up, my dear Count, for it is already late!" And the Monk Robak called out with a threatening mien: "Enough of this; hurry up!" Thus the orders of the Judge and the Monk separated the tender pair and drove them from the room.

Meanwhile Thaddeus had embraced his uncle with tears and was kissing Robak's hand. Robak, pressing the lad's brow to his breast and lying his palms crosswise on his head, gazed aloft and said: "My son, may God be with you!" Then he began to weep. But Thaddeus was already beyond the threshold.

"What, brother?" asked the Judge, "will you tell him nothing? not even now? Shall the poor lad still remain in ignorance, now that he is going to leave us!"

"No, nothing!" said the Monk, after a long interval of weeping, his face covered by his hands. "Why should the poor fellow know that he has a father who has hidden [pg 262] himself from the world as a scoundrel and a murderer? God sees how I longed to tell him, but of that consolation I will make an offering to God, to expiate my former sins."

"Then," said the Judge, "it is now time for you to think of yourself. Pray reflect that a man of your age, in your weak condition, would be unable to emigrate along with the others. You have said that you know a little house where you must hide; tell me where it is. We must hasten, the waggon is waiting, ready harnessed; would it not be better to go to the woods, to the forester's hut?"

"Early to-morrow morning will be time enough," said Robak, nodding his head. "Now, my brother, send for the priest to come here as quickly as may be with the viaticum; send off every one but the Warden, and shut the door."

The Judge carried out Robak's instructions and sat down on the bed beside him; but Gerwazy remained standing, resting his elbow on the pommel of his sword, and leaning his bent brow on his hands.

Robak, before beginning to speak, riveted his gaze on the face of the Warden and remained mysteriously silent. But as a surgeon first lays a gentle hand on the body of a sick man before he makes a cut with the knife, so Robak softened the expression of his sharp eyes, which he allowed to hover for a long time over the eyes of Gerwazy; finally, as if he wished to strike a blind blow, he covered his eyes with his hand and said with a powerful voice:—

"I am Jacek Soplica."

At these words the Warden turned pale, bowed down, and, with half his body bent forward, remained fixed in this position, hung upon one foot, like a stone flying [pg 263] from on high but checked in its course. He raised his eyelids and opened wide his mouth with its threatening white teeth; his mustaches bristled; his sword dropped from his hands, but he caught it near the floor with his knees and held the pommel with his right hand, gripping it convulsively: the long black blade of the sword stretched out behind him and shook back and forth. And the Warden was like a wounded lynx, about to spring from a tree into the very face of a hunter: it puffs itself into a ball, growls, flashes fire from its bloody eyeballs, twitches its whiskers and lashes its tail.

"Pan Rembajlo," said the Monk, "I am no longer alarmed by the wrath of men, for already I am under the hand of God. I adjure thee in the name of Him who saved the world, and on the cross blessed His murderers and accepted the prayer of the robber, that you relent, and hear in patience what I have to say. I have myself declared my name; to ease my conscience I must gain or at least beg forgiveness. Hear my confession; then you will do with me as you wish."

Here he joined his two hands as though in prayer; the Warden drew back amazed, smote his hand on his brow and shrugged his shoulders.

And the Monk began to tell of his former intimacy with the Horeszko and of the love between him and the Pantler's daughter, and of the enmity between the two men that thence arose. But he spoke confusedly; often he mixed accusations and complaints in his confession, often he interrupted his speech as though he had ended, and then began anew.

The Warden, who was thoroughly familiar with the story of the Horeszkos, straightened out in his mind the whole tale, though it was sadly tangled, and could fill up the gaps in it; but the Judge entirely failed to understand [pg 264] many points. Both listened attentively, bending their heads forward; but Jacek spoke more and more slowly, and often interrupted himself.

* * * * * * * *

"You already know, my dear Gerwazy, how often the Pantler used to invite me to banquets; he would propose my health, and many a time he cried, raising his beaker aloft, that he had no better friend than Jacek Soplica. How he would embrace me! All who saw it thought that he shared his very soul with me. He a friend? He knew what then was passing within my soul!

* * * * * * * *

"Meanwhile the neighbourhood was already whispering; gossips would say to me: 'Ah, Pan Soplica, your suit is vain; the threshold of a dignitary is too high for the feet of Jacek the Cup-Bearer's son.' I laughed, pretending that I mocked at magnates and their daughters, and that I cared nothing for aristocrats; that if I often visited them, I did it out of mere friendship, and that I would never marry outside my own station in life. And yet these jests pricked my soul to the quick: I was young and daring, and the world was open to me in a land where, as you know, one born a simple gentleman may be chosen king just as freely as the most powerful lord. Once Tenczynski asked in marriage a daughter of a royal house, and the King gave her to him without shame. 173 Are not the Soplicas of equal merit with the Tenczynskis, through their blood, through their ancient crest, and through their faithful service to the Commonwealth!

* * * * * * * *

"How easily a man may ruin the happiness of others in a single instant; and in a long lifetime he cannot [pg 265] restore it! One word from the Pantler, and how happy we should have been! Who knows? Perhaps we should be living still; perhaps he too, with his belovèd child—with his fair Eva—and with her grateful husband, would have grown old in peace! perhaps he would have rocked to sleep his grandchildren! But now? He has destroyed us both—and he himself—and that murder—and all the consequences of that crime, all my sufferings and transgressions! I have no right to accuse him, I am his slayer; I have no right to accuse him, I forgive him from my heart—but he too——

* * * * * * * *

"If he had but once openly refused me—for he knew our feelings—if he had not received my visits, then who knows? Perhaps I should have gone away, have become enraged, have cursed him, and finally have left him in peace. But he, the proud and cunning lord, formed a new plan; he pretended that it had never even entered his head that I could strive for such a union. But he needed me, I had influence among the gentry and every one in the district liked me. So he feigned not to notice my love; he welcomed me as before and even insisted that I should come more often; but whenever we were alone together, seeing my eyes darkened with tears and my heart over-full and ready to burst forth, the sly old man would suddenly throw in some indifferent word about lawsuits, district diets, or hunting——

* * * * * * * *

"Ah, often over the winecups, when he was in a melting mood, when he clasped me so closely and assured me of his friendship, since he needed my sabre or my vote at the diet, and when in return I was forced to clasp him in friendly wise, then anger would so boil up within me that I would turn the spittle within my [pg 266] lips and clasp my sword hilt with my hand, longing to spit upon this friendship and to draw the sword at once. But Eva, noticing my glance and my bearing, would guess, I know not how, what was passing within me, and would gaze at me imploringly, and her face would turn pale; and she was so fair and meek a dove, and she had so gentle and serene a glance!—so angel-like that—I know not how—but I lacked the courage to anger or alarm her—and I held my peace. And I, a roistering champion famous through all Lithuania, before whom the greatest lords had been wont to tremble, who had not lived a day without a battle, who would not have allowed the Pantler, no, not the King himself, to do me wrong; I, who was driven to fury by the least disagreement—I, then, though angry and drunken, held my peace like a lamb!—as though I had suddenly beheld the consecrated Host! 174

* * * * * * * *

"How many times did I wish to open my heart and even to humble myself to implore him; but when I looked into his eyes and met his gaze cold as ice, I felt shame for my emotion; I hastened once more to discourse as coldly as I might of suits at law and of the district diets, and even to jest. All this, to be sure, was from pride, in order not to debase the name of the Soplicas, in order not to lower myself before a magnate by a vain request and receive a refusal—for what gossip there would have been among the gentry, if they had known that I, Jacek——

* * * * * * * *

"The Horeszkos refuse a wench to a Soplica! They serve me, Jacek, with black soup!

"Finally, not knowing myself what way to turn, I bethought me of gathering together a little company [pg 267] of gentry, and of leaving forever this district and my Fatherland; of going off somewhere or other, to Moscow or to the land of the Tatars, and beginning a war. I rode over to bid the Pantler farewell, in the hope that when he saw his faithful partisan, his former friend, a man almost of his own household, with whom he had caroused and made war for so many long years, now bidding him farewell and riding off to the ends of the earth—that the old man might be moved and show me at least a trace of a human soul, as a snail shows its horns!

"Ah! if one has at the bottom of his heart the faintest spark of feeling for a friend, that spark will break forth when he bids him farewell, like the last flame of life before a man expires! The coldest eye, when for the last time it touches the brow of a friend, will often shed a tear!

* * * * * * * *

"The poor girl, hearing that I was about to leave the country, turned pale, and fell in a swoon, almost dead; she could not speak, but from her eyes there streamed a flood of tears—I learned how dear I was to her.

* * * * * * * *

"I remember that for the first time in my life I shed tears, for joy and for despair; I forgot myself, I went mad; I was ready once more to fall at her father's feet, to cling like a serpent about his knees, to cry out, 'Dear father, take me for your son or slay me!' Then the Pantler, sullen, cold as a pillar of salt, polite and indifferent, began a discourse—of what? of what? Of his daughter's wedding! At that moment? O Gerwazy, dear friend, consider; you have a human heart!

"The Pantler said: 'Pan Soplica, a wooer has just come to me on behalf of the Castellan's175 son; you are my friend, what do you say to that? You know, sir, [pg 268] that I have a daughter, fair and rich—and the Castellan of Witepsk! That is a low, parvenu seat in the Senate; what do you advise me, brother?' I have entirely forgotten what I said in reply to that, probably nothing at all—I mounted my horse and fled!"

* * * * * * * *

"Jacek!" cried the Warden, "you are clever at finding excuses! Well? They do not lessen your guilt! For it has happened many a time ere now that a man has fallen in love with the daughter of a lord or king, and has tried to capture her by force; has planned to steal her away or to avenge himself openly—but so stealthily to kill him! a Polish lord, in Poland, and in league with the Muscovites!"

"I was not in league with them," answered Jacek in a voice full of sorrow.

"Seize her by force? I might have; from behind gratings and locks I would have snatched her; I would have shattered this castle of his into dust! I had behind me Dobrzyn and four other hamlets. Ah, would that she had been such as our plain gentlewomen, strong and vigorous! Would that she had not dreaded flight and the pursuit and could have borne the sound of clashing arms! But the poor child! Her parents had shielded her so carefully that she was frail and timid! She was but a little spring caterpillar—the larva of a butterfly! And to snatch her thus, to touch her with an armed hand, would have been to kill her. I could not! No!

"To avenge myself openly, and tumble the castle into ruins by an assault, I was ashamed, for they would have said that I was avenging myself for my rejection! Warden, your honest heart cannot feel what hell there is in wounded pride.

"The demon of pride began to suggest to me better [pg 269] plans: to take a bloody revenge, but to hide the reason for my vengeance; to frequent the castle no more and to root out my love from my heart; to dismiss Eva from my memory and to marry another; and then later to find some pretext for a quarrel, and to take vengeance.

"At first I thought that I had succeeded in overcoming my heart, and I was glad of that fancied change, and—I married the first poor girl that I met! I did evil, and how cruelly was I punished for it! I loved her not, Thaddeus's poor mother, my most devoted wife and the most upright soul—but I was strangling in my heart my former love and my anger. I was like a madman; in vain I forced myself to work at farming or at business; all was of no avail. Possessed by the demon of vengeance, morose and passionate, I could find no comfort in anything in the world—and thus I passed from one sin to another; I began to drink.

"And so in no long time my wife died of grief, leaving me that child; and despair consumed me!

* * * * * * * *

"How ardently I must have loved that poor girl! for so many years! Where have I not been! And yet I have never been able to forget her, and still does her belovèd form stand before mine eyes as if painted! I drank, but I have not been able to drink down her memory for one instant; nor to free myself from it, though I have traversed so many lands! Now I am in the dress of God's servant, on my bed, and bleeding—I have spoken of her so long—at this moment to speak of such things! God will forgive me! You must learn now in what sorrow and despair I committed——

"That was but a short time after her betrothal. Everywhere the talk was of nothing but her betrothal; [pg 270] they said that when Eva took the ring from the hand of the Wojewoda she swooned, that she had been seized with a fever, that she had symptoms of consumption, that she sobbed continually; they conjectured that she was secretly in love with some one else. But the Pantler, calm and gay as ever, gave balls in his castle and assembled his friends; me he no longer invited—in what way could I be useful to him? My scandalous life at home, my misery, my disgraceful habits had brought upon me the contempt and mockery of the world! Me, who once, I may say, had made all the district tremble! Me, whom Radziwill had called 'my dear'! Me, who, when I rode forth from my hamlet, had led with me a train more numerous than a prince's! And when I drew my sabre, then many thousand sabres had glittered round about, striking terror to the lords' castles,—But now the very children of the peasant boors laughed at me! So paltry had I quickly made myself in the eyes of men! Jacek Soplica! He who knows the feeling of pride——"

Here the Bernardine grew weak and fell back on the bed, and the Warden said, deeply moved:—

"Great are the judgments of God! It is the truth! the truth! So is it you? and are you Jacek? the Soplica? in a monk's cowl? Have you been living a beggar's life! You, whom I remember when you were strong and rosy, a handsome gentlemen, when lords flattered you, when women went mad over you! The mustachioed champion! That was not so long ago! it is grief that has aged you thus! How could I fail to recognise you from that shot, when you hit the bear with so sure an aim? For our Lithuania had no better marksman than you, and next to Maciek you were also the foremost swordsman! It is the truth! Once the gentlewomen sang of you:—
[pg 271]
When Jacek twirls his whisker, men tremble far and near;
'Gainst whom he knots his whisker, that man feels mortal fear—
Though he be Prince Radziwill, to fight he will not dare.
You tied a knot against my lord! Unhappy man! And is it you? Fallen to such a state! The mustachioed Jacek a monkish alms-gatherer! Great are the judgments of God! And now! ha! you cannot escape the penalty; I have sworn, he who has shed a drop of the Horeszkos' blood——"

Meanwhile the Monk had raised himself to a sitting posture on the bed; and he thus concluded:—

"I rode around the castle; who can tell the names of all the devils that filled my head and heart! The Pantler? Is he slaying his own child as he has already slain and ruined me?—I rode up to the gate; a demon enticed me there. Look how he revels! Every day a drinking bout in the castle! How many candles there are in the windows, what music peals through the halls! And shall not this castle crash down upon his bald head?

"Think of vengeance, and a demon will at once furnish you a weapon. Hardly had I thought of it, when the demon sent the Muscovites. I stood gazing; you know how they stormed your castle.
* * * * * * * *
"For it is false that I was in any league with the Muscovites.
* * * * * * * *
"I gazed; various thoughts passed through my head: at first with a stupid laugh I gazed as a child upon a burning house; then I felt a murderous joy, expecting that speedily it would begin to blaze and totter; at times I was prompted to leap in and save her—even the Pantler——
* * * * * * * *

[pg 272]
"Your defence, as you know, was vigorous and prompt. I was amazed; the Muscovites kept falling close by me; the beasts aimed poorly.—At the sight of their overthrow hatred again overcame me.—That Pantler a victor! And shall he prosper thus in his every purpose? And shall he triumph even over this fearful assault? I was riding away, smitten with shame.—Day was just dawning; suddenly I beheld him and recognised him; he stepped out on the balcony and his diamond buckle glittered in the sun; proudly he twirled his mustache and proudly gazed around; and it seemed to me that he mocked at me above all others, that he had recognised me and that thus he pointed his hand at me, scoffing and threatening,— I seized a carbine from a Muscovite; I barely raised it to my shoulder, scarcely aimed—it went off! You know the rest!

"Cursed firearms! He who slays with the sword must take his stand and press on; he parries and flourishes; he may disarm his enemy and check his sword halfway. But with these firearms it is enough to hold the gun; an instant, a single spark——
* * * * * * * *
"Did I flee when you aimed at me from above? I levelled my eyes at the two barrels of your gun. What despair! A strange grief pinned me to the earth! Why, Gerwazy, ah why did you miss at that time? You would have done me a kindness!—evidently as a penance for my sin I must needs——"

Here his breath failed him once more.

"God knows," said the Warden, "I sincerely wished to hit you! How much blood did you shed by your one shot! How many disasters have fallen upon us and upon [pg 273] your family, and all of them through your guilt alone, Pan Jacek! And yet to-day, when the yagers aimed at the Count (the last of the Horeszkos, though in the female line), you preserved him; and when the Muscovites shot at me you threw me on the ground, so that you have been the saviour of us both. If it is true that you are a monk, in holy orders, then your habit shields you from my penknife.

Farewell, I will set foot no more upon your threshold; our account is clear—let us leave the rest to the Lord."

Jacek stretched out his hand—but Gerwazy started back.

"Without dishonour to my noble blood," he said, "I cannot touch a hand denied by such a murder, committed for private vengeance, and not pro publico bono ."

But Jacek, sinking from the pillows into the bed, turned to the Judge and grew more and more pale; he eagerly asked for the parish priest, and cried to the Warden:—

"I implore you to remain; in a moment more I shall finish; hardly have I strength to conclude—Warden—I shall die this night."

"What, brother?" cried the Judge, "I have seen your wound; it is trifling: why do you say this? Send for the priest! Perhaps it has been ill tended: I will send for the doctor; he is at the apothecary's."

"It is too late, brother," interrupted the Monk. "In the same place I have an earlier gunshot wound; I received it at Jena. It was ill healed, and now it has been irritated—there is gangrene there already. I am familiar with wounds; see how black the blood is, like soot; a doctor could do nothing. But this is a trifle; we die but once; to-morrow or to-day we must yield [pg 274] up our souls. Warden, thou wilt forgive me; I must die!
* * * * * * * *

"There is merit in refusing to betray your country, though your own people proclaim you a traitor! Especially for a man who had such pride as mine!
* * * * * * * *

"The name of traitor clove to me like a pestilence. The neighbours turned their faces from me, my former friends fled from me, the timid greeted me from afar and turned aside; even a mere peasant boor or a Jew, though he bowed, would, as he passed by, smite me with a sneering laugh. The word 'traitor' rang in my ears and echoed through my house and over my fields; that word from morn till dark hovered before me like a spot before a sick man's eye. And yet I was *not*

a traitor to my country.

"The Muscovites showed by acts of violence that they regarded me as one of their partisans: they gave the Soplicas a considerable part of the dead man's estates; later the Targowica confederates wished to bestow an office upon me.176 If I had then consented to turn Muscovite!—Satan counselled it—I was already influential and rich; but if I had become a Muscovite?—The foremost magnates would have sought my favour; even my brother gentlemen—even the mob, which is so ready to disparage those of its own number, is prone to forgive those happier men who serve the Muscovites! I knew this, and yet—I could not.
* * * * * * * *

"I fled from my country! Where have I not been! what have I not suffered!
* * * * * * * *

"At last God deigned to reveal to me the one true [pg 275] remedy: I must reform myself and repair as much as possible what——
* * * * * * * *

"The Pantler's daughter and her husband the Wojewoda had been transported to some place in Siberia; there she died young, leaving here behind her a daughter, little Zosia. I had her brought up.
* * * * * * * *

"Perchance I slew him more through stupid arrogance than through disappointed love; so I humbly became a monk. I, once proud of my birth, I who was once a warlike hero, I bowed my head, I became a gatherer of alms, and took the name of Robak, the Worm, since like a worm in the dust——

"The evil example that I had set my countrymen, that invitation to treason, I must redeem by setting a good example, by blood and by self-sacrifice.

"I have fought for my country: where? how? I shall never tell; not for earthly glory have I run so often upon shot and steel. I like better to remember, instead of my famous, warlike exploits, my quiet, useful acts, and my sufferings, which no one——

"Often have I succeeded in penetrating into this land, bearing orders from the generals, or collecting information, or concluding agreements—the men of Galicia know this monkish cowl—and in Great Poland they know it too! For a year I toiled in a Prussian fortress, chained to a wheelbarrow; thrice the Muscovites have cut up my back with stripes, and once they had me on the road to Siberia; later the Austrians buried me in the dungeons of Spielberg, at hard labour, in carcer durum —but by a miracle the Lord God delivered me and granted that I should die among my own people, with the sacraments.
[pg 276]
"Perchance even now, who knows? Perchance I have sinned anew! Perchance I have hastened too much the insurrection, exceeding the commands of my generals. The thought that the house of the Soplicas should be the first to take up arms, and that my kindred should raise the first banner of the Warhorse in Lithuania!—That thought ... seems pure.——

"You have longed for vengeance? You have it now, for you have been the instrument of God's punishment! With your sword God cut short my plans. You have tangled the thread of the plot that had been spun for so many years! The great aim that absorbed my whole life, my last worldly feeling upon earth, which I fondled and cherished like my dearest child—that you have slain before the father's eyes, and I have forgiven you I You!——"

"Even so may God forgive you too!" interrupted the Warden. "Father Jacek, if you are now about to take the sacrament, remember that I am no Lutheran or schismatic! I know that whoever saddens the last moments of a dying man, commits sin. I will tell you something that will surely comfort you. When my late master had fallen wounded, and I was kneeling by him, bending over his breast; when, wetting my sword in his wound, I vowed vengeance, my lord shook his head and stretched out his hand towards the door, towards the place where you were standing, and drew a cross in the air; he could not speak, but he made a sign that he forgave his murderer. I understood well, but I was so furious with rage that I have never said even a word of that cross."

Here the sufferings of the sick man made further speech impossible and a long hour of silence followed. They were awaiting the priest. The thunder of hoofs [pg 277] was heard, and the Tavern-Keeper, out of breath, knocked at the chamber door; he brought an important letter, which he showed to Jacek. Jacek gave it to his brother and bade him read it aloud. The letter was from Fiszer, 177 who was then Chief of Staff of the Polish army under Prince Joseph. It brought the news that in the Privy Council of the Emperor war had been declared, and that the Emperor was already proclaiming it over the whole world; that a General Diet had been convoked in Warsaw, and that the assembled representatives of Masovia would solemnly decree the union of Lithuania with the Grand Duchy.

Jacek, as he listened, repeated prayers in a low voice, and, clasping to his breast the consecrated candle, raised to Heaven his eyes, now kindled with hope, and shed a flood of last joyous tears. "Now, O Lord," he said, "let thy servant depart in peace!" All kneeled; and then a bell rang at the door, a token that the priest had arrived with the body of our Lord.

Night was just departing, and across the milky sky were streaming the first rosy beams of the sun: they entered through the window panes like diamond arrows, and fell upon the bed; they surrounded the head of the sick man, wreathing with gold his face and his temples, so that he shone like a saint in a fiery crown. [pg 278]

BOOK XI.—THE YEAR 1812

ARGUMENT

Spring omens—The entrance of the armies—Religious services—Official rehabilitation of the late Jacek Soplica—From the talk between Gerwazy and Protazy a speedy ending of the lawsuit may be inferred—A love affair between an uhlan and a girl—The quarrel over Bobtail and Falcon is at last settled—Thereupon the guests gather for the banquet—The presentation of the betrothed couples to the generals.

Memorable year! Happy is he who beheld thee in our land! The folk still call thee the year of harvest, but the soldiers the year of war; old men still love to tell tales of thee and poets still dream of thee. Thou hadst long been heralded by the marvel in the sky and preceded by a vague rumour among the folk; with the coming of the spring sun the hearts of the Lithuanians were seized with a certain strange foreboding, as if the end of the world were approaching—by a certain yearning and joyous expectation.

In the spring, when the cattle were driven forth for the first time, men noticed that, though famished and lean, they did not run to the young corn 179 that already made gay the fields, but lay down on the ploughed land, and, drooping their heads, either lowed or chewed the cud of their winter food.

The villagers too, as they ploughed for the spring grain, did not show their wonted joy in the end of the long winter; they did not sing songs, but worked lazily, as though forgetful of the sowing and the harvest. As they harrowed, at every step they checked their oxen and their [pg 279] nags, and gazed anxiously towards the west, as though from this direction some marvel were about to appear. And they regarded anxiously the birds, which were returning home; for already the stork had flown back to its native pine and had spread its white wings, the early standard of spring; and after it the swallows, coming on in noisy regiments, gathered above the waters, and from the frozen earth collected mud for their tiny houses. At evening in the thickets one could hear the calling of the woodcocks as they rose from the earth; and flocks of wild geese honked over the forest and, wearied, settled noisily down to feed; and in the depths of the dark heaven the cranes kept up a continuous clamour. Hearing this, the night watchmen would ask in dread whence came such disorder in the winged kingdom, and what storm had driven forth these birds so early.

And now new swarms, like flocks of finches, plover, and starlings, swarms of bright plumes and pennons shone bright upon the hills and came down into the meadows. It was cavalry! In strange array, and arms never seen before, came regiment after regiment; and straight across the country, like melted snows, the iron-shod ranks flowed along the roads. From the forests emerged black shakos, a row of bayonets glittered, and the infantry, countless as ants, swarmed forth.

All were turned towards the north; you would have said that at that time, coming from the Sunny South 180 and following the birds, men too were entering our land, driven on by the force of some instinct that they could not comprehend.

Steeds, men, cannon, eagles flowed on day and night; here and there fires glowed in the sky; the earth trembled, in the distance one could hear the rolling of thunder.—
[pg 280]
War! war! There was no corner in the Lithuanian land to which its roar did not reach; amid dark forests, the peasant, whose grandfathers and kinsmen had died without seeing beyond the boundaries of the wood, who understood no other cries in the sky than those of the winds, and none on earth except the roaring of beasts, who had seen no other guests than his fellow-woodsmen, now beheld how a strange glare flamed in the sky—in the forest there was a crash—that was a cannon ball that had wandered from the battlefield and was seeking a path in the wood, tearing up stumps and cutting through boughs. The hoary, bearded bison trembled in his mossy lair and bristled up his long shaggy mane; he half rose, resting on his forelegs, and, shaking his beard, he gazed in amazement at the sparks suddenly glittering amid the brushwood: this was a stray bombshell that twirled and whirled and hissed, and at last broke with a roar like thunder; the bison for the first time in his life was terrified and fled to take refuge in deeper hiding.

"A battle! Where? In what direction?" asked the young men, as they seized their arms; the women raised their hands in prayer to Heaven. All, sure of victory, cried out with tears in their eyes: "God is with Napoleon and Napoleon is with us!"

O spring! Happy is he who beheld thee then in our country! Memorable spring of war, spring of harvest! O spring, happy is he who beheld how thou didst bloom with corn and grass, but glittered with men; how thou wert rich in events and big with hope! I see thee still, fair phantom of my dream! Born in slavery and chained in my swaddling bands, I have had but one such spring in my whole life.

Soplicowo lay close by the highway along which two generals were pressing forward from the Niemen. Our [pg 281] own Prince Joseph and Jerome, King of Westphalia, 181 had already occupied Lithuania from Grodno to Slonim, when the King issued orders to give the army three days of repose. But the Polish soldiers, despite their hardships, murmured because the King would not permit them to march on; so eager were they to overtake the Muscovites at the earliest possible moment.

The main staff of the Prince had halted in the town near by, but in Soplicowo was a camp of forty thousand men, and with them Generals Dombrowski, 182 Kniaziewicz, 183 Malachowski, 184 Giedrojc, 185 and Grabowski, 186 with their staffs.

As it was late when they arrived, each man chose quarters wherever he could, either in the old castle or in the mansion; soon orders had been issued and guards stationed, and each weary man went to his chamber for sleep. As night drew on all became quiet, both camp, mansion, and field; one could see only the patrols wandering about like shadows, and here and there the flickering of the camp fires; one could hear only the watchwords being passed about from post to post in the army.

All slept, the master of the house, the generals, and the soldiers; the eyes of the Seneschal alone were not closed in sweet slumber. For on the morrow the Seneschal had to arrange a banquet by which he would fain make famous the house of the Soplicas for ever and ever; a banquet worthy of guests so dear to Polish hearts, and in keeping with the great solemnity of the day, which was both a church holiday and a family holiday; on the morrow the betrothals of three couples were to take place. Moreover, General Dombrowski had made known that evening that he wished to have a Polish dinner.
[pg 282]
Though the hour was late, the Seneschal had gathered cooks from the neighbourhood with all possible speed; there were five of them working under his direction. As head cook he had girt him with a white apron, donned a nightcap, and tucked up his sleeves to the elbows. In one hand he held a fly-flapper, and with it he drove away insects of all sorts, which were settling greedily on the dainties; with the other hand he put on his well-wiped spectacles, took a book from his bosom, unwrapped it, and opened it.

This book was entitled The Perfect Cook . 187 Herein were described in detail all the dishes peculiar to the Polish table: with its aid the Count of Tenczyn was wont to give those banquets in the Italian land at which the Holy Father Urban VIII. marvelled; 188 by its aid, later on, Karol My-dear-friend Radziwill, 189 when he entertained King Stanislaw at Nieswiez, arranged that memorable feast the fame of which still lives throughout Lithuania in popular tales.

What the Seneschal read, understood, and proclaimed, that straightway did the skilful cooks carry out. The work seethed: fifty knives clattered on the tables; scullions black as demons rushed about, some carrying wood, others pails of milk and wine; they poured them into kettles, spiders, and stew-pans, and the steam burst forth. Two scullions sat by the stove and puffed at the bellows; the Seneschal, the more easily to kindle the fire, had given orders to have melted butter poured on the wood—this bit of extravagance is permitted in a well-to-do household. The scullions stuffed bundles of dry brushwood into the fire; others of them placed upon spits immense roasts of beef and venison, and haunches of wild boars and of stags; still others were plucking whole heaps of birds of all sorts— [pg 283] clouds of down flew about, and grouse, heath cocks, and hens were stripped bare. But there were very few hens: since the attack that bloodthirsty Buzzard Dobrzynski had made on the hencoop at the time of the foray, when he had annihilated Zosia's establishment, without leaving a bit for medicine, 190 Soplicowo, once famous for its poultry, had not yet managed to blossom out again with new birds. For the rest, there was a great abundance of all the sorts of meats that could be gathered from the house and from the butchers' shops, from the woods and from the neighbours, from near and from far: you would have said that the only thing lacking was bird's milk. The two things that a generous man requires in order to give a feast were united at Soplicowo: plenty and art.

Already the solemn day of the Most Holy Lady of Flowers 191 was approaching; the weather was lovely, the hour early; the clear sky was extended about the earth like a calm, hanging, concavo-convex sea. A few stars shone from its depths, like pearls from the sea bottom, seen through waves; on one side a little white cloud, all alone, drifted along and buried its wings in the azure, like the vanishing pinions of a guardian angel, who, detained through the night by the prayers of men, has been belated, and is hastening to return to his fellow-denizens of heaven.

Already the last pearls of the stars had grown dim and been extinguished in the depths of the sky, and the centre of the sky's brow was growing pale; its right temple, reposing on a pillow of shadow, was still swarthy, but its left grew ever rosier; but farther off the horizon line parted like a broad eyelid, and in the centre one could see the white of an eye, one could see the iris and the pupil—now a ray darted forth and circled [pg 284] and shimmered over the rounded heavens, and hung in the white cloud like a golden arrow. At this beam, at this signal of day, a cluster of fires flew forth, crossing one another a thousand times on the sphere of the skies—and the eye of the sun rose up—still somewhat sleepy, it blinked and trembled and shook its gleaming lashes; it glittered with seven tints at once: at first sapphire, it straightway turned blood red like a ruby, and yellow as a topaz; next it sparkled transparent as crystal, then was radiant as a diamond; finally it became the colour of pure flame, like a great moon, or like a twinkling star: thus over the measureless heaven advanced the solitary sun.

To-day from the whole neighbourhood the Lithuanian populace had gathered before sunrise around the chapel, as if to hear some new marvel proclaimed. This gathering was due in part to the piety of the folk and in part to curiosity; for to-day at Soplicowo the generals were to attend service, those famous captains of our legions, whose names the folk knew and honoured as those of patron saints; all whose wanderings, cam-paigns, and battles were the people's gospel throughout Lithuania.

Now some officers and a throng of soldiers arrived. The folk surrounded them and gazed upon them, and they could hardly believe their eyes when they beheld their fellow-countrymen wearing uniforms, and carrying arms—free, and speaking the Polish language!

The mass began. The little sanctuary could not contain the entire throng; the folk kneeled on the grass, gazing at the door of the chapel, and bared their heads. The white or yellow hair of the Lithuanian folk was gilded like a field of ripe grain; here and there a maiden's fair head, decked with fresh flowers or with [pg 285] peacock's feathers, and with ribbons flowing loose from her braided hair, blossomed among the men's heads like a corn-flower or poppy amid the wheat. The kneeling, many-coloured throng covered the plain, and at the sound of the bell, as though at a breath of wind, all heads bent down like ears of corn on a field.

To-day the village girls had brought to the altar of the Virgin Mother the first tribute of spring—fresh sheaves of greenery; everything was decked with nosegays and garlands—the altar, the image, and even the belfry and the galleries. Sometimes a morning zephyr, stirring from the east, would tear down the garlands and throw them upon the brows of the kneeling worshippers, and would spread fragrance abroad as from a priest's censer.

When the mass and the sermon were over in the church, there came forth at the head of the whole gathering the Chamberlain, who had recently been unanimously chosen Marshal of the Confederacy 192 by the electoral assembly of the district. He wore the uniform of the wojewodeship, a tunic embroidered with gold, a kontusz of gros-de-Tours with a fringe, and a massive brocade belt, on which hung a sabre with a hilt of lizard skin. At his neck shone a large diamond pin; his cap was white, and on it was a large tuft of costly feathers, the crests of white herons. (Only on festival days is worn so rich an ornament, every little feather of which is worth a ducat.) Thus adorned, he stepped up on a mound before the church; the villagers and soldiers crowded around him: he spoke:—

"Brothers, the priest has proclaimed to you from the pulpit the liberty that the Emperor-King has already restored to the Kingdom, and is now restoring to the Duchy of Lithuania, to all Poland; you have heard [pg 286] the official decrees and the letters convening a General Diet. I have only a few words to say to the company on a matter that pertains to the Soplica family, the lords of this district.

"All the neighbourhood remembers the crime committed here by the deceased Pan Jacek Soplica; but, since you all know of his sins, it is time to proclaim his merits, also, before the world. Here are present the generals of our armies, from whom I have heard all that I tell you. This Jacek did not die at Rome, as was reported, but only changed his former way of life, his calling, and his name; and all his offences against God and his country he has blotted out by his holy life and by great deeds.

"It was he who at Hohenlinden,193 when General Richepanse, half vanquished, was already preparing to retreat, not knowing that Kniaziewicz was on the way to his rescue—it was he, Jacek, called Robak, who amid spears and swords brought to Richepanse from Kniaziewicz letters announcing that our men were attacking the enemy in the rear. Later, in Spain, when our uhlans had taken the fortified ridge of Somosierra, 194 he was wounded twice by the side of Kozietulski! Following this, as an emissary, with secret instructions, he traversed various quarters of our land, in order to watch the currents of popular feeling and to found and build up secret societies. Finally, at Soplicowo, in the home of his fathers, while he was paving the way for an insurrection, he perished in a foray. The news of his death arrived in Warsaw just at the moment when His Majesty the Emperor deigned to bestow on him as a reward for his former heroic deeds the knightly badge of the Legion of Honour.

"Therefore, taking into consideration all these [pg 287] matters, I, as representative of the authority of the wojewodeship, proclaim to you with my confederate's staff of office that Jacek by faithful service and by the favour of the Emperor has removed the blot of infamy from his name, and has won back his honour, taking once more his place in the ranks of true patriots. So whoever dares to speak a word at any time to the family of the deceased Jacek of the offence that he long since atoned for, that man will be liable, as a penalty for such a taunt, to gravis notæ macula , 195 according to the words of the statutes, which thus punish both militem and skartabell 196 if he spread calumny against a citizen of the Commonwealth—and since general equality before the law has now been proclaimed, therefore Article 3 is likewise binding on townsfolk and serfs. 197 This decree of the Marshal the Scribe will enter in the acts of the General Confederation, and the Apparitor will proclaim it.

"As for the cross of the Legion of Honour, the fact that it arrived late does not derogate from its glory; if it could not serve Jacek as an adornment, let it serve as a memorial of him: I hang it on his grave. For three days it will hang there, then it will be deposited in the chapel, as a votum for the Virgin."

So saying, he took the badge from its case and hung on the modest cross that marked the grave a red ribbon knotted into a cockade, and a starry white cross with a golden crown; the rays of the star shone in the sunlight like the last gleam of Jacek's earthly glory. Meanwhile the kneeling folk repeated the Angelus, praying for the eternal repose of the sinner; the Judge walked about among the guests and the throng of villagers and invited all to the banquet at Soplicowo.

But on the bench of turf before the house two old [pg 288] men had taken their seats, each holding on his knees a tankard full of mead. They gazed into the garden, where amid the buds of bright-coloured poppy stood an uhlan like a sunflower, wearing a glittering head-dress adorned with gilded metal and with a cock's feather; near him a little maid in a garment green as the lowly rue raised eyes blue as forget-me-nots towards the eyes of the youth. Farther on girls were plucking flowers among the beds, purposely turning away their heads from the lovers, in order not to embarrass their talk together.

But the old men, as they drank their mead and passed from hand to hand a bark snuffbox, continued their chat.

"Yes, yes, my dear Protazy," said Gerwazy the Warden. "Yes, yes, my dear Gerwazy," said Protazy the Apparitor. "Yes, yes indeed," they repeated in unison over and over again, nodding their heads in time to the words; finally the Apparitor spoke:—

"That our lawsuit has a strange conclusion I do not deny; however, there are precedents. I remember lawsuits in which worse outrages were committed than in ours, and yet marriage articles ended the whole trouble: in this way Lopot was reconciled to the Borzdobohaty family, the Krepsztuls with the Kupsces, Putrament with Pikturna, Mackiewicz with the Odynieces, and Turno with the Kwileckis. What am I saying! The Poles used to have worse broils with Lithuania than the Horeszkos with the Soplica family; but when Queen Jadwiga198 took the matter under advisement, then that difficulty too was settled out of court. It is a good thing when the parties have maidens or widows to give in marriage; then a compromise is always ready at hand. The longest suits are ordinarily [pg 289] with the Catholic clergy or with close kindred, for then the cases cannot be concluded by marriage. Hence come the endless quarrels between the Lechites and the Russians, who proceed from Lech and Rus, 199 two born brothers; hence also there were so many prolonged lawsuits between the Lithuanians and the Knights of the Cross, until Jagiello finally won. Hence finally that famous lawsuit of the Rymszas and the Dominicans long pendebat on the calendar, until finally Father Dymsza, the syndic of the convent, won the case: whence the 'proverb, the Lord God is greater than Lord Rymsza. And I may add, mead is better than the penknife."

So saying, he drank off a tankard to the health of the Warden.

"True, true!" replied Gerwazy with emotion. "Strange have been the fortunes of our beloved Kingdom and of our Lithuania! They are like a true married pair! God joined them, and the devil divides them; God has his own and the devil has his own! Ah, dear brother Protazy, that our eyes should see this— that these brethren from the Kingdom should visit us once more! I served with them years ago, and remember that bold confederates came from their country! If only my deceased lord the Pantler had lived to see this hour! O Jacek, Jacek!— but why should we lament? Now Lithuania will soon be reunited to the Kingdom, and therewith all is forgiven and forgotten."

"And it is strange," said Protazy, "that in regard to this Zosia, for whose hand our Thaddeus is now suing, a year ago there was an omen, as it were a sign from Heaven."

"Panna Sophia she should be called," interrupted the Warden, "for she is now grown up, and is no [pg 290] longer a little girl; besides that, she comes of the blood of dignitaries; she is the granddaughter of the Pantler."

"Well, it was an omen prophetic of her fate," Protazy concluded; "I beheld the omen with my own eyes. A year ago our servants were sitting here on a holiday, drinking mead, and we saw— whack! there fell from the eaves two sparrows fighting, both old males. One, which was somewhat the younger, had a grey throat, the other a black one; they continued to scuffle about the yard, turning over and over, until they were buried in dust. We gazed at them, and meanwhile the servants whispered to one another that the black one must stand for the Horeszko, and the other for the Soplica. So, whenever the grey one was on top, they would cry, 'Vivat Soplica; foh, the Horeszko cowards!' but when it fell, they shouted, 'Get up, Soplica; don't give in to the magnate— that's shameful for a gentleman!' So we laughed and waited to see which would beat; but suddenly little Zosia, moved with pity for the birds, ran up and covered those warriors with her tiny hand: they still fought in her hands till the feathers flew, such was the fury of those little scamps. The old wives, looking at Zosia, quietly passed the word about, that it would certainly be that girl's destiny to reconcile two families long at variance. So I see that the old wives' omen has to-day come true. To be sure, at that time they had in mind the Count, and not Thaddeus."

To this the Warden replied: "There are strange things in the world; who can fathom them all! I too will tell you, sir, something which, though not so marvellous as that omen, is nevertheless hard to understand. You know that in old days I should have been glad to drown the Soplica family in a spoonful of water; and yet of this young fellow Thaddeus I was always immensely [pg 291] fond, from his childhood up. I took nonce that whenever he got into a fight with the other lads he always beat them; so, every time that he came to the castle, I kept stirring him up to difficult feats.

He succeeded in everything, whether he set out to dislodge the doves from the tower, or to pluck the mistletoe from the oak, or to tear down a crow's nest from the highest pine: he was equal to anything. I thought to myself—that boy was born under a happy star; too bad that he is a Soplica! Who would have guessed that in him I was to greet the owner of the castle, the husband of Panna Sophia, Her Grace my Lady!"

Here they broke off their conversation, but, deep in thought, they continued to drink; one could only hear now and then these brief words, "Yes, yes, Gerwazy" ; "Yes, Protazy."

The bench adjoined the kitchen, the windows of which were standing open and pouring forth smoke as from a conflagration; at last between the clouds of smoke, like a white dove, flashed the shining nightcap of the head cook. The Seneschal, putting his head out of the kitchen window, above the heads of the old men, listened in silence to their talk, and finally handed them some biscuits in a saucer, with the remark:—

"Have something to eat with your mead, and I will tell you a curious story of a quarrel that seemed likely to end in a bloody fight, when Rejtan, hunting in the depths of the forests of Naliboki, played a trick on the Prince de Nassau. This trick he nearly atoned for with his own life; I made up the gentlemen's quarrel, as I will tell you."

But the Seneschal's story was interrupted by the cooks, who inquired whom he would have set the table.

The Seneschal withdrew, and the old men, having [pg 292] finished their mead, turned their thoughtful eyes towards the centre of the garden, where that handsome uhlan was talking with the young lady. At that moment the uhlan, taking her hand in his left (his right hung in a sling, so that he was evidently wounded), addressed the lady with these words:—

"Sophia, you positively must tell me this; before we exchange rings, I must be sure of it. What does it matter that last winter you were prepared to give me your promise? I did not accept your promise then, for what did I care for such a forced promise? I had then stayed in Soplicowo but a very short time, and I was not so vain as to flatter myself that by my mere glance I could awaken love in you. I am no braggart; I wished by my own merits to win your regard, even though I might have to wait long for it. Now you are so gracious as to repeat your promise—how have I ever deserved such favour? Perhaps you are taking me, Zosia, not so much from attachment, as because your uncle and aunt are urging you to do so; but marriage, Zosia, is a very serious matter: take counsel of your own heart and do not hearken to any one's authority, either to your uncle's threats or to your aunt's entreaties. If you feel for me nothing but kindness, we may postpone this betrothal for a time; I do not wish to bind your will: let us wait, Zosia. There is no reason for haste, especially since, yesterday evening, I received orders to remain here in Lithuania as instructor in the local regiment, until I am healed of my wounds. Well, my beloved Zosia?"

Raising her head, and looking timidly into his eyes, Zosia replied:—

"I do not now remember perfectly what happened so long ago; I know that everybody told me that I [pg 293] must marry you. I always assent to the will of Heaven and the will of my elders. " Then, lowering her eyes, she added: "Before your departure, if you remember, when Father Robak died on that stormy night, I saw that you were dreadfully sorry to leave us. You had tears in your eyes: those tears, I tell you truly, fell deep into my heart; since then I have trusted your word, that you were fond of me. Whenever I have uttered a prayer for your success, I have always had before my eyes the picture of you with those great shining tears. Later the Chamberlain's wife went to Wilno and took me there for the winter; but I longed for Soplicowo and for that little room where you met me for the first time one evening by the table, and where you later bade me farewell. In some strange way the memory of you, like seeds of kale planted in the fall, all through the winter sprouted in my heart, so that, as I tell you, I continually longed for that little room; and something whispered to me that I should find you there again; and so it has happened. While thinking of this, I often had your name on my lips as well—this was at Wilno in the carnival season; the girls said that I was in love. So now, if I love any one, it must surely be you."

Thaddeus, happy at such a proof of affection, took her arm and pressed it to him, and they left the garden for the lady's chamber, for that room that Thaddeus had occupied ten years before.

At this moment the Notary was tarrying there in marvellous array, and proffering his services to his betrothed lady: he bustled about and handed her signet rings, little chains, gallipots and bottles and powders and patches; gay at heart, he gazed in triumph on the young damsel. The young damsel had finished making her toilet, and was sitting before the mirror taking counsel of the [pg 294] Graces; but the maids were still toiling over her, some with curling irons in their hands were freshening the limp ringlets of her tresses, others, on their knees, were working at a flounce.

While the Notary was thus tarrying with his betrothed, a scullion rapped on the window to attract his attention; they had caught sight of a rabbit. The rabbit, stealing out of the willows, had whisked over the meadow and leapt into the garden amid the growing vegetables; there it was seated, and it was an easy matter to fright it from the cabbage patch and to course it, stationing the hounds on the narrow path that it must take. The Assessor ran up, pulling Falcon by the collar; the Notary hurried after him, calling to Bobtail. The Seneschal made them both stand with their dogs near the fence, while he himself with his fly-flapper set out for the garden, and by trampling, whistling, and clapping his hands greatly terrified the poor beast. The huntsmen, each holding his hound by the collar, pointed their fingers to the spot from which the hare was to appear, and made a soft smacking sound with their lips; the hounds pricked up their ears, snuffed the wind with their muzzles and trembled impatiently, like two arrows set on one string. All at once the

Seneschal shouted, "At him," and the hare darted from behind the fence into the meadow, the hounds after him; and speedily, without making a single turn, Falcon and Bobtail together fell upon the grey rabbit from opposite sides at the same instant, like the two wings of a bird, and buried their teeth like talons in his back. The rabbit gave one cry, like a newborn babe, pitifully! The huntsmen ran up; it already lay breathless, and the hounds were tearing the white fur beneath its belly.

The huntsmen were patting their dogs, but meanwhile [pg 295] while the Seneschal, drawing the hunting-knife that hung at his girdle, cut off the feet and said:—

"To-day each dog shall receive an equal fee, for they have gained equal glory; equal was their fleetness and equal was their toil; worthy is the palace of Pac, and worthy is Pac of the palace;200 worthy are the huntsmen of the hounds, and worthy are the hounds of the huntsmen. Thus is ended your long and furious quarrel; I, whom you appointed your judge and stakeholder, at last give my verdict: you both have triumphed. I return your stakes; let each man keep his own, and do you both sign the treaty."

At the summons of the old man the huntsmen turned beaming faces on each other and joined their long parted right hands. Then the Notary spoke:—

"My stake was a horse with its caparison; I also agreed before the district authorities to deposit my ring as a fee for the judge; a forfeit once pledged cannot be withdrawn. Let the Seneschal accept the ring as a reminder of this incident, and let him have engraved on it either his own name or, if he prefers, the armorial bearings of the Hreczechas; the carnelian is smooth, the gold eleven carats fine. The uhlans have now commandeered my horse for their troop, but the caparison remains in my possession; every expert praises this caparison, that it is strong and comfortable, and pretty as a picture. The saddle is narrow, in the Turko-Cossack style; in front it has a pommel, and in the pommel are set precious stones; the seat is covered with a damask pad. And when you leap into your place, you rest on that soft down as comfortably as in a bed; and when you start to gallop" —here the Notary Bolesta, who, as is well known, was extremely fond of gestures, spread out his legs as though he were leaping [pg 296] on a horse, and then, imitating a gallop, he swayed slowly to and fro— "and when you start to gallop, then light flashes from the housing as though gold were dripping from your charger, for the side bands are thickly set with gold and the broad silver stirrups are gilded; on the straps of the bit and on the bridle glitter buttons of mother of pearl, and from the breastplate hangs a crescent shaped like Leliwa,201 that is, like the new moon. This whole splendid outfit was captured, as rumour reports, in the battle of Podhajce, 202 from a certain Turkish noble of very high station. Accept it, Assessor, as a proof of my esteem."

Happy in his gift, the Assessor replied:—

"My stake was the gift that I once received from Prince Sanguszko—my elegant dog-collars, covered with lizard-skin, with rings of gold, and my leash woven of silk, the workmanship of which is as precious as the jewel that glitters upon it. That outfit I wanted to leave as an inheritance for my children; I shall surely have children, for you know that I am to be married to-day. But, my dear Notary, I beg you humbly that you will deign to accept that outfit in exchange for your rich caparison, and as a reminder of the quarrel that was prolonged for so many years and has finally been concluded in a manner honourable to us both.—May harmony flourish between us!"

So they returned home, to proclaim at table that the quarrel between Bobtail and Falcon had been concluded.

There was a report that the Seneschal had raised that rabbit in the house and slyly let it out into the garden, in order to make the huntsmen friends by means of too easy a prey. The old man played his trick so mysteriously that he completely fooled all Soplicowo. A scullion, some years later, whispered a word of this, [pg 297] wishing to embroil once more the Assessor and the Notary; but in vain did he spread abroad reports slanderous to the hounds—the Seneschal denied the story, and nobody believed the scullion.

The guests were already assembled in the great hall of the castle, and were conversing around the table as they awaited the banquet, when the Judge entered in the uniform of a wojewoda, escorting Thaddeus and Sophia. Thaddeus, raising his left hand to his forehead, saluted his superior officers with a military bow. Sophia, lowering her eyes and blushing, greeted the guests with a curtsy (she had been taught by Telimena how to curtsy gracefully). On her head she wore a wreath, as a betrothed maiden; for the rest, her costume was the same that she had worn that morning in the chapel, when she brought in her spring sheaf for the Virgin Mary. She had reaped once more, for the guests, a fresh sheaf of greenery, and with one hand she distributed flowers and grasses from it; with the other she adjusted on her head her glittering sickle. The leaders, kissing her hands, took the posies; Zosia curtsied once more to all in turn, her cheeks glowing.

Then General Kniaziewicz took her by the shoulders, and, imprinting a fatherly kiss on her brow, lifted the girl aloft and set her on the table; all clapped their hands and shouted "Bravo!" being charmed by the girl's figure and bearing, and more particularly by her Lithuanian village attire; since for these famous captains, who in their roving life had wandered so long in foreign lands, there was a marvellous charm in the national costume, which reminded them both of the years of their youth and of their loves of long ago: so almost with tears they gathered around the table and gazed eagerly upon her. Some asked Zosia to raise her [pg 298] head and show her eyes; others begged her to be so kind as to turn around—the bashful girl turned around, but covered her eyes with her hands. Thaddeus looked on gaily and rubbed his hands.

Whether some one had counselled Zosia to make her appearance in such garments, or whether she knew by instinct (for a girl always guesses by instinct what is becoming to her), suffice it to say that this morning for the first time in her life Zosia had been scolded for obstinacy by Telimena, since she had refused to put on fashionable attire: at last by her tears she had prevailed on them to let her remain in this village costume.

She wore a long white underskirt and a short gown of green camlet with a pink border; the bodice was also of green, laced crosswise with pink ribbons from the waist to the neck; under it her bosom took refuge like a bud beneath leaves. On her shoulders shone the full white sleeves of the shirt, like the wings of a butterfly stretched for flight; at the wrist they were gathered and fastened with a ribbon; her throat was also encircled by the close-fitting shirt, the collar of which was fastened with a pink knot. Her earrings were artistically carved out of cherry stones; in their making Buzzard Dobrzynski had taken huge pride; they represented two hearts with dart and flame, and had been a present to Zosia when Buzzard was paying his court to her. About her collar hung two strings of amber beads, and on her temples was a wreath of green rosemary; the ribbons that decked her tresses Zosia had thrown back over her shoulders. On her brow, as is the custom with reapers, she had fastened a curved sickle, freshly polished by cutting grasses, bright as the new moon above the brow of Diana.

All admired and clapped their hands. One of the [pg 299] officers took from his pocket a portfolio containing bundles of papers; he undid them, sharpened his pencil, moistened it with his lips, gazed at Zosia, and began to draw. Hardly had the Judge beheld the papers and pencils, when he recognised the artist, though he had been greatly changed by his colonel's uniform, his rich epaulets, his truly uhlan-like bearing, his blackened mustache, and a small Spanish beard. The Judge recognised the Count: "How are you, Your Excellency? So you keep a travelling painter's kit even in your cartridge box!" In very truth it was the young Count. He was a soldier of no long standing, but since he had a large income and had fitted out a whole troop of cavalry at his own expense, and had borne himself admirably in the very first battle, the Emperor had to-day just appointed him a colonel. So the Judge greeted the Count and congratulated him on his promotion, but the Count paid no attention, and continued to draw diligently.

In the meantime a second betrothed pair had entered. The Assessor, once in the service of the Tsar, had entered that of Napoleon; he had a company of gendarmes under his command, and, although he had been in office hardly twelve hours, he had already donned a dark blue uniform with Polish facings, and dragged behind him a curved sabre, and clinked his spurs. By his side, with dignified steps, walked his belovèd, dressed with great magnificence, Tekla Hreczecha: for the Assessor had long ago abandoned Telimena, and, the more deeply to wound that coquette, he had turned his heart's devotion to the Seneschal's daughter. The bride was not over young, she had perhaps already seen half a century go by; but she was a good housekeeper and a dignified and well-to-do person, for, aside [pg 300] from her ancestral village, her dowry had been increased by a little sum presented to her by the Judge.

For the third pair they waited vainly, a long time. The Judge grew impatient and sent servants; they returned and reported that the third bridegroom, the Notary, when looking for the rabbit, had lost his wedding ring, and was now looking for it in the meadow; meanwhile the Notary's lady was still at her dressing-table, and, though she was herself hurrying and was being aided by the serving women, she had been absolutely unable to finish her toilet: she would scarcely be ready by four o'clock. [pg 301]

BOOK XII.—LET US LOVE ONE ANOTHER!

ARGUMENT

The last old-Polish banquet—The state centrepiece—Explanation of its figures—Its transformations—Dombrowski receives a present—More of Penknife—Kniaziewicz receives a present—The first official act of Thaddeus on receiving his inheritance—Remarks of Gerwazy—The concert of concerts—The polonaise—Let us love one another!

Finally with a crash the doors of the hall were thrown wide open, and the Seneschal entered, wearing a cap, and with his head held high; he did not greet the company nor take his place at the table, for to-day the Seneschal emerged in a new character, as Marshal of the Court; he bore a wand in sign of office, and with this wand he indicated to each in turn his place and showed the guests their seats. First of all, as the highest in authority in the wojewodeship, the Chamberlain-Marshal took the place of honour, a velvet chair with ivory arms; next him on the right sat General Dombrowski, and on the left Kniaziewicz, Pac, 203 and Malachowski. Amid this company the Chamberlain's wife had her seat; farther on other ladies, officers, magnates, country gentry, and neighbours, men and women alternately, all took places in order as the Seneschal indicated.

The Judge, with a bow, withdrew from the banquet; in the yard he was entertaining a throng of peasants, whom he had gathered at a table a furlong in length; he himself sat at one end and the parish priest at the [pg 302] other. Thaddeus and Sophia did not take seats at the table; being occupied with serving the peasants, they ate as they walked. Such was the ancient custom—that new owners of a farm, at the first feast, should wait on the common folk.

Meanwhile the guests, as in the castle hall they awaited the bringing in of the food, gazed with amazement at the great centrepiece, the metal and the workmanship of which were equally precious. There is a tradition that Prince Radziwill the Orphan 204 had this set made to order in Venice, and had it decorated in Polish style according to his own ideas. The centrepiece had later been carried off in the time of the Swedish wars, 205 and had found its way in some mysterious manner into this country gentleman's mansion; today it had been brought forth from the treasury and it now occupied the middle of the table, forming an immense circle, like a coach wheel.

The centrepiece, which was coated from rim to rim with froth and sugar white as snow, counterfeited marvellously well a winter landscape. In the centre a huge grove of confections showed dark; on the sides were houses which seemed to form peasant villages and hamlets of gentry, and which were coated, not with hoar frost, but with sugary froth; the edges were decorated with little porcelain figures in Polish costumes: like actors on a stage, they were evidently representing some striking event; their gestures were artistically reproduced, the colours were individual; they lacked only voice—for the rest they seemed to be alive.

"What is it that they represent?" asked the curious guests; whereupon the Seneschal, raising his wand, spoke as follows (meanwhile brandy was being served, in preparation for dinner):—
[pg 303]
"With your permission, honoured gentlemen and guests, those persons whom you see there in countless numbers represent the progress of a Polish district diet, its consultations, voting, triumphs, and disputes; I myself guessed the meaning of this scene, and I will explain it to the company.

"There on the right may be seen a numerous assembly of gentry: they have evidently been invited to a banquet, preceding the diet; the board is waiting ready set, but no one is showing the guests their seats; they are standing in groups, and each group is deep in discussion. Notice that in the centre of each group stands a man from whose parted lips, wide-open eyes, and restless hands you may see that he is an orator and is expounding something, that he is explaining it with his finger and marking it on his palm. These orators are recommending their candidates with various success, as may be seen from the bearing of the brother gentlemen.

"You may be sure that there in the second group the gentry are listening with attention: this good man has tucked his hands into his belt and has pricked up his ears; that other is holding his hand to his ear and is silently twirling his mustache; he is evidently gathering in the words and storing them up in his memory. The orator takes solid comfort in seeing that his hearers are converted; he strokes his pocket, for he already has their votes in his pocket.

"But in the third gathering the situation is quite different: here the orator must catch his auditors by their belts—notice how they are pulling away and turning aside their ears; notice how this auditor bristles with wrath; he has raised his arms and is threatening the orator and stopping his mouth; he has evidently [pg 304] heard praise showered on his opponent. That other man has bent down his brow like a bull; you might think him about to toss the orator on his horns. This party are drawing their sabres, and those others have started to flee.

"One gentleman stands silent and alone between the groups; he is evidently a non-partisan and is timidly hesitating for whom to give his vote! He does not know, and is at odds with himself; he leaves it to chance—he has lifted up his hands and extended his thumbs; with his eyes shut he aims nail against nail; evidently he will trust his vote to fortune; if the thumbs meet, he will cast an affirmative ballot, but if they miss he will deposit a negative.

"On the left is another scene, a convent refectory, transformed into the assembly hall of the gentry. The older men are seated in a row on benches; the younger are standing and looking curiously over their heads towards the centre; in the centre stands the Marshal, holding the urn in his hands; he is counting the balls, and the gentry devour them with their eyes; he has just shaken out the last one: the Apparitors raise their hands and announce the name of the elected official.

"One gentlemen has no respect for the general concord: see, he has thrust in his head from the window of the refectory kitchen; see his wide-open eyes, how insolently he stares; he has opened his mouth as though he wanted to eat up the whole roomful: it is easy to guess that this gentlemen has shouted '*Veto!*' See how at that sudden challenge to a quarrel the throng is crowding to the door; they are evidently on their way to the kitchen; they have drawn their swords, and a bloody fight is sure to break out.

"But there in the corridor, sirs, pray notice that [pg 305] reverend old priest advancing in his chasuble; that is the Prior bringing the Host from the altar, while a boy in a surplice rings a bell and asks all to give way. The gentry at once sheathe their sabres, cross themselves, and kneel; but the priest turns in the direction whence a clink of arms is still heard: soon he will arrive, and at once he will calm and reconcile all.

"Ah, you young men, do not remember this, how among our turbulent, self-willed gentry, always under arms though they were, no police were ever needed: while the true faith flourished, laws were respected; there was liberty with order and glory along with plenty I In other lands, I hear, the government maintains soldiers and all sorts of policemen, gendarmes, and constables. But if the sword alone guards the public security, then I shall never believe that liberty can exist in those lands."

Suddenly, tapping his snuffbox, the Chamberlain said:—

"Seneschal, I pray you, postpone these stories until later; this diet is a curious thing, to be sure, but we are hungry; pray, sir, have them bring in the dinner."

Bending down his wand to the floor, the Seneschal replied:—

"Your Excellency, pray grant me this indulgence; I will speedily finish with the last scene of the district diets. Here is the new Marshal, borne out of the refectory on the shoulders of his partisans; see how the brother gentlemen are throwing up their caps and standing with open mouths—vivats! But there on the other side lingers the outvoted candidate, all alone, with his cap pulled down over his gloomy brow; his wife is waiting in front of her house, and has guessed what is going on. Poor woman, now she is fainting in the [pg 306] arms of her maid! Poor woman, she was to have received the title of Right Honourable, but now she is left just Honourable for three more years!"

Here the Seneschal concluded his description, and gave a sign with his wand; immediately lackeys began to enter in pairs, bringing the different dishes: the beet soup called royal, and the old-Polish broth, artistically prepared, into which the Seneschal in marvellous and mysterious wise had thrown several pearls and a piece of money; such broth purifies the blood and fortifies the health; after it came other dishes—but who could describe them all! Who would even comprehend those dishes of kontuz, arkas , and blemas , 206 no longer known in our times, with their ingredients of cod, stuffing, civet, musk, caramel, pine nuts, damson plums! And those fish! Dry salmon from the Danube, sturgeon, Venetian and Turkish caviare, pikes and pickerel a cubit long, flounders, and capon carp, and noble carp! Finally a culinary mystery: an uncut fish, fried at the head, baked in the middle, and with its tail in a ragout with sauce.

The guests did not ask the names of the dishes, nor were they halted by that curious mystery; they ate everything rapidly with a soldier's appetite, filling their glasses with the generous Hungarian wine.

But meanwhile the great centrepiece had changed its colour, 207 and, stripped of its snow, had already turned green; for the light froth of sugared ice, slowly warmed by the summer heat, had melted and disclosed a foundation hitherto hidden from the eye: so the landscape now represented a new time of year, shining with a green, many-coloured spring. Various grains came forth, as if yeast were making them grow; gilded ears of saffron wheat were seen in rich profusion, also rye, clad in [pg 307] leaves of picturesque silver, and buckwheat, made artistically of chocolate, and orchards blooming with pears and apples.

The guests had scant time to enjoy the gifts of summer; in vain they begged the Seneschal to prolong them. Already the centrepiece, like a planet in its appointed revolution, was changing the season of the year; already the grain, painted with gold, had gathered warmth from the room, and was slowly melting; already the grasses were growing yellow and the leaves were turning crimson and were falling; you might have said that an autumn wind was blowing; finally those trees, gorgeous an instant before, now stood naked, as if they had been stripped by the winds and the frost; they were sticks of cinnamon, or twigs of laurel that counterfeited pines, being clad in caraway seeds instead of needles.

The guests, as they drank their wine, began to tear off the branches, stumps, and roots, and to chew them as a relish. The Seneschal walked about the centrepiece, and, full of joy, turned triumphant eyes upon the guests.

Henryk Dombrowski feigned great amazement, and said:—

"My friend the Seneschal, are these Chinese shadows? Or has Pinety208 given you his demons as servants? Do such centrepieces still exist among you, here in Lithuania, and do all men feast in this ancient fashion? Tell me, for I have passed my life abroad."

"No, Your Excellency the General," said the Seneschal with a bow, "these are no godless arts! This is only a reminder of those famous banquets that used to be given in the mansions of our ancient magnates, when Poland enjoyed happiness and power! All that I have done I learned by reading in this book. You ask [pg 308] me whether this custom has been preserved everywhere in Lithuania. Alas, new fashions are already creeping in even among us! Many a young gentleman exclaims that he cannot stand the expense; he eats like a Jew, grudging his guests food and drink; he is stingy with the Hungarian wine, and drinks that devilish, adulterated, fashionable Muscovite champagne; then in the evening he loses as much money at cards as would suffice for a banquet for a hundred gentlemen and brothers. Even—for what I have in my heart I will to-day speak out frankly; let not the Chamberlain take it ill of me—when I was getting that wonderful centre-*piece from the treasure room, then even the Chamberlain, even he made fun of me, saying that this was a tiresome, antiquated contrivance—that it looked like a child's plaything and was unfit for such famous men as we have with us to-day! Judge!—even you, Judge, said that it would bore the guests! And yet, so far as I may infer from the amazement of the company, I see that this is fine art, that it was worthy of being seen! I doubt whether a like occasion will ever again return for entertaining at Soplicowo such dignitaries. I see, General, that you are an expert at banquets; pray accept this book: it will be of use to you some day when you are giving a feast for a company of foreign monarchs, or perhaps one even for Napoleon himself. But permit me, before I tender the book to you, to relate by what chance it fell into my hands."

Suddenly a murmur arose outside the door, and many voices shouted in unison, "Long live Cock-on-the-Steeple!" A throng pushed into the hall, with Maciej at their head. The Judge led the guest by the hand to the table and gave him a high seat among the leaders, saying:—

[pg 309]

"Pan Maciej, unkind neighbour, you come very late, when dinner is almost over."

"I eat early," replied Dobrzynski; "I did not come here for food, but only because I was overpowered by curiosity to see close at hand our national army. Of this much might be said; it is neither fish, flesh, nor fowl. These gentlemen caught sight of me and brought me here by force; and you, sir, are compelling me to seat myself at your table—I thank you, neighbour."

With these words he turned his plate

bottom upwards, as a sign that he would not eat, and relapsed into glum silence.

"Pan Dobrzynski," said General Dombrowski to him, "are you that famous swordsman of the Kosciuszko times, that Maciej, called Switch! Your fame has reached me. And pray tell me, is it possible that you are still so hale, so vigorous! How many years have gone by! See, I have grown old; see, Kniaziewicz too has grizzled hair; but you might still enter the lists against young men. And your switch doubtless blooms as it did long ago; I have heard that recently you birched the Muscovites. But where are your brethren? I should beyond measure like to see those penknives and razors of yours, the last relics of ancient Lithuania."

"After that victory, General," said the Judge, "almost all the Dobrzynskis took refuge in the Grand Duchy, and must have entered one or other of the legions."

"Why certainly," answered a young squadron commander, "I have in the second company a mustachioed scarecrow, Sergeant-Major Dobrzynski, who calls himself Sprinkler, but whom the Masovians call the Lithuanian bear. If you bid me, General, we will have him brought in."
[pg 310]
"There are several other natives of Lithuania here," said a lieutenant. "One such soldier is known under the name of Razor; another carries a blunderbuss and rides with the sharp-shooters; there are likewise two grenadiers named Dobrzynski in the chasseur regiment."

"Well, but I want to know about their chief," said the General, "about that Penknife of whom the Seneschal has told me so many marvels, worthy of one of the giants of old times."

"Penknife," said the Seneschal, "though he did not go into exile, nevertheless feared the result of an investigation, and hid himself from the Muscovites; all winter the poor fellow roamed about the forests, and he has only recently come forth from them. In these times of war he might have been good for something, for he is a valorous man, only he is unfortunately a trifle bowed by age. But here he is."

Here the Seneschal pointed towards the vestibule, where servants and peasants were standing crowded together. Above the heads of all a shining bald pate showed itself suddenly like the full moon; thrice it emerged and thrice it vanished in the cloud of heads; the Warden was bowing as he strode forward, until finally he made his way out of the press, and said:—

"Your Excellency the Hetman of the Crown—or General—never mind which is the correct title—I am Rembajlo, and I present myself at your summons with this my penknife, which, not by its setting nor by its inscriptions but by its temper, has won such fame that even Your Excellency knows of it. If it knew how to speak, perchance it would say somewhat in praise even of this old arm, which, thank God, has served long and faithfully the Fatherland and likewise the family of the [pg 311] Horeszkos: of which fact the memory is still famous among men. My boy, rarely does a bookkeeper on an estate mend pens so deftly as this penknife cleaves heads: it were long to count them! And noses and ears without number! But there is not a single nick upon it, and no murderous deed has ever stained it, but only open war, or a duel. Only once!— may the Lord give him eternal rest!— an unarmed man, alas, fell beneath its edge! But even that, God is my witness, was pro publico bono."

"Show it to me," said General Dombrowski with a laugh. "That is a lovely penknife, a real headsman's sword!"

He gazed with amazement on the huge blade, and passed it on to the other officers; all of them tried it, but hardly one of the officers could lift that blade on high. They said that Dembinski, 209 famous for his strength of arm, could have brandished the broadsword, but he was not there. Of those present only the squadron commander Dwernicki, 210 and Lieutenant Rozycki, 211 the leader of a platoon, managed to swing the iron pole: thus the blade was passed for trial from hand to hand along the line.

But General Kniaziewicz, the tallest of stature, proved to be also the stoutest of arm. Seizing the huge blade, he swung it as lightly as a common sword and flashed it like lightning over the heads of the guests, recalling to their minds the tricks of the Polish school of fencing, the cross stroke, the mill, the crooked slash, the downright blow, the stolen slash, and the attitudes of counterpoint 212 and tierce, which he knew likewise, for he had been trained in the School of Cadets.

While he was still laughing and fencing, Rembajlo had kneeled and embraced him about the knees, and [pg 312] was groaning out between his tears, at every turn of the sword:—

"Beautiful! General, were you ever a confederate? Beautiful, splendid! That is the Pulawskis' 213 thrust! Thus Dzierzanowski 214 bore himself! That is Sawa's thrust! Who can so have trained your arm except Maciej Dobrzynski! But that? General, that is my invention; in Heaven's name, I do not wish to boast, but that stroke is known only in Rembajlo hamlet, and from my name it is called My-boy's slash. Who can have taught it to you? That is my stroke, mine!"

He rose and clasped the General in his arms.

"Now I can die in peace! There still exists a man who will fondle my darling child; for I have long been grieving, both day and night, at the thought that after my death this my blade might rust away! Now it will not rust! Your Excellency the General, forgive me!—throw away those spits, those German swordlets; it is shameful for a gentleman's son to wear that little cane! Take instead a sabre such as befits a gentleman: now I lay at your feet this my penknife, which is the most precious thing that I possess in all the world. I have never had a wife, I have never had a child: it has been both wife and child to me; from my embrace it has never departed; from dawn till dark have I petted it; it has slept by night at my side! And since I have grown old, it has been hanging on the wall above my couch, like God's commandments over the Jews! I thought to have it buried in my grave along with my arm; but I have found an owner for it. May it be your servant!"

The General, half laughing, and half touched with emotion, replied:—

"Comrade, if you give up to me your wife and child, [pg 313] you will be left for the rest of your life very solitary and old, a widower and without children! Tell me how I may recompense you for this precious gift, and with what I may sweeten your childless widowhood!"

"Am I Cybulski," 215 answered the Warden mournfully, "who gambled away his wife, playing marriage with the Muscovites, as the song relates?—I am quite content that my penknife will still gleam before the world in such a hand. Only remember, General, to give it a long strap, well let out, for the blade is long; and always hew from the left ear with both hands—then you will cut through from head to belly."

The General took the penknife, but since it was very long and he could not wear it, the servants put it away in an ammunition waggon. As to what became of it there are various tales, but no one knew with certainty, either then or later.

Dombrowski turned to Maciek:—

"What have you to say, comrade? Can it be that you are not glad at our coming? Why are you silent and glum? How can your heart help leaping up when you see the gold and silver eagles, and when the trumpeters trumpet Kosciuszko's reveille close to your ear? Maciek, I thought that you were more of a fighting man: if you do not seize your sabre and mount your horse, at least you will gaily drink with your colleagues to the health of Napoleon and the hopes of Poland!"

"Ha!" said Maciej, "I have heard and I see what is going on! But, sir, two eagles never nest together! Lords' favour, hetman, rides a piebald steed!216 The Emperor a great hero! On that subject we could expend much talk! I remember that my friends the Pulawskis used to say, as they gazed on Dumouriez, 217 [pg 314] that Poland needed a Polish hero, no Frenchman or Italian either, but a Piast, 218 a Jan or a Jozef, or a Maciek—that's all. The army! They say it is Polish! But these fusileers, sappers, grenadiers , and cannoneers! You hear, in that crowd, more German than native titles! 219 Who can understand them! And then you must certainly have with you Turks or Tatars or Schismatics, or men of God knows what faith: I have seen it myself; they are assaulting the peasant women in the villages, plundering the passers-by, pillaging the churches! The Emperor is bound for Moscow! That is a long road if he has set out without the blessing of God. I have heard that he has already incurred the bishop's curse; 220 all this is——"

Here Maciej dipped some bread in his soup, munched it, and did not finish his last phrase.

Maciek's speech did not suit the taste of the Chamberlain, and the young men began to murmur; the Judge interrupted the wrangling, by announcing the arrival of the third betrothed couple.

It was the Notary; he announced himself as the Notary, but nobody recognised him. He had hitherto worn the Polish costume, but now his future wife, Telimena, had forced him by a clause in the marriage articles to renounce the kontusz; 221 so the Notary willy-nilly had assumed French garb. The dress coat had evidently deprived him of half his soul; he strode along as if he had swallowed a walking-stick, stiffly and straight forward; like a crane, he dared not look to the right or the left. His expression was composed, and yet from his expression one could see that he was in torture; he did not know how to bow or where to put his hands, he, who was so fond of gestures! He tucked his hands into his belt—there was no belt—he only stroked himself [pg 315] self on the stomach; he noticed his mistake, was greatly confused, turned red as a lobster, and hid both his hands in the same pocket of his dress coat. He advanced as if running the gauntlet, amid whispers and banter, feeling as ashamed of his dress coat as of a dishonourable deed; at last he met the eyes of Maciek, and trembled with fright.

Maciej had hitherto lived on very friendly terms with the Notary; but now he turned on him so sharp and furious a glance that the Notary grew pale and began to button his coat, thinking that Maciej would tear it off him with his glance. Dobrzynski merely repeated twice over in a loud voice, "Idiot!" and was so fearfully disgusted with the Notary's change of garb that he at once rose from the table; slipping out without saying good-bye, he mounted his horse and returned to the hamlet.

But meanwhile the Notary's fair sweetheart, Telimena, was spreading abroad the gleams of her beauty and of her toilet, from top to toe of the very latest style. What manner of gown she wore, and what her coiffure was like, it were vain to write, for the pen could never express it; only the pencil could portray those tulles, muslins, laces, cashmeres, pearls and precious stones—and her rosy cheeks and lively glances!

The Count at once recognised her, and, pale with astonishment, rose from the table and looked about him for his sword.

"And is it thou!" he cried, "or do my eyes deceive me? Thou? In my presence? Dost clasp another's hand? O faithless being, O traitorous soul! And dost thou not hide thy face for shame beneath the earth? Art thou so unmindful of thy vows so lately made? Ah, man of easy faith! Why have I worn these ribbons! [pg 316] But woe to the rival who so contemns me! Only across my body shall he advance to the altar!"

The guests arose; the Notary was in frightful distress; the Chamberlain was making hurried efforts to reconcile the rivals, but Telimena, taking the Count aside, whispered to him:—

"The Notary has not yet taken me as his wife: if you have anything against his doing so, answer me this, and answer me right off, short and to the point: do you love me, have you not yet changed your affections, are you ready to marry me right off; right off, to-day? If you agree, I will give up the Notary."

"O woman beyond my comprehension!" said the Count, "formerly in thy feelings thou wast poetic; but now thou seemest altogether prosaic. What are your marriages except chains that bind only the hands and not the spirit? Believe me, there are proffers of love even without an avowal of it, and there are duties even without an engagement! Two burning hearts at the two ends of the earth converse together like stars with trembling beams. Who knows? Perhaps for this very reason the earth so aspires towards the sun, and is thus ever dear to the moon—that they gaze upon each other eternally, and run towards each other by the shortest path, but can never draw near to each other!"

"Enough of that," she interrupted; "by the grace of God I am no planet, Count! Enough, Count, I am a woman. I know what's coming; make an end to all this chatter. Now I warn you; if you utter one word to break off my marriage, then, as God is in Heaven, I will jump at you with these nails and——"

"I will not disturb your happiness, madam," said the Count, and he turned away his eyes, full of grief [pg 317] and contempt; and, in order to punish his faithless sweetheart, he chose the Chamberlain's daughter as the object of his constant flames.

The Seneschal was eager to make peace between the estranged young men by citing wise examples, so he began to recount the story of the wild boar of the forests of Naliboki, and of the quarrel between Rejtan and the Prince de Nassau; 222 but meanwhile the guests had finished eating their ices and were going outside the castle into the yard, to enjoy the fresh air.

There the peasantry were just finishing their banquet, and pitchers of mead were going the rounds; the musicians were already tuning their instruments and summoning people to dance. They looked for Thaddeus, who was standing some distance away and whispering something of pressing moment to his future wife:—

"Sophia, I must take counsel with you in a very important matter; I have already asked my uncle's opinion, and he is not opposed. You know that a considerable portion of the villages that I am to be the owner of, according to the law ought to have descended to you. These serfs are not my subjects, but yours; I should not venture to dispose of their affairs without the consent of their lady. Now, when we ourselves possess once more our beloved Fatherland, shall the peasants by that happy change gain only this much, that they receive another lord? To be sure, they have hitherto been governed with kindness, but after my death God knows to whom I may leave them; I am a soldier, and we both are mortal; I am a man, and I fear my own caprices: I shall act with greater security if I renounce my own authority and give over the fate of the villagers into the protection of the law. Being free ourselves, let us make the villagers free likewise; [pg 318] let us grant them as their own the possession of the land on which they were born, which they have gained by bloody toil, and from which they nourish us all and make us all rich. But I must warn you that the grant of these lands will lessen our income; we must live in moderate circumstances. I from my youth am wonted to a frugal life; but you, Sophia, spring from a mighty line, and have passed your early years in the capital—will you consent to live in a village, far from the great world, like a country girl?"

In reply Zosia said modestly,—

"I am a woman, authority does not belong to me. You will be my husband; I am too young to give advice—whatever you arrange, I agree to with all my heart! If by freeing the villagers you become poorer, then, Thaddeus, you will be all the dearer to my heart. Of my family I know little, and to it I am quite indifferent; I remember only that I was poor and an orphan, and that I was taken in as a daughter by the Soplicas, that I was brought up in their house and married from it. Of the country I am not afraid: if I have lived in a great city, that was long ago; I have forgotten it, and have always loved the country. Believe me, that my hens and roosters have given me more amusement than all those St. Petersburgs, If at times I have longed for amusement and for society, that was from childishness; I know now that the city wearies me. I convinced myself last winter, after a short stay in Wilno, that I was born for a country life; in the midst of gaieties I longed once more for Soplicowo. And I am not afraid of work, for I am young and strong; I know how to walk about the place and wear a bunch of keys: you will see how quickly I shall learn how to manage the household!" [pg 319]

While Zosia was speaking these last words, Gerwazy came up to her, amazed and glum.

"I know it already," he said, "the Judge has already been speaking of this liberty! But I do not understand what that has to do with peasants! I am afraid that there may be something a trifle German in this! Why, liberty is not a peasant's affair, but a gentleman's! To be sure, we are all derived from Adam, but I have heard that the peasants proceed from Ham,223 the Jews from Japhet, and we gentry from Shem; hence we are lords over both, as the elder brothers. But now the parish priest gives us different teaching from the pulpit—he says that so it was under the old law; but that when once Christ our Lord, though he sprang from the blood of kings, was born among Jews in a peasant's stable, from that time on he has made equal all classes of men and brought in peace among them. Well, so be it, since it can't be otherwise! Especially if, as I hear, Your Excellency my Lady Sophia has agreed to everything; it is for you to give orders and for me to obey them: authority belongs to you alone. Only I warn you that we must not grant merely an empty liberty, in words alone, like that under the Muscovites, when the late Pan Karp freed his serfs and the Muscovite starved them to death with a triple tax. 224 So it is my advice that according to the ancient custom we make the peasants nobles and proclaim that we bestow on them our own coats of arms. You, my lady, will bestow on some villages the Half-Goat; to others let Pan Soplica give his Star and Crescent. 225 Then will even Rembajlo recognize the peasant as his equal, when he beholds him an honourable gentleman, with a coat of arms. The Diet will confirm the act.

"But, sir, do not make anxious your

lady wife by [pg 320] saying that the giving up of the lands will make you both so extremely poor; God forbid that I should see the hands of a dignitary's daughter hardened with housewifely labour. There is a way of preventing this: in the castle I know of a certain chest in which lies the table service of the Horeszkos and with it various rings, necklaces, bracelets, rich plumes, caparisons, and marvellous swords—the Pantler's treasures, hidden from plunderers, in the ground; to Pani Sophia, as his heiress, they belong; I have guarded them in the castle like the eyes in my head, keeping them from the Muscovites, and from you, my Soplica friends. I have likewise a good-sized pouch of my own thalers, saved from my earnings, and likewise from the gifts of my masters; I had intended, when the castle should be returned to us, to devote some pennies to the repairing of the walls—to-day it turns out that they will be needed for the new style of farming. And so, Pan Soplica, I am moving to your abode; I shall live with my lady, on her bounty, and shall rock to sleep a third generation of Horeszkos; I will train my lady's child to use the penknife, if it is a son—and she will have a son, for wars are coming on, and in time of war sons are always born."

Hardly had Gerwazy spoken these last words, when Protazy approached with dignified steps; he bowed, and took from the bosom of his kontusz a huge panegyric, two and a half sheets long. 226 It had been composed in rime by a young subaltern, who once had been a famous writer of odes in the capital; he had later donned a uniform, but, retaining even in the army his devotion to letters, he still continued to make verses. The Apparitor read aloud full three hundred of them; at last, when he came to the place:—
[pg 321]
Thou whose fair eyes
Rouse in us painful joys and blissful sighs;
When on Bellona's ranks thy glance descends,
All spears are broken and each buckler bends:

To-day soft Hymen conquers cruel Mars;
Thy gentle hand the hissing serpents tears }
From Discord's hydra front, emblem of dreadful wars— }
Thaddeus and Sophia began to clap vigorously, as if in applause, but really because they did not wish to hear further. Now at the Judge's bidding the parish priest mounted the table and proclaimed Thaddeus's determination to the villagers.

Hardly had the peasants heard this news, when they leapt towards their young master and fell at the feet of their lady. "The health of our masters!" they shouted with tears, and Thaddeus shouted, "The health of our fellow citizens, free Poles, our equals!" "I propose the health of the common people!" said Dombrowski—the people shouted: "Long live the generals, vivat the army, vivat the people, vivat all classes!" With a thousand voices, one health thundered after another.

Buchmann alone did not deign to share in the general joy; he praised the project, but would have preferred to change it slightly, and first of all to appoint a legal commission, which should—but the shortness of the time prevented them from adopting Buchmann's advice, for in the yard of the castle the officers and ladies, the privates and the village girls were already standing in couples: "the polonaise!" they all shouted with one breath. The officers were bringing up the army musicians, but the Judge whispered in the General's ear:—

"Pray give orders for the band to restrain itself for a while longer. You know that to-day sees the betrothal of my nephew, and it is the ancient custom of our family to celebrate betrothals and marriages with village music. [pg 322] Look, there stand the player of the dulcimer, the fiddler, and the bagpiper, all worthy musicians—already the fiddler is making mouths, and the bagpiper is bowing and begging with his eyes that I will have them begin—the poor fellows will weep. The common folk will not know how to skip to other music; so let them begin and let the folk have their fun; afterwards we will listen to your excellent band."

He made a sign. The fiddler tucked up the sleeve of his coat, squeezed tightly the finger board, rested his chin on the tailpiece, and sent his bow over the fiddle like a race horse. At this signal, the bagpipers, who were standing close by, blew into their sacks and filled their cheeks with breath, making a quick motion with their arms as though flapping their wings; you might have thought that the pair would fly off on the breeze, like the chubby children of Boreas. But there was no dulcimer.

There were many players of the dulcimer, but none of them dared to perform in Jankiel's presence. (Jankiel had been spending the whole winter no one knows where; now he had suddenly made his appearance along with the General Staff.) Everybody knew that no one could compare with him in playing that instrument, either in skill, taste, or talent. They begged him to play and offered him the dulcimer; the Jew refused, saying that his hands had grown stiff, that he was out of practice, that he did not dare to, that he was embarrassed by the men of high station; with many a bow he was stealing away. When Zosia saw this, she ran up, and with one white hand proffered him the hammers with which the master was wont to sound the strings; with the other hand she stroked the old man's grey beard, and said with a curtsy:—
[pg 323]
"Jankiel, be so good; you see this is my betrothal; play for me, Jankiel. Haven't you often promised to play at my wedding?"

Jankiel, who was beyond measure fond of Zosia, nodded his beard as a sign that he did not refuse. So they led him into the centre of the company and put his instrument on his knees; he gazed on it with delight and pride, like a veteran called back to active service, when his grandsons take down from the wall his heavy sword: the old man laughs, though it is long since he has had a sword in his hand, for he feels that his hand will not yet betray the weapon.

Meanwhile two of his pupils were kneeling by the dulcimer, tuning the strings afresh and twanging them as a test of their work. Jankiel with half-closed eyes sat silent and held the hammers motionless in his fingers.

He lowered them, at first beating a triumphal measure; then he smote the strings more briskly, as with a torrent of rain: all were amazed, but that was only a test, for he suddenly broke off and lifted both hammers aloft.

He played anew; now the strings trembled with motions as light as though the wing of a fly were sounding on the string, giving forth a gentle, hardly audible buzzing. The master fixed his gaze on the sky, awaiting inspiration; he looked down and surveyed the instrument with a haughty eye, he raised his hands and lowered them together, and smote with both hammers at once; the auditors were amazed.—

All at once from many strings there burst forth a sound as though a whole janissaries' band had become vocal with bells and cymbals and drums. 227 The Polonaise of the Third of May 228 thundered forth! The rippling notes breathed of joy, they poured joy into one's ears; the [pg 324] girls wanted to dance and the boys could not stand still—but the notes carried the thoughts of the old men back into the past, to those happy years when the Senate and the House of Deputies, after that great day of the Third of May, celebrated in the assembly hall the reconciliation of King and Nation; when they danced and sang, "Vivat our beloved King, vivat the Diet, vivat the people, vivat all classes!"

The master kept quickening the time and playing with greater power, but suddenly he struck a false chord like the hiss of a snake, like the grating of iron on glass—it sent a shudder through every one, and mingled with the general gaiety an ill-omened foreboding. Disturbed and alarmed, the hearers wondered whether the instrument might not be out of tune, or the musician be making a blunder. Such a master had not blundered! He purposely kept touching that traitorous string and breaking up the melody, striking louder and louder that angry chord, confederated against the harmony of the tones; at last the Warden understood the master, covered his face in his hands, and cried, "I know, I know those notes; that is Targowica!" And suddenly the ill-omened string broke with a hiss; the musician rushed to the treble notes, broke up and confused the measure, abandoned the treble notes, and hurried his hammers to the bass strings.

One could hear louder and louder a thousand noises, measured marching, war, an attack, a storm; one could hear the reports of guns, the groans of children, the weeping of mothers. So finely did the wonderful master render the horrors of a storm that the village girls trembled, calling to mind with tears of grief the Massacre of Praga, 229 which they knew from song and story; they were glad when finally the master thundered [pg 325] with all the strings at once, and choked the outcries as though he had crushed them into the earth.

Hardly did the hearers have time to recover from their amazement, when once more the music changed: at first there were once more light and gentle hummings; a few thin strings complained together, like flies striving to free themselves from the spider's web. But more and more strings joined them; now the scattered tones were blended and legions of chords were united; now they advanced measuredly with harmonious notes, forming the mournlful melody of that famous song of the wandering soldier who travels through woods and through forests, ofttimes fainting with woe and with hunger: at last he falls at the feet of his faithful steed, and the steed with his foot digs a grave for him. A poor old song, yet very dear to the Polish troops! The soldiers recognized it, and the privates crowded about the master; they hearkened, and they remembered that dreadful season when over the grave of their country they had sung this song and departed for the ends of the earth; they called to mind their long years of wandering, over lands and seas, over frosts and burning sands, amid foreign peoples, where often in camp they had been cheered and heartened by this folk song. So thinking, they sadly bowed their heads!

But they raised them straightway, for the master was playing stronger and higher notes; he changed his measure, and proclaimed something quite different from what had preceded. Once more he looked down and measured the strings with his eye; he joined his hands and smote with the two hammers in unison: the blow was so artistic, so powerful, that the strings rang like brazen trumpets, and from the trumpets a well-known song floated to the heavens, a triumphal march, [pg 326] "Poland has not yet perished; march, Dombrowski, to Poland!" —And all clapped their hands, and all shouted in chorus, "March, Dombrowski!"

The musician seemed amazed at his own song; he dropped the hammers from his hands and raised his arms aloft; his fox-skin cap dropped from his head to his shoulders; his uplifted beard waved majestically; his cheeks glowed with a strange flush; in his glance, full of spirit, shone the lire of youth. At last, when the old man turned his eyes on Dombrowski, he covered them with his hands, and from under his hands gushed a stream of tears.

"General," said he, "long has our Lithuania awaited thee—long, even as we Jews have awaited the Messiah; of thee in olden times minstrels prophesied among the folk; thy coming was heralded by a marvel in the sky. Live and wage war, O thou our—"

As he spoke, he sobbed; the honest Jew loved his country like a Pole! Dombrowski extended his hand to him and thanked him; Jankiel, doffing his cap, kissed the leader's hand.

It was time to begin the polanaise.— The Chamberlain stepped forward, and, lightly throwing back the flowing sleeves of his kontusz and twirling his mustache, he offered his arm to Zosia; with a polite bow he invited her to lead off in the first couple. Behind the Chamberlain a long line of couples formed; the signal was given and the dance began—he was its leader.

Over the greensward glittered his

crimson boots, the light gleamed from his sabre and his rich girdle shone; he advanced slowly, with seeming carelessness—yet in every step and every motion one could read the feelings and the thoughts of the dancer. He stopped, as if he wished to question his lady; he bent his head down [pg 327] towards her as if wishing to whisper in her ear; the lady averted her head, was bashful, would not listen; he doffed his white cap and bowed humbly; the lady deigned to gaze upon him, but still kept a stubborn silence; he slackened his pace, followed her glances with his eyes, and at last he laughed.—Happy in her reply, he advanced more quickly, gazing down at his rivals; now he hung his white cap with its heron's plumes over his brow, now he shook it above his brow; at last he cocked it over his ear and twirled his mustache. He strode on; all felt envious of him and pressed upon him in pursuit; he would have been glad to steal away from the throng with his lady; at times he stood still, courteously raised his hand, and humbly begged them to pass by; sometimes he meditated withdrawing adroitly to one side; he often changed his course, and would have been glad to elude his comrades, but they importunately followed him with swift steps, and encircled him from all sides in the evolutions of the dance: so he grew angry, and laid his right hand on his sword hilt, as if to say: "I care not for you; woe to those who are jealous of me!" He turned about with a haughty brow and with a challenge in his eye, and made straight for the throng; the throng of dancers did not dare withstand him, but retired from his path—and, changing their formation, they started again in pursuit of him.—

Cries rang out on all sides: "Ah, perhaps he is the last—watch, watch, you young men—perhaps he is the last who can lead the polonaise in such fashion!" And the couples followed one another merrily and uproariously; the circle would disperse and then contract once more! As when an immense serpent twines into a thousand folds, so there was seen a perpetual change [pg 328] amid the gay, parti-coloured garments of the ladies, the gentlemen, and the soldiers, like glittering scales gilded by the beams of the western sun and relieved against the dark pillows of turf. Brisk was the dance and loud the music, the applause, and the drinking of healths.

Corporal Buzzard Dobrzynski alone neither listened to the band, nor danced, nor made him merry; with his hands behind him he stood glum and sullen and called to mind his old-time wooing of Zosia; how he had loved to bring her flowers, to plait little baskets, to gather birds' nests, to make little earrings. Ungrateful girl! Though he had wasted upon her so many lovely gifts, though she had fled from him, though his father had forbidden him, yet how many times he had sat on the wall just to see her through the window, and had stolen into the hemp in order to watch how she tended her little flower garden, picked cucumbers, or fed the roosters! Ungrateful girl! He drooped his head; finally he whistled a mazurka; then he jammed his casque down over his ears and went to the camp, where the sentinels were standing by the cannon: there, to distract his mind, he began a game of cribbage with the private soldiers, and sweetened his sorrow with the cup. Such was the constancy of Dobrzynski to Zosia.

Zosia was dancing merrily: but, though she was in the first couple, from a distance she could hardly be seen; on the broad surface of the turf-spread court, in her green gown and decked with garlands and with flowery wreaths, she circled amid the grasses and flowers unseen in her flight, guiding the dance as an angel guides the motion of the stars by night: you could guess where she was, for towards her all eyes were turned and all arms stretched out; towards her the tumult pressed. In vain did the Chamberlain strive to [pg 329] remain by her side; his envious rivals had already pressed him out of the first couple: nor did the happy Dombrowski long enjoy his triumph; he yielded her to a second, but a third was already hastening up; and he, too, at once pressed aside, departed without hope. At last Zosia, by this time wearied, met Thaddeus as she passed down the line; and, fearing further change, and wishing to remain with him, she brought the dance to an end. She went to the table to pour wine for the guests.

The sun was already setting, the evening was warm and quiet; the circle of the heavens, here and there strewn with little clouds, was azure on high, but rosy in the west; the little clouds foretold fine weather, being light and shining—here like flocks of sheep sleeping on the greensward, there of somewhat smaller size, like coveys of teal. In the west was a cloud in shape like the drapery curtains of a couch, transparent and with many folds, pearly at the summit, gilded on the margin, purple in the centre; it still burned and glowed with the western gleams; at last it slowly turned yellow, then pale and grey; the sun dropped its head, drew the cloud about it, and sighing a single time with a warm breath—it fell asleep. 230

But the gentlefolk continued to drink and to propose the healths of Napoleon, the Generals, Thaddeus, and Zosia; finally of all three betrothed pairs in turn, of all the guests present with them, of all those that had been invited, of all the friends that any one alive could remember, and of all the dead whose memory had remained holy.
And I was there among the guests, and there drank wine and mead;
And what I saw and heard I wrote, that all of you might read. 231
[pg 331]

NOTES

[Such of the following notes as are not enclosed in brackets are by Mickiewicz himself. They include the entire commentary that the poet published with Pan Tadeusz . The other notes are either by the translator or culled from the following books or suggested by them:—

Mickiewicz, Pisma , wyd. Kallenbach (Brody, 1911), tom v. (This includes a "glossary" to Pan Tadeusz by Franciszek Jerzy Jaroszynski.)

Mickiewicz, Master Thaddeus; or, The Last Foray in Lithuania; translated by Maude Ashurst Biggs, with notes by the translator and Edmond S. Naganowski (London, 1885).

Mickiewicz, Œuvres poétiques complètes, trad. Christien Ostrowski, ed. 4 (Paris, 1859).

Mickiewicz, Herr Thaddäus, übersetzt von Siegfried Lipiner, ed. 2 (Leipzig, 1898).

It was difficult to draw the line between direct quotation and mere utilization of material. In particular, the translator's indebtedness to Jaroszynski is much greater than the quotation marks here used would indicate.]

Introductory Note

[The following summary of a few important events in Polish history, and of some of the leading features of Polish society and institutions, may be of assistance to readers of Pan Tadeusz.

The Polish Commonwealth was formed by the union of two separate states, Poland proper on the west, with a population predominantly Polish, and Lithuania on the east, with a population Lithuanian in the north (Lithuania proper) and Russian in the rest of its territory. After being long at odds with each other [pg 332] and with the German Knights of the Cross, these two states were united in 1386 by the marriage of Queen Jadwiga of Poland to the heathen Prince Jagiello of Lithuania, who thereupon accepted Christianity (p. 288). They remained under the dominion of the Jagiellos until the last of the male line of that house, Zygmunt August (compare note 64), died childless in 1572, and the throne became elective. The union was at first very loose, depending only on the person of the sovereign, but it became constantly closer, until in 1569 the two states agreed to have a common Œiet, sitting at Warsaw. Lithuania retained until the last, however, its separate officials, treasury, and army (compare pp. 171 and 310, and note 29). A constant stream of colonisation flowed east from Poland (called the Crown or the Kingdom) into Lithuania (p. 168), until the gentry of that country became Polish, while the peasantry remained either Lithuanian or Russian.

In the Polish Commonwealth the towns were of small importance; their inhabitants, though personally free, had almost no political rights. The country population was divided into the szlachta, or freemen, who fought the battles of the country and in whom was vested the entire political power, and the chlopi, or peasants, who were serfs, and cultivated the estates of the szlachta. The szlachta, who formed about a tenth of the population of the country, were legally all of equal rank (p. 100); as a matter of fact, differences of property created great social and even (in practice) political distinctions between them. Some of them, possessed of mere patches of land, lived a life little different from that of the peasants (p. 167). Still others entirely lost their land and became attached, even as menial servants, to the households of their richer neighbours. (Thus Gerwazy was a servant, though not quite a menial, of the Pantler.) The great land owners (or magnates), by gathering around them hordes of gentle-born, landless dependents, were able to support private armies, and to exercise a preponderating influence on the affairs of the country. Hence the Constitution of May 3, 1791, excluded szlachta not holding land from the right to vote.—In English works on Poland the words szlachta and szlachcic have usually been rendered as nobility and noble; in the present volume the terms gentry and gentleman are used, which, though far from satisfactory, are at all events somewhat less misleading.

The adoption of the elective instead of the hereditary principle in Poland after the extinction of the Jagiello line led to frequent civil wars, and was one cause of the country's decline in power during the seventeenth and eighteenth centuries. The King was elected for life by the whole body of the gentry, and every gentleman was theoretically eligible to the crown (p. 264). Poland's peculiar parliamentary system also contributed to its decay. Laws were made by a Diet of which the upper house, or Senate, was formed by the bishops, wojewodas (see note 26), castellans (see [pg 333] note 38), and ministers, while the lower house was composed of deputies elected by district diets (p. 303). A unanimous vote was required on all measures; more than this, any one deputy by his veto could dissolve the Diet, even in the last moments of its session, and undo all the work previously accomplished. This law of the liberum veto, and the elective nature of the royal office, offered countless opportunities for foreign nations to interfere in the affairs of the Commonwealth. The district diets, besides electing deputies to the General Diet, instructed them how to vote, and chose local officials (p. 75); they also were bound by the rule of the liberum veto (pp. 182, 304). Under such a constitution the only practical means of reform was through armed rebellion. Hence rebellions, or confederacies, were legalised in Poland; a number of citizens might combine together, choose a marshal (pp. 180, 182, 285), and seek to overthrow the established order; in case of success they became the government, in case of failure they were not liable to punishment. A diet held by a confederacy was not subject to the liberum veto, but adopted decisions by a majority vote.

In the seventeenth century, not to speak of civil troubles, Poland was devastated by disastrous wars, in particular with the Cossacks and with the Swedes (1655-60; pp. 169, 302). The great victory of Jan Sobieski, the warrior king, over the Turks in 1683, when he went to the relief of Vienna, was the last military triumph of old Poland (pp. 167, 170, 200, 201).

During the eighteenth century Poland sank to a condition of disgraceful dependence on Russia. In 1764 Catharine II. caused her favourite, Stanislaw Poniatowski, to be elected King. In 1768 Polish patriots, in a convulsive effort to throw off the Russian ascendancy, organised the Confederacy of Bar, which maintained a desperate struggle for four years. The Confederacy was crushed by Russia, and soon after its defeat followed the first partition of Poland (1772), by which Russia received a large share of the former Lithuanian provinces. A Diet, convoked under the forms of a confederacy, in order to avoid dissolution by the liberum veto, was obliged to sanction this partition. The desperate opposition of Rejtan, the deputy from the district of Nowogrodek (that is, from the region of which Mickiewicz was a native), Korsak, and other patriots, was of no avail (pp. 3, 139, 140).

After the disaster of the first partition the patriotic party in Poland made efforts to save their country, which culminated in the Four Years' Diet (1788-92). The labours of this Diet, which again was convoked under the forms of a confederacy, culminated in the Constitution of May 3, 1791. This measure, which was drawn up in secret and rushed through the Diet at a time when most of its probable opponents were absent, transformed Poland from an aristocratic republic into a constitutional hereditary monarchy, abolished the liberum veto, and secured religious [pg 334] toleration. Amid great enthusiasm the King took the oath to the new order of government (p. 324).

In the next year, however, a group of upholders of the old anarchic state of affairs, one of whose leaders was Ksawery Branicki (p. 200), formed with the support of Russia a confederacy which was proclaimed at Targowica (pp. 274, 324), a small town in the Ukraine, and the object of which was the undoing of the work of the Four Years' Diet. The Russian armies entered the country and overcame the resistance of the Polish troops, two of the foremost leaders of which were Prince Joseph Poniatowski, the nephew of the King, and Kosciuszko. Then followed the second partition of Poland (1793), by which the territory of the Commonwealth was reduced to about one third of its original dimensions. In the next year occurred a popular revolt, of which Kosciuszko assumed the leadership, and which, despite a brilliant victory at Raclawice (p. 252), near Cracow, and some other successes, was soon quelled by the allied powers, Russia, Prussia, and Austria. In a battle at Maciejowice (p. 252) Kosciuszko was defeated, and, severely wounded, was himself taken prisoner by the Russians. The final episode of the war was the fall of Warsaw. Suvorov, the Russian commander, captured by storm Praga, a suburb of the city, and gave over its inhabitants to massacre (pp. 3, 324). In the following year, 1795, the remnant of the Polish kingdom was divided among the three allies.

Even now not all the Poles despaired of their country's fate. The idea arose of transferring to France the headquarters of Polish interests and of forming bodies of Polish troops that should fight for France against the common enemies of France and Poland and thereby prepare themselves for service in the restoration of Poland. The leader of this movement, and the most noted general of the new Polish Legions, was Jan Henryk Dombrowski, who had won fame in the war of 1794. The Legions' first field of activity was in northern Italy, where they supported the struggle of Lombardy for independence. Here arose (1797) the famous Song of the Legions, "Poland has not yet perished, while we still live" (pp. 3, 97, 325, 326). In the next year (1798) Dombrowski aided the French in the capture of Rome, and Kniaziewicz was put in command of the garrison on the Capitol (p. 31). In 1800 a new Polish force won laurels at Marengo and Hohenlinden (p. 286). In return for these services Bonaparte did nothing whatever for the restoration of Poland. The legions were sent oversea to reduce the negro insurrection in the island of San Domingo, where the greater part of them perished (1803; p. 31).

In 1806, after his victory at Jena (p. 176), Napoleon summoned the Poles to his standards. A large force was organised, under the command of Prince Joseph Poniatowski and Dombrowski. In the succeeding war, which includes the siege and capture of Dantzic (p. 116) and the battle of Preussisch-Eylau (p. 251),
[pg 335]
Napoleon decisively defeated the Russians at Friedland (1807) and soon after concluded the Peace of Tilsit (p. 161). By this treaty there was created, out of a portion of the Polish lands received by Prussia at the different partitions, a new state, known as the Grand Duchy of Warsaw, and ruled by the King of Saxony as a constitutional monarch under the protection of Napoleon. The Niemen divided this new state from the portion of Poland under the rule of Russia (pp. 31, 255).

The new Grand Duchy had to furnish troops in aid of Napoleon. In 1808 the Polish light cavalry, led by Kozietulski, won glory by the capture of Somosierra, a defile leading to Madrid (p. 286).

In 1809, after a war with Austria, in which he received valuable aid from the Poles, Napoleon increased the Grand Duchy of Warsaw by lands taken from that country. Tardy and ungenerous though his action had been, he had thus done something to justify the hopes of the Poles that he would one day reconstitute their Commonwealth as a whole. Hence it will be clear with what enthusiasm Poland, and still more Lithuania, awaited the outcome of a great war between Napoleon and Russia, such as was evidently approaching in the year 1811. The Poles believed Napoleon to be unconquerable, and trusted that when he had defeated Russia he would proclaim the reunion of Lithuania with the Grand Duchy of Warsaw; then Poland would live once more (pp. 160, 277).

The actual outcome of the war was a crushing blow to Polish hopes. Napoleon's invasion of Russia resulted in his utter defeat; after his flight home his army was defeated at Leipzig (1813), where Prince Joseph Poniatowski met his death. Two years later, at the Congress of Vienna, the greater portion of Poland was given over to Russia, to be governed as a constitutional state. Such it remained, in name at least, until the desperate insurrection of 1831, the failure of which ended all pretence of Polish self-government under Russian rule. To drown the grief and despair with which that tragedy had filled his mind Mickiewicz turned back in the next year (when he began Pan Tadeusz) to the scenes of his childhood, to the days full of hope and joyful expectation that had preceded Napoleon's attack on Russia.]

1 In the time of the Polish Commonwealth the carrying out of judicial

decrees was very difficult, in a country where the executive authorities had almost no police at their disposal, and where powerful citizens maintained household regiments, some of them, for example the Princes Radziwill, even armies of several thousand. So the plaintiff who had obtained a verdict in his favour had to apply for its execution to the knightly order, that is to the gentry, with whom rested also the executive power. Armed kinsmen, friends, and neighbours set out, verdict in hand, in company with the apparitor, and gained possession, often not without bloodshed, [pg 336] of the goods adjudged to the plaintiff, which the apparitor legally made over or gave into his possession. Such an armed execution of a verdict was called a zajazd [foray]. In ancient times, while laws were respected, even the most powerful magnates did not dare to resist judicial decrees, armed attacks rarely took place, and violence almost never went unpunished. Well known in history is the sad end of Prince Wasil Sanguszko, and of Stadnicki, called the Devil.—The corruption of public morals in the Commonwealth increased the number of forays, which continually disturbed the peace of Lithuania. [The rendering of zajazd by foray is of course inexact and conventional; but the translator did not wish to use the Polish word and could find no better English equivalent.]

2 Every one in Poland knows of the miraculous image of Our Lady at Jasna Gora in Czenstochowa. In Lithuania there are images of Our Lady, famed for miracles, at the Ostra [Pointed] Gate in Wilno, the Castle in Nowogrodek, and at Zyrowiec and Boruny.

3 [See p. 332.]

4 [Tadeusz (Thaddeus) Kosciuszko (1746-1817). This most famous Polish patriot was a native of the same portion of Lithuania as Mickiewicz. He early emigrated to America and served with distinction in the Revolutionary War. On his later career see p. 334. After the failure of the insurrection of 1794 Kosciuszko was imprisoned for two years in St. Petersburg; in 1796, on the death of Catharine, he was released by Paul. He thereafter lived in retirement, first in France and then in Switzerland, resisting all the attempts of Napoleon to draw him into his service. At the Congress of Vienna he made fruitless efforts in behalf of Poland. His memory is probably more reverenced by the Polish people than that of any other man. His remains rest in the cathedral at Cracow, and on the outskirts of the city is a mound of earth 150 feet high raised as a monument to him.]

5 [Czamarka (diminutive of czamara) in the original; see note 82.]

6 [See p. 333. Rejtan had taken part in the Confederacy of Bar. Owing to the disasters to Poland he lost his reason, and in 1780 he killed himself.]

7 [A soldier and poet, of a Wilno family. As a colonel of engineers he fought in the war of 1792. He prepared and led the insurrection in Wilno in 1794, and perished at the siege of Praga in the same year.]

8 [See p. 333. Korsak was a deputy to the Four Years' Diet, and a leader in Kosciuszko's insurrection. He perished by the side of Jasinski.]

9 The Russian government in conquered countries never immediately overthrows their laws and civil institutions, but by its edicts it slowly undermines and saps them. For example, in Little Russia the Lithuanian Statute, modified by edicts, was [pg 337] maintained until the most recent times. Lithuania was allowed to retain its ancient organisation of civil and criminal courts. So, as of old, rural and town judges are elected in the districts, and superior judges in the provinces. But since there is an appeal to St. Petersburg, to many institutions of various rank, the local courts are left with hardly a shadow of their traditional dignity.

10 The Wojski (tribunus) was once an officer charged with the protection of the wives and children of the gentry during the time of service of the general militia. But this office without duties long ago became merely titular. In Lithuania there is a custom of giving by courtesy to respected persons some ancient title, which becomes legalised by usage. For instance, the neighbours call one of their friends Quartermaster, Pantler, or Cup-bearer, at first only in conversation and in correspondence, but later even in official documents. The Russian government has forbidden such titles, and would like to cover them with ridicule and to introduce in their place the system of titles based on the ranks in its own hierarchy, to which the Lithuanians still have great repugnance. [The present translator has followed Ostrowski's example in rendering wojski as seneschal, "ne pouvant mieux faire."]

11 [See p. 334 and note 176.]

12 The Chamberlain, once a noted and dignified official, Princeps Nobilitatis, under the Russian government has become merely a titular dignitary. Formerly he was still judge of boundary disputes, but he finally lost even that part of his jurisdiction. Now he occasionally takes the place of the Marshal, and appoints the komomicy or district surveyors.

13 ["The outer garment of the ancient Polish costume, a sort of loose frock or coat, falling below the knees, and secured by a girdle round the waist. The effect was remarkably picturesque and graceful." —M. A. Biggs. A characteristic feature of the kontusz was the turned-back upper false sleeves.]

14 The Apparitor (wozny) or Bailiff, who was chosen from among the landed gentry by the decree of a tribunal or court, carried summonses, proclaimed persons in legal possession of property adjudged to them, made inquests, called cases on the court's calendar, etc. Usually this office was assigned to one of the minor gentry.

15 [See p. 334 and note 176.]

16 [A Lithuanian dish of beet leaves and cream, served with ice. Mickiewicz later repeats this passage in true Homeric fashion: see pp. 85, 133.]

17 [An allusion to a tale told by Suetonius, Life of Vespasian, §23.]

18 The buzzard is a bird resembling a hawk. It is well known how a flock of small birds, particularly swallows, will pursue a hawk. Hence the proverb, to fly as after a buzzard.
[pg 338]

19 [The reference is to the plica polonica, a disease of the hair in which it becomes matted and twisted together. It is common in certain parts of Poland, as its name indicates.]

20 [Robak is the Polish word for *worm* .]

21 [Plat is the Russian word for *rascal* . Compare p. 235 .]

22 Among the Russian peasantry numerous stories are current in regard to the incantations of Bonaparte and Suvorov.

23 The *assessors* form the rural police of a district. According to the edicts, they are in part elected by the citizens, in part appointed by the government; these last are called the *crown assessors* . Judges of appeal are also called *assessors* , but there is no reference to them here.

24 One class of *notaries* (rejenci aktowi) have charge of certain government bureaus; others (rejenci dekretowi) record verdicts: all are appointed by the clerks of the courts.

25 [See p. 333 .]

26 Joseph, Count Niesiolowski, the last Wojewoda of Nowogrodek, was president of the revolutionary government during Jasinski's insurrection. [A wojewoda was the chief dignitary of a Polish province or wojewodeship . The office had very slight duties, and was rather a title of distinction than an administrative position. It was particularly valued because it conferred a seat in the Senate.]

27 Jerzy Bialopiotrowicz, the last Secretary of the Grand Duchy of Lithuania, took an active part in the Lithuanian insurrection under Jasinski. He was judge of the state prisoners at Wilno. He was a man highly honoured in Lithuania for his virtues and his patriotism.

28 [According to a mythical story current in Poland, three brothers, Lech, Czech, and Rus, were the founders of the Polish, Bohemian, and Russian nations. Compare p. 289 .]

29 At Sluck there was a famous factory for making gold brocade and massive belts, which supplied all Poland. It was perfected by the efforts of Tyzenhaus. ["Antoni Tyzenhaus, 1733-85, first Grand Secretary, later Under-Court-Treasurer of Lithuania, a man who did much for the elevation of the economic condition and of the state of education in Lithuania, for a long time an unwavering partisan of King Stanislaw August." —Jaroszynski. Compare p. 173 .]

30 [In the original, Golden Altar , a title of numerous Polish books of devotion in the eighteenth and nineteenth centuries.]

31 The Court Calendar (Trybunalska Wokanda) was a long, narrow little book, in which were entered the names of the parties to suits in the order of the defendants. Every advocate and apparitor had to own such a calendar.

32 [The reference is of course to the golden eagles of Napoleon joined with the silver eagles of Poland. The Polish coat-of-arms shows a white eagle on a red field.]
[pg 339]

33 [Jan Henryk Dombrowski (1755-1818): see p. 334 . He took part in almost all the wars of Napoleon; in 1812 he was stationed in White Russia and had an active share in the campaign only towards its close.]

34 General Kniaziewicz, as messenger of the Italian army, delivered to the Directory the captured standards. [Otton-Karol Kniaziewicz (1762-1842). He, like Dombrowski, had taken part in Kosciuszko's insurrection.]

35 Prince Jablonowski, in command of the Legion of the Danube, died in San Domingo, and almost all his legion perished there. Among the Polish emigrants there are a few veterans who survived that unhappy expedition, among others General Malachowski. [see p. 281 and note 184 .]

36 An organ was ordinarily set in the gallery of the old castles.

37 ["The health of the Primate of Poland (Archbishop of Gnesen) was drunk after that of the King, because he was the highest dignitary in the Kingdom. Between the death of one sovereign and [the] election of his successor, he was Interrex." —M. A. Biggs.]

38 [The office of castellan was next in dignity to that of wojewoda ; except for some very slight military duties the post was purely titular, but it was prized because it entitled the holder to a seat in the Senate.]

39 Black soup, served at table to a young man suing for a young woman's hand, signified a refusal. [Naganowski states that it is "a thickish soup, made chiefly of the blood of a duck or goose, vinegar, and spice."]

40 [See p. 333 .]

41 [The bracketed passage was inserted by the translator.]

42 These barges (wiciny) are large boats on the Niemen, with which the Lithuanians carry on trade with the Prussians, freighting grain down the river and receiving colonial wares in return for it.

43 [Zrazy in the original. "A national dish, prepared as follows: Take good and tender beef, mince it fine, add a little butter, spice, onions, salt, pepper, egg, bread-crumbs, make small pats or cakes of the compound; fried, boiled, or stewed." —M. A. Biggs.]

44 [Son of a bitch.]

45 [Goat-strangler.]

46 [The north-western part of old Poland, including the portion now incorporated in Prussia.]

47 Prince Dominik Radziwill, a great lover of hunting, emigrated to the Grand Duchy of Warsaw, and equipped at his own cost a regiment of cavalry, which he commanded in person. He died in France. With him became extinct the male line of the Princes of Olyka and Nieswiez, the most powerful lords in Poland and in all probability in Europe.
[pg 340]

48 Mejen distinguished himself in the national war under Kosciuszko. Mejen's ramparts are still shown near Wilno.

49 [Kite.]

50 [The translator has omitted the phrase, "called little grand-mothers."]

51 [The translation of this poem by Miss M. A. Biggs contains a note "supplied by Dr. Rostafinski of Cracow" as to the scientific names of the different mushrooms mentioned by Mickiewicz.

(1) " Lisica [fox-mushroom]. Cantarellus cibarius (Chantarelle).

(2) Borowik [pine-lover]. Boletus edulis (called in Lithuania Bovinus).

(3) Rydz [orange-agaric]. Agaricus deliciosus .

(4) Muchomor [fly-bane]. Amanita muscaria , or Agaricus muscarius (fly-agaric). This is the Siberian fungus, with remarkable intoxicating properties.

(5) Surojadki [leaf-mushrooms]. A species of the Russula . Those quoted by Mickiewicz seem to be Russula nitida, R. alutacea , and R. emetica .

(6) Kozlak . Two species of Boletus ; one B. luteus , the other (mentioned in the text) B. luridus {poisonous) .

(7) Bielaki [whities], Agaricus piperatus and Agaricus vellereus .

(8) Purchawki [puffball]. Lycoperdon bovista .

(9) Lejki [funnels]. The word does not signify any particular sort of fungus; it may be that the poet created the name a forma . The shape suggests Agaricus chloroides ."]

52 A well-known Lithuanian folk-song tells of the mushrooms marching to war under the lead of the pine-lover . In this song the qualities of the edible mushrooms are described.

53 [Zosia is the diminutive of Zofia (Sophia).]

54 [Telimena's last words are taken almost literally from a popular song, Serce nie sluga .]

55 [The Breughels were a famous family of Dutch painters of the sixteenth and early seventeenth centuries. Pieter had a bent towards diabolic scenes, whence he received the title "hell Breughel" (Van der Helle); Jan, his younger brother, was a master in the painting of landscapes, flowers, flies, etc. Apparently the Count's learning did not extend to the father of these two brothers, who was also a famous painter.]

56 A noted genre painter; some years before his death he began to paint landscapes. He died recently in St. Petersburg.

57 [The Polish points the contrast by a rime: "the uproar was not funereal , but dinnerial ."]

58 [This translation of the Polish matecznik is of course purely conventional: compare pp. 105 -107 .]
[pg 341]
59 The breed of small, strong English dogs, called bulldogs [literally, leeches], is used for hunting big game, particularly bears.

60 The sprawnik or kapitan sprawnik is the chief of the rural police. The strapczy is a sort of government attorney. These two officials, who have frequent opportunities for misusing their authority, are greatly hated by the people generally. [These offices, and the names of them, are Russian, not Polish. Strapczyna would be the name given to the wife of a strapczy .]

61 [The paragraph here inclosed in brackets is not found in the editions of Pan Tadeusz published during the lifetime of Mickiewicz. It occurs in his manuscript, among many other passages that he did not choose to print; in the edition of 1858 it was added to the printed text. It has been included here, though with some hesitation, because the succeeding narrative did not seem quite clear without it. It seemed needless to record other variant readings, even in these notes; they are of little interest except to special students of the work of Mickiewicz.]

62 According to the tradition, Grand Prince Giedymin had a dream on the mountain of Ponary of an iron wolf, and by the counsel of the wajdelota [bard] Lizdejko founded the city of Wilno.

63 [Witenes and Mindowe (also called Mendog) were early princes of Lithuania. Giedymin (died 1341) was the founder of the power of that nation, and the father of Olgierd and Kiejstut. One son of Kiejstut was Witold, famous as a warrior and prince. One son of Olgierd was Jagiello: see p. 332 . Lizdejko is said to have been the last high priest of heathen Lithuania.]

64 Zygmunt August [1548-72] was raised to the throne of the Grand Duchy of Lithuania according to the ancient rites; he girt on him the sword and crowned himself with the soft cap (kolpak). He was a great lover of hunting.

65 In the district of Rosieny, on the estate of Paszkiewicz, the Rural Secretary, grew an oak known under the name of Baublis, which was formerly, in pagan times, honoured as a sacred tree. In the interior of this decayed giant Paszkiewicz has founded a cabinet of Lithuanian antiquities.

66 Not far from the parish church of Nowogrodek grew some ancient lindens, many of which were felled about the year 1812.

67 [Jan Kochanowski (1530-84) was the greatest poet of Poland up to the time of Mickiewicz. Czarnolas was his country estate, on which he passed in retirement the closing years of his life. In a famous epigram he tells of the charms of his linden tree:—

"Seat thyself underneath my leaves, O guest,
And rest.
I promise thee that the sharp-beaming sun
Here shall not run,
But 'neath the trees spread out a heavy shade:
[pg 342]
Here always from the fields cool winds have played;
Here sparrows and the nightingales have made
Charming lament.
And all my fragrant flowers their sweets have spent
Upon the bees; my master's board is lent
That honey's gold.
And I with gentle whisperings can fold
Sweet sleep upon thee. Yea, 'tis true I bear
No apples; yet my Lord speaks me as fair
As the most fruitful trees
That graced the Gardens of Hesperides. "
Translated by Miss H. H. Havermate and G. R. Noyes .]

68 See Goszczynski's poem, The Castle of Kaniow . [This poem, by Seweryn Goszczynski (1803-76) was published in 1828. The reference is probably to the following passage: "Does that prattling oak whisper in his ear sad tales of the disasters of this land, when beneath its sky the gloomy vulture of

slaughter extended a dread shadow with bloody wings, and after it streamed clouds of Tatars?"]

69 ["Those used for the candles regularly lit by the Jews on Friday at sunset, to avoid the 'work' of kindling light or fire on the Sabbath."—M. A. Biggs.]

70 Kolomyjkas are Ruthenian songs resembling the Polish mazurkas. [Ostrowski states that these are popular airs that are sung and danced at the same time. Naganowski adds that the first word is derived from the town of Kolomyja in Galicia. Mazurka is "merely the feminine form of Mazur," a Masovian.]

71 [Dombrowski's march, "Poland has not yet perished." Compare pp. 325, 326, 334.]

72 [See note 42.]

73 [The Jews in Poland, though not persecuted, formed a separate class, without share in the government of the country. They were separated from the Poles by religion, customs, and language. Yet instances of intermarriage and assimilation were not uncommon. Compare p. 100.]

74 The pokucie is the place of honour, where formerly the household gods were set, and where still the Russians hang their sacred pictures (ikons). Here a Lithuanian peasant seats any guest whom he desires to honour.

75 [July mead (lipcowy miod) perhaps might better be called lindenflower mead. The Polish name of July, lipiec, is derived from lipa, a linden tree. See the epigram quoted in note 67.]

76 [See note 2. Since Czenstochowa was in the Grand Duchy of Warsaw, Robak finds occasion to hint at the reunion of Lithuania and the Kingdom.]

77 [The reference is to the Eastern (Orthodox) Church, the state church of Russia.]

78 [Compare p. 319.]
[pg 343]

79 [An old jingle expressing the equality before the law of all members of the Polish gentry.]

80 [Maciej Stryjkowski (1547-83) wrote a famous chronicle that is one of the sources for the early history of Lithuania.

"Polish heraldry is comparatively simple beside that of other countries. The use of family names was unknown till the fifteenth century; before that the different branches of one stock were only recognised by one common escutcheon. One might belong to the stock of the arrow, the two daggers, the horseshoe, the double or triple cross, etc. There were only 540 of these escutcheons for the whole of Poland. A great number of families were grouped together under each one of these signs; we shall often find a man described as being of such and such a crest."—M. A. Biggs.

"It may be added that a wealthy and powerful nobleman often rewarded his retainers and famuli by 'admitting them to his escutcheon,' i.e. obtaining for them a diploma of honour from the King, ratifying the knightly adoption. Hence it is common to hear of the greatest and most ancient Polish families having the same armorial bearings with some very obscure ones."—Naganowski. Compare p. 319.]

81 [See p. 334.]

82 ["The tarataika is species of capote; the czamara a long frock-coat, braided on the back and chest like a huzzar's uniform, and with tight sleeves. The sukmana is a sort of peasant's coat made of cloth, the wearing of which by Kosciuszko indicated his strong democratic tendencies, and sympathy with the lower classes."—M. A. Biggs.

83 The beaks of large birds of prey become more and more curved with advancing age, and finally the upper part grows so crooked that it closes the bill, and the bird must die of hunger. This popular belief has been accepted by some ornithologists.

84 It is a fact that there is no instance of the skeleton of a dead animal having been found.

85 Birdies (ptaszynki) are guns of small calibre, used with a small bullet. A good marksman with such a fowling-piece can hit a bird on the wing.

86 ["It may be interesting to know that one of the yet surviving friends and schoolfellows of Mickiewicz, Ignatius Domejko, the present Rector of the University of Santiago (Chili), related during his stay in Warsaw last year (1884) that he challenged the young poet, then at Wilno, to find a proper name riming with Domejko. Mickiewicz improvised a verse riming Domejko with Dowejko. It is not, however, quite certain whether there was actually a family of that name." —Naganowski.]

87 Little leaves of gold lie at the bottom of bottles of Dantzic brandy. [The city, formerly under Polish rule, was annexed to Prussia at the time of the Second Partition, 1793.]
[pg 344]

88 ["The bigos was not of course prepared then and there on the spot. It is usually made in large quantities, put into barrels, and stored in cellars. The oftener it is heated the more savoury it is." —M. A. Biggs.]

89 [See p. 333.]

90 Queen Dido had a bull's hide cut into strips, and thus enclosed within the circuit of the hide a considerable territory, where she afterwards built Carthage. The Seneschal did not read the description of this event in the Aeneid, but in all probability in the scholiasts' commentaries.

N.B.—Some places in the fourth book are by the hand of Stefan Witwicki.]

91 Once in the Diet the deputy Philip, from the village of Konopie (hemp), obtaining the floor, wandered so far from the subject that he raised a general laugh in the chamber. Hence arose the proverb: "He has bobbed up like Philip from the hemp."

92 [There is here an untranslatable pun in the original; niemiec, the Polish word for *German*, is derived from niemy, *dumb*.]

93 [In the original: "And the Word became——" "These words of the Gospel of St. John are often used as an exclamation of astonishment." —M. A. Biggs.]

94 ["Of all spoils the most important were the spolia opima, a term applied to those only which the commander-in-chief of a Roman army stripped

in a field of battle from the leader of the foe."— Smith's Dictionary of Antiquities. They were awarded but three or four times in the course of Roman history.]

95 [In the original there is here an internal jingle between klucznik (warden) and puszczyk (screech owl).]

96 [This festival furnished the subject and the title for Mickiewicz's greatest poem, next to Pan Tadeusz. The poet's own explanation of it is in part as follows: "This is the name of a festival still celebrated among the common folk in many districts of Lithuania, Prussia, and Courland. The festival goes back to pagan times, and was formerly called the feast of the goat (koziel), the director of which was the kozlarz, at once priest and poet. At the present time, since the enlightened clergy and landowners have been making efforts to root out a custom accompanied by superstitious practices and often by culpable excesses, the folk celebrate the forefathers secretly in chapels or in empty houses not far from the graveyard. There they ordinarily spread a feast of food, drink, and fruits of various sorts and invoke the spirits of the dead. The folk hold the opinion that by this food and drink and by their songs they bring relief to souls in Purgatory."]

97 [See note 1]

98 [The original here has a delightful pun. Gerwazy misunderstands his lord's high-flown word wassalow (vassals) as wonsalow (mustachioed champions). A long mustache was the dearest [pg 345] adornment of a Polish gentleman; compare Gerwazy's description of Jacek on pages 43 and 115, where wonsal is the title given him in the original.]

99 [The last three names might be translated, Cuttem, Slashem, Whackem.]

100 [The buzdygan or mace was the staff of office of certain subordinate officers in the Polish army, as the bulawa was that of the hetmans or generals. Each was a short rod with a knob at the end, but the knob on the bulawa was round, that on the buzdygan was pear-shaped, with longitudinal notches.]

101 [See note 82.]

102 In Lithuania the name okolica or zascianek is given to a settlement of gentry, to distinguish them from true villages, which are settlements of peasants. ["These zascianki were inhabited by the poorest of the lesser nobility, who were in fact peasants, but possessed of truly Castilian pride. The wearing of a sword being restricted to nobles, it was not unusual to see such zasciankowicze, or peasant nobles, following the plough bare-footed, wearing an old rusty sword hanging at their side by hempen cords."—Naganowski. In this volume hamlet has been arbitrarily chosen as a translation for the name of these villages of gentry.]

103 [See page 334.]

104 Kisiel is a Lithuanian dish, a sort of jelly made of oaten yeast, which is washed with water until all the mealy parts are separated from it: hence the proverb. [The literal translation of the Polish line is simply: "To the Horeszkos he is merely the tenth water on the kisiel."]

105 [See pp. 334, 335.]
106 [See p. 332.]
107 [See p. 335.]

108 [The arms of Lithuania (called the "Pursuit") are a horse-man in full career, with sword uplifted to strike. The Bear is the coat-of-arms of Zmudz, a portion of Lithuania, on the Baltic]

109 [Wilno (Vilna).]

110 [A French statesman and historian, in the years 1810-12 Napoleon's representative at Warsaw.]

111 ["A convicted slanderer was compelled to crawl under the table or bench, and in that position to bark three times like a dog, and pronounce his recantation. Hence the Polish word odszczekac, to bark back, generally used to express recanting."—M. A. Biggs.]

112 After various brawls this man was seized at Minsk, and shot, in accordance with a court decree.

113 When the King was to assemble the general militia, he had a pole set up in each parish with a broom or bundle of twigs tied to the top. This was called *sending out the twigs*. Every grown man of the knightly order was obliged, under pain of loss of the privileges of gentle birth, to rally at once to the Wojewoda's [pg 346] standard. [The twigs symbolised the King's authority to inflict punishment. The reign of Jan III. Sobieski was 1674-96.]

114 ["The district of Dobrzyn in Masovia, that exclusively Polish region the central point of which is Warsaw. The inhabitants of it are called Masovians; hence this name is also applied to the men of Dobrzyn who emigrated from Masovia to Lithuania." —Lipiner.]

115 [Bartlomiej is the Polish form of Bartholomew; Maciej and Maciek (a diminutive) are variant forms of Matyasz (Matthias).]

116 By-names are really sobriquets.

117 [Krolik, Maciej's nickname, means both rabbit and little king or kinglet.]

118 [See p. 333.]

119 [See note 29.]

120 [Maciej had naturally joined the Confederates of Bar, who opposed the King because of his subserviency to the Russians. "But when the King later declared himself for the patriotic party… it is no wonder that our Maciek took sides with the crown, the power of which then needed strengthening. He supported Tyzenhaus, because of the latter's beneficial activity in the most important direction, that of the economic welfare of the country. After the King's contemptible desertion to the camp of the Confederates of Targowica, all noble and patriotic men in Poland had of course to oppose him. Thus the King, and not Maciek, was the real Cock-on-the-Steeple, and our man of Dobrzyn was really always on the side of those who fought for 'the good of the country.' "—Lipiner.]

121 [The last Under-Treasurer of Lithuania. He took part in Jasinski's insurrection: compare p. 3 and note 7.]

122 Alexander Count Pociej, on his return to Lithuania after the war, assisted those of his fellow-countrymen who were emigrating abroad, and sent considerable sums to the treasury of the Legions.

123 [The opening line of a popular

hymn by Franciszek Karpinski (1741-1825).]

124 [This form of greeting is still used by the common people in Poland.]

125 [Joseph Grabowski, a landed proprietor of the Grand Duchy of Posen, was a colonel of the General Staff during the Napoleonic wars, and later played an important part in the public life of the Grand Duchy. At Lukow, near Obiezierz, in 1831, he entertained Mickiewicz and his brother Franciszek.]

126 [See note 46 .]

127 [See p. 334 .]

128 [A proverbial phrase; compare p. 283 .]

129 [Also often called Baptist.]

130 [See note 20 .]

[pg 347]

131 [See p. 333 .]

132 ["The 'contracts' of Kiev and Minsk were famous fairs, held in those cities at stated times, for the conclusion of agreements of all sorts."—Jaroszynski. As these are the only contracts of which Maciej has heard, the word, as used by the eloquent student of Rousseau, naturally puzzles him. (Adapted from Naganowski.)]

133 ["In 1568 a Polish gentleman named Pszonka founded on his estate, Babin, near Lublin, a satiric society, called the Babin Republic. It scourged contemporary manners in a peculiar fashion, sending to every man who became noted for some crime or folly a diploma by virtue of which he was admitted to the 'Republic' and had an office conferred on him. Thus, for example, a quack was appointed physician, a coward general, and a spendthrift steward."—Lipiner.]

134 [See p. 333 .]

135 ["Klejnot , here translated jewel , also means escutcheon .]

136 ["The order of the Piarists attained, after the expulsion of the Jesuits in 1773, great influence over the education of youth, and initiated, mainly by the efforts of Konarski, an improved system of education. While the Jesuits had laid the main stress upon Latin, the Piarists substituted French as the groundwork of education. This was an improvement upon the previous system, but it had the effect of inducing an aping of French manners and customs in literature and social life, till the reaction in favour of Polish nationality." —M. A. Biggs (slightly altered).]

137 [Literally, "of Marymont flour. " Marymont is a village near Warsaw, which is (or was) famous for its flour.]

138 [The epithet in the original is Sak , a sack; glupi jak sak, "stupid as a sack," is a Polish proverb. As an equivalent, the archaic *Buzzard* seemed preferable to the grotesque modern *Donkey* .]

139 [Lele and Polele, or Lelum and Polelum, were reputed to be twin brothers in the Polish pagan mythology. Slowacki introduces them into his drama Lilla Weneda .]

140 [See p. 332 .]

141 [Berenice's hair. (Jaroszynski.)]

142 The constellation known among astronomers as Ursa Major .]

143 It was the custom to hang up in churches any fossil bones that might be discovered; the people regard them as the bones of giants.

144 The memorable comet of the year 1811.

145 ["When the plague is about to strike upon Lithuania, the eye of the seer divines its coming; for, if one may believe the bards, often in the desolate graveyards and meadows the Maid of Pestilence rises to sight, in a white garment, with a fiery crown on her temples; her brow towers over the trees of Bialowieza, [pg 348] and in her hand she waves a bloody kerchief."—Mickiewicz, Konrad Wallenrod .]

146 Father Poczobut, an ex-Jesuit, and a famous astronomer, published a work on the Zodiac of Denderah, and by his observations aided Lalande in calculating the motions of the moon. See the biography of him by Jan Sniadecki.

147 [Jan Sniadecki (1756-1830) was a man of real distinction both as an astronomer and as one of the intellectual leaders of Poland. During Mickiewicz's student days he was professor at the University of Wilno. The young poet disliked him, as a representative of the cold, rationalistic tradition of the eighteenth century.]

148 [At Jassy, in Roumania, peace was concluded in 1792 between Russia and Turkey. The poet represents Branicki and his comrades as rushing to the protection of the Russian armies: compare p. 334 .]

149 [Fvlmen Orientis Joannes III. rex Poloniarvm ter maximus. Calissii typis Collegij Societatis Jesv. 1684.]

150 [Rubinkowski, Jan Kaz. Janina zwycieskich tryumfow Jana III. Poznan, S. J. 1739.]

151 [Adam Kazimierz Czartoryski (1734-1823), a cousin of Stanislaw Poniatowski, and one of the leading men of his time in Poland.]

152 [See p. 3 and note 6 .]

153 [See note 29 .]

154 [See p. 171 and note 121 .]

155 Properly Prince de Nassau-Siegen [1745-1808], a famous warrior and adventurer of those times. He was a Muscovite admiral and defeated the Turks in the bay [of the Dnieper, near Ochakov]; later he was himself utterly defeated by the Swedes. He spent some time in Poland, where he was granted the rights of a citizen. The combat of the Prince de Nassau with the tiger [in Africa!] was noised abroad at the time through all the newspapers of Europe.

156 [Thaddeus, though he may catch a glimpse of this scene through the keyhole, apparently does not hear the conversation, if one may judge by his later ignorance: compare p. 261 .]

157 [In the original Switezianka , a nymph that apparently Mickiewicz himself invented as an inhabitant of the Switez, a small lake near his home. One of his ballads is entitled Switezianka , another Switez .]

158 [The Polish "short mile" was of 15,000 feet, or somewhat less than three English miles; the "long mile" was of 22,500 feet.]

159 [A sort of Polish Puck. He figures prominently in Slowacki's tragedy Balladyna .]

160 [See note 21 . The name of Plut's birthplace might be translated Skinnem .]

[pg 349]

161 The Yellow Book , so called from its binding, is the barbarous book of

Russian martial law. Frequently in time of peace the government proclaims whole provinces as being in a state of war, and on the authority of the Yellow Book confers on the military commander complete power over the estates and lives of the citizens. It is a well-known fact that from the year 1812 to the revolution [of 1831] all Lithuania was subject to the Yellow Book , of which the executor was the Grand Duke the Tsarevich [Constantine].]

162 [Joseph Baka (1707-80), a Jesuit, wrote Reflections on Inevitable Death, Common to All . His short doggerel rimes, which breathe a jovial gaiety, were long extremely popular. In recent times suspicion has been cast on Baka's authorship of the work. (Adapted from Jaroszynski.)]

163 A Lithuanian club is made in the following way. A young oak is selected and is slashed from the bottom upwards with an axe, so that bark and bast are cut through and the wood slightly wounded. Into these notches are thrust sharp flints, which in time grow into the tree and form hard knobs. Clubs in pagan times formed the chief weapon of the Lithuanian infantry; they are still occasionally used, and are called nasieki , gnarled clubs.

164 After Jasinski's insurrection [compare p. 3 and note 7], when the Lithuanian armies were retiring towards Warsaw, the Muscovites had come up to the deserted city of Wilno. General Deyov at the head of his staff was entering through the Ostra Gate. The streets were empty; the townsfolk had shut themselves in their houses. One townsman, seeing a cannon loaded with grapeshot, abandoned in an alley, aimed it at the gate and fired. This one shot saved Wilno for the time being; General Deyov and several officers perished; the rest, fearing an ambuscade, retired from the city. I do not know with certainty the name of that townsman.

165 Even later still forays (zajazdy) occurred, which, though not so famous, were still bloody and much talked of. About the year 1817 a man named U[zlowski] in the wojewodeship of Nowogrodek defeated in a foray the whole garrison of Nowogrodek and took its leaders captive.

166 [A town not far from Odessa, captured from the Turks in 1788 by Potemkin.]

167 [Izmail was a fortress in Bessarabia, captured from the Turks by Suvorov in 1790, after a peculiarly bloody siege. (Byron chose this episode for treatment in Don Juan , cantos vii and viii.) Mickiewicz makes Rykov give the name as Izmailov; Rykov is a bluff soldier, not a stickler for geographical nomenclature.]

168 [In Italy, near Modena, memorable for the victory of the Russians and Austrians over the French in 1799.]

169 Evidently Preussisch-Eylau. [In East Prussia: see p. 334 .]

170 [Alexander Rimski-Korsakov (1753-1840), a Russian [pg 350] general sent in 1799 to Switzerland in aid of Suvorov; he was beaten on September 25, before uniting with Suvorov, and was in consequence for a time dismissed from the service.]

171 [A village not far from Cracow, where on April 4, 1794, Kosciuszko with an army of 6000, among them 2000 peasants, armed with scythes, defeated a body of 7000 Russians.]

172 [See p. 334 .]

173 [Jan Tenczynski, an ambassador from Poland to Sweden, gained the love of a Swedish princess. On his journey to espouse her he was captured by the Danes, in 1562, and he died in confinement in Copenhagen in the next year. His memory has been honoured in verse by Kochanowski and in prose by Niemcewicz.]

174 [Compare p. 305 .]

175 [See note 38 .]

176 Apparently the Pantler was slain about the year 1791, at the time of the first war. [In the chronology of this poem there is serious confusion. From Jacek's narrative (pp. 269 -272) it is plain that Thaddeus was born shortly before the death of the Pantler. At the time of the action of the poem he is about twenty years old (p. 21), and he was born at the time of Kosciuszko's war against the Russians (p. 6), which would be naturally interpreted as 1794, the date of the war in which Kosciuszko was the dictator. All this would be consistent with the original plan of Mickiewicz, to have the action take place in 1814 (see Introduction, p. xiv); it conflicts with the chronology of the completed poem, the action of which is placed in the years 1811-12. Apparently Mickiewicz inserted the note above in a vain attempt to restore consistency. The "first war" could be none other than that following the Constitution of May 3, 1791, in which Prince Joseph Poniatowski and Kosciuszko were leaders. But this war did not begin until after the proclamation of the Confederacy of Targowica, which was on May 14,1792.]

177 [A former adjutant of Kosciuszko; he perished in the war of 1812.]

178 A certain Russian historian describes in similar fashion the omens and the premonitions of the Muscovite people before the war of 1812.

179 Run [the Polish word here used] is the winter corn when it comes up green.

180 Wyraj [the Polish word here used] in the popular dialect means properly the autumn season, when the migratory birds fly away; to fly to wyraj means to fly to warm countries. Hence figuratively the folk applies the word wyraj to warm countries and especially to some fabulous, happy countries, lying beyond the seas.

181 [Prince Joseph Poniatowski (compare pp. 334 -335) and Jerome Bonaparte (1784-1860),the youngest brother of Napoleon.]

182 [See pp. 31 and 334 , and note 33 .]

[pg 351]

183 [See pp. 31 and 334 , and note 34 .]

184 [Kazimierz Malachowski (1765-1845); he lived to share in the insurrection of 1831. Compare note 35 .]

185 [Romuald Giedrojc (1750-1824); in 1812 he organised the army in Lithuania.]

186 [Michal Grabowski (1773-1812), killed at the siege of Smolensk.]

187 A book now very rare, pub-

lished more than a hundred years ago by Stanislaw Czerniecki.

188 That embassy to Rome has been often described and painted. See the preface to The Perfect Cook : "This embassy, being a great source of amazement to every western state, redounded to the wisdom of the incomparable gentleman [Ossolinski] as well as to the splendour of his house and the magnificence of his table—so that one of the Roman princes said: 'To-day Rome is happy in having such an ambassador.' " N.B.—Czerniecki himself was Ossolinski's head cook. [The information given by Mickiewicz does not quite agree with that furnished by Estreicher, Bibliografia Polska (Cracow, 1896), xiv. 566, 567. Czerniecki was apparently the head cook of Lubomirski, Wojewoda of Cracow, etc., not of Ossolinski.]

189 [Karol Radziwill (1734-90), called My-dear-friend from a phrase that he constantly repeated, the richest magnate of his time in Poland and one immensely popular among the gentry, led a gay and adventurous life. In 1785 he entertained King Stanislaw at Nieswiez; this reception cost him millions.]

190 [Compare p. 177 and note 128 .]

191 [The festival of the Annunciation, March 25.]

192 In Lithuania, on the entrance of the French and Polish armies, confederacies were formed in each wojewodeship and deputies to the Diet were elected.

193 It is a well-known fact that at Hohenlinden the Polish corps led by General Kniaziewicz decided the victory. [At Hohenlinden in Bavaria the French under Moreau defeated the Austrians, December 3, 1800; compare p. 334.]

194 [See p. 335 .]

195 [A brand of deep disgrace. The Chamberlain is of course quoting from the Latin text of the law.]   196 [Militem (soldier) here signifies a full-fledged gentleman, of ancient lineage. Skartabell (a word of uncertain etymology) was a term applied to a newly created noble, who was not yet entitled to all the privileges of his order.]

197 [The Constitution of May 3, 1791 (see p. 333), conferred many political rights on the inhabitants of the Polish cities and took the peasants "under the protection of the law," though it did not set them free.]

198 [See p. 332 .]

199 [See note 28 .]

[pg 352]

200 ["The finest palace in Warsaw was beyond dispute that of General Pac, who died in exile at Smyrna." —Ostrowski. The proprietor of the palace seems to have been present at Soplicowo at this very time: see p. 301 .]

201 [This was a Polish escutcheon characterised by a golden crescent and a six-pointed golden star. It was borne by the Soplicas: see p. 319 .]

202 [A village in eastern Galicia, the scene of a battle in 1667 between the Turks and the Poles under Sobieski.]

203 [See p. 295 and note 200 .]

204 Radziwill the Orphan travelled very widely, and published an account of his journey to the Holy Land. [Mikolaj Krzysztof Radziwill was converted from Calvinism to Catholicism. In 1582-84 he made a pilgrimage to the Holy Land and Egypt, on which he wrote a book.]

205 [See p. 333 .]

206 [Jaroszynski explains kontaz as a sort of sausage, arkas as a cold dish of milk, cream, and yolks of eggs, and blemas (the same word as *blancmange*) as almond jelly.]

207 In the sixteenth, and at the beginning of the seventeenth century, at the time when the arts flourished, even banquets were directed by artists, and were full of symbols and of theatrical scenes. At a famous banquet given in Rome for Leo X. there was a centre-piece that represented the four seasons of the year in turn, and that evidently served as a model for Radziwill's. Table customs altered in Europe about the middle of the eighteenth century, but remained unchanged longest in Poland.

208 Pinety [Pinetti?] was a conjurer famous throughout Poland, but when he visited the country I do not know.

209 [Henryk Dembinski (1791-1864) took part in the Napoleonic wars, the insurrection of 1831, and the Hungarian insurrection of 1849.]

210 [Joseph Dwernicki (1778-1857), a member of the Legions, who in 1804 fitted out a squadron at his own cost. In 1826 he was made a general, and distinguished himself in the insurrection of 1831.]

211 [Samuel Rozycki entered the army in 1806; he took part in the insurrection of 1831.]

212 [The translator cannot find that *counterpoint* is a term of fencing, but does not know how else to render kontrpunkt .]

213 [The Pulawski family were among the organisers and most prominent leaders of the Confederacy of Bar. Joseph Pulawski was the first commander-in-chief of its armed forces. His son Kazimierz won fame as a leader after his father's death. Later, in 1777, he came to America, and distinguished himself by his services to the cause of the revolutionists. He was killed in 1779 at the attack on Savannah.]

214 [Michal Dzierzanowski, a Confederate of Bar and an adventurer [pg 353] famous in the eighteenth century; he took part in almost all the wars of his time. He died in 1808. The Cossack Sawa was one of the most active leaders in the Confederacy of Bar.]

215 The mournful song of Pani Cybulski, whom her husband gambled away at cards to the Muscovites, is well known in Lithuania.

216 [That is, is fickle. The translator is here indebted to Miss Biggs's version.]

217 [Charles Francois Dumouriez (1739-1823) was an agent of the French government sent to support the Confederacy of Bar. He later became prominent in the affairs of his own country.]

218 [The Piasts were the first royal dynasty of Poland. In later times the name was used to denote any candidate for the Polish throne who was of native birth.]

219 [The italicised words are of foreign origin in the original text. For old Maciek everything not Polish is Muscovite or German. Gerwazy has the

same way of thinking: compare p. 318.]

220 [Doubtless Maciek had heard of the excommunication of Napoleon by Pius VII. in 1809.]

221 The fashion of adopting the French garb raged in the provinces from 1800 to 1812. The majority of the young men changed their style of dress before marriage at the desire of their future wives. [On the kontusz see note 13.]

222 The story of the quarrel of Rejtan with the Prince de Nassau, which the Seneschal never concluded, is well known in popular tradition. We add here its conclusion, in order to gratify the curious reader.—Rejtan, angered by the boasting of the Prince de Nassau, took his stand beside him at the narrow passage that the beast must take; just at that moment a huge boar, infuriated by the shots and the baiting, rushed to the passage. Rejtan snatched the gun from the Prince's hands, cast his own on the ground, and, taking a pike and offering another to the German, said: "Now we will see who will do the better work with the spear." The boar was just about to attack them, when the Seneschal Hreczecha, who was standing at some distance away, brought down the beast by an excellent shot. The gentlemen were at first angry, but later were reconciled and generously rewarded Hreczecha.

223 [Compare p. 100.]

224 The Russian government recognises no freemen except the gentry (szlachta). Peasants freed by landowners are immediately entered in the rolls of the Emperor's private estates, and must pay increased taxes in place of the dues to their lords. It is a well-known fact that in the year 1818 the citizens of the province of Wilno adopted in the local diet a project for freeing all the peasants, and appointed a delegation to the Emperor with that aim in view; but the Russian government ordained that the project [pg 354] should be quashed and no further mention made of it. There is no means of setting a man free under the Russian government except to take him into one's family. Accordingly many have had the privileges of the gentry conferred on them in this way as an act of grace or for money.

225 [Compare p. 296, and note 201.]

226 ["Before the inauguration of a better taste by Mickiewicz and other great writers, the so-called French or Classical school of literature in Poland produced a quantity of panegyrics or complimentary verses in honour of great personages, with stale classical images, and strained, far-fetched metaphors, destitute of real poetry. Our author has seized this happy opportunity of satirising the faults of classicism."—M. A. Biggs.]

227 ["Janissaries' music, a type of extraordinarily noisy Turkish martial music, was fashionable in eastern Europe in the eighteenth century, and was introduced into Poland."—Jaroszynski.]

228 [See p. 333.]

229 [See p. 334.]

230 ["Readers who have already observed into what close connection Mickiewicz loves to bring the phenomena of nature and the affairs of men, will not find it difficult, nor will they regard it as a forced interpretation, to understand the clouds, which at the close of the poem. he paints with such disproportionate breadth and with such apparent minuteness, as something quite different from mere external reality. They will have no difficulty in seeing in that western cloud, which was adorned with gold and pearl, but in the centre was blood-red, Napoleon, the great warrior of the west; or, if they prefer, the hopes of Poland that were linked to him. We are in the year 1812: both the aureole of that name, and the hopes and rejoicing that it aroused, we may recognise in the gleaming, but fleeting picture, which 'slowly turned yellow, then pale and grey,' and behind which the sun fell asleep with a sigh. Thus in this passage, as well as earlier, in the words of Maciek (page 314), the poet gives us warning of the great tragedy which was soon to overwhelm not only Lithuania and Poland but the world."—Lipiner.]

231 [This concluding couplet imitates the conventional ending of a Polish fairy tale.]

THE TEMPLE PRESS LETCHWORTH
ENGLAND

***